MATERIAL BEINGS

Peter van Inwagen

MATERIAL BEINGS

Cornell University Press

Ithaca and London

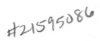

First published in 1990 by Cornell University Press.

International Standard Book Number 0-8014-1969-7
Library of Congress Catalog Card Number 90-55125
Printed in the United States of America
Librarians: Library of Congress cataloging information
appears on the last page of the book.

♾ The paper in this book meets the minimum requirements
of the American National Standard for Information Sciences—
Permanence of Paper for Printed Library Materials, ANSI Z39.48-1984.

To my mother
and the memory of my father

Contents

MATERIAL BEINGS

Preface

The theory of material things presented in this book has seemed to many of the philosophers who have read the book in manuscript to be a very strange one. This reaction seems to be based on a single consequence of the theory: that there are no tables or chairs or any other visible objects except living organisms. Let us call this consequence of the theory "the Denial." It is the Denial that evokes what David Lewis (who knows them well) has called the incredulous stares. The first thing I want to do in this Preface is to make clear the nature of the Denial—of my denial that there are any of the things the medievals called "substances existing by art" (tables, statues, houses) or "substances existing by accident" (sticks, stones, severed limbs). I want to do this because, or so I judge, all the attempts I have heard at articulations of the incredulity behind the stares involve misrepresentations of the Denial. No doubt many philosophers who understand the Denial perfectly will find it incredible, but I prefer informed incredulity to uninformed incredulity. I have gone into the nature of the Denial very carefully in Section 10, but what I have said there seems to have escaped the attention of many readers of the manuscript. I fear that it is also likely to escape the attention of many readers of the book. I propose, therefore, to try to attract attention to the content of Section 10 by giving a brief exposition of it here at the very beginning of the book.

The key to understanding the Denial is an analogy: My denial that there are tables and chairs should be understood by analogy to Copernicus' denial that the sun moves.

Here is a brief sketch of this analogy, which is developed systematically in Section 10 and extended and applied in incidental passages in the succeeding sections. I say (A): imagine Copernicus saying (B):

(A) Nonphilosophers, people immersed in the business of ordinary life, hardly ever say things like "There are chairs." But they do say

1

things like "Some of her chairs are very good nineteenth-century copies of Chippendales." My position is that the proposition that someone who had no interest in metaphysics might express by uttering or writing the latter sentence in ordinary circumstances is consistent with the proposition that I, when I am talking or writing about metaphysics, express by uttering or writing the sentence 'There are no chairs'.

(B) Nonastronomers, people immersed in the business of ordinary life, hardly ever say things like "The sun moves." But they do say things like "It was cooler in the garden after the sun had moved behind the elms." My position is that the proposition that someone who had no interest in astronomy might express by uttering or writing the latter sentence in ordinary circumstances is consistent with the proposition that I, when I am talking or writing about astronomy, express by uttering or writing the sentence 'The sun does not move'.

I will not develop this analogy here. But I would ask readers who object to the Denial to attempt, first, to articulate their objections with care, and, secondly, to try to transform these objections—using the contrasted theses (A) and (B) above as a model for the transformation—into objections to the Copernican denial that the sun moves. Since (I believe it will transpire) the objections that result from this exercise will not render the Copernican denial implausible, I would ask the critics of the Denial to explain why their objections to that thesis nevertheless render it implausible. This, I suppose, amounts to a request for an argument to show that the Denial and Copernicus' denial that the sun moves differ in some way that diminishes the force of my analogy. I do not make this request as an expression of a complacent confidence that any forthcoming argument must be a bad one. I make this request because I think that such arguments, if they can be given, will be very helpful in evaluating objections to the Denial.

Having completed the first task that I want to accomplish in this Preface, I now will explain what has led me to a theory that has such an odd consequence. What is it that leads me to accept a theory that commits me to the Denial? I have come to hold the theory presented in this book because it is a sort of vector sum or resultant of a great many of my metaphysical convictions. This metaphor can be pressed a bit. One might know a lot, even all there is to know, about the forces acting on a body and still not know how that body will move—not till one has calculated the direction and magnitude of the sum of those forces. I want now to lay out the metaphysical convictions whose "vector sum" has determined the final direction my theorizing has taken. (One aspect of the "vector sum" metaphor needs qualification. A set of vectors has a unique sum. But it may well be that there is more than one theory that is consistent with my metaphysical convictions. It might be better to view my convictions not as "forces" but as "constraints." The theory presented in the book should be viewed from that perspective as a theory that satisfies those constraints; the only one I am aware of at present, and, in all probability, the one I should find most attractive if others should come to light.) Some of these convictions will turn up in various places in the book as premises of arguments; others are implicit in the way I present arguments, examples, and analogies, and, perhaps, implicit in what I do *not* do, paths I do not explore. Here I attempt to isolate them and present them in systematic order. It would not be accurate to say that all ten of the "convictions" that I am about to record are unargued-for presuppositions of the book. Some of them I argue for in the body of the book, and one of them—number (9), anticonventionalism—I present a rather lengthy argument for here. It would be better to say that they are propositions that I should have accepted even if I had been able to think of no arguments for them. But even this careful generalization is not exactly right, for my faith in one of these propositions is not as robust as it once was. I touch on my recent tendency to apostasy in the next paragraph.

(1) In this book I presuppose a "classical" or "absolute" view of the identity relation. Some of the central arguments of the book would have quite large holes in them if, for example, the following were possible: x and y are both persons and both living organisms, but x and y are the same organism and different persons. To my chagrin, however, while I was engaged in making a long series of revisions of the first draft, I acquired—owing to reflection on matters quite unrelated to the metaphysics of material objects—a certain sympathy with the idea of "relative identity." But not everything can be discussed in one book, and I have done almost nothing to soften the stern "classical" line on identity that I unreflectively took when writing the first draft. (In Section 16, I have very briefly indicated how an allegiance to relative identity might affect one's perspective on certain matters.) There is, after all, so much to be said for the classical or "absolute" view of identity that it seems a reasonable candidate for a view that can be presupposed without argument. The reader who is committed to a "relative" view of identity may regard the conclusions of this book as hypothetical: given that we accept the classical view of identity as one of the constraints on our theorizing about material things, our theories will have such-and-such a character.

(2) Material things endure through time and (typically) change with the passage of time. They are not extended in time. "Temporal extent" is not one of the dimensions that figure in determining the size of an object. People and cats and whatever other things there are that endure and change are three-dimensional objects. (Or, at any rate, they have only as many dimensions as space has. I don't mean to quarrel with the "super-string" theorists who postulate nine spatial dimensions.) And this is not to say that they are three-dimensional "slices" of four-dimensional objects, for that would imply that the cat sleeping here today and the cat that slept here yesterday are numerically distinct objects (albeit they are "gen-identical")—but today's cat and yesterday's cat are one and the same. I do not object to the relativistic reification of "space-time" as a physically real four-dimensional continuum. But I insist that distinct regions of space-time are in some cases "occupied" by numerically the same three-dimensional object. (I have developed this idea in "Four-Dimensional Objects," *Nous* 24 [1990]: 245–55). The original plan of this book included an appendix devoted to the case against the thesis that people and cats and such are four-dimensional objects, extended in time as well as in space. Owing to considerations of both time and space, however, I have had to abandon this plan. Again, those who are committed to the thesis whose falsity I presuppose (in this case "four-dimensionalism") may regard the conclusions of the book as hypothetical: *given* that we accept "three-dimensionalism" as one of the constraints on our theorizing about material things, our theories will have such-and-such a character.

(3) The book adheres to standard logic as an ideal. Considerations having to do with the vagueness of material things will force us in the final sections of the book to accept certain revisions of standard logic. But I have not regarded this unfortunate consequence of the vagueness of material things as providing me with a license to abandon (say) the Principle of the Transitivity of Identity whenever that might help with the problem at hand. I have tried to construct a theory that violates the constraints of standard logic only in extreme cases; and I have regarded it as important to construct a theory according to which our everyday adventures (as opposed to bizarre adventures imagined by a philoso-pher or a science-fiction writer) do not involve such extreme cases and thus conform to the requirements of standard logic. I believe that, as a physical theory ought not to tell us that we cannot employ Euclidean geometry when we are designing suspension bridges, so a metaphysical theory ought not to tell us that we cannot employ standard logic when we reason about the commonplace.

(4) I have not adopted a counterpart-theoretical understanding of modal statements about individuals—not even to deal with extreme

cases. The reason I have not done this is that, when you come right down to it, I simply do not like counterpart theory. But this constraint, unlike most of the other constraints in the list I am giving, could be abandoned without requiring much revision of what is said in most of the book. And it would certainly make matters much simpler: most of the worries expressed in Section 14 about "counterfactual identity" would simply disappear, and the few positive things I have been able to say about counterfactual identity could be "built into" the similarity measure that defines the counterpart relation. Anyone who is comfortable with counterpart theory should feel to produce his own counterpart-theoretical version of my theses about counterfactual identity.

(5) I assume in this book that matter is ultimately particulate. I assume that every material thing is composed of things that have no proper parts: "elementary particles" or "mereological atoms" or "metaphysical simples." I suppose that questions about whether two objects are composed of or constituted by the same "quantity" or "parcel" of matter—or "the same matter" *tout court*—make sense only in the case of composite objects, and that in that case these questions must be understood as asking whether the composite objects are composed of the same ultimate parts. Thus, in my view, there is no notion of sameness of *matter* that is prior to or independent of the notion of sameness of *objects*.

(6) I suppose that *two* objects cannot be composed of exactly the same (proper) parts at the same time. Some philosophers maintain that a man and "his body" (or a gold statue and "the gold of which it is made") are numerically distinct objects that occupy the same space at the same time. But this must entail that the atoms that compose the man (the statue) simultaneously compose a distinct object, the body (the gold). I must therefore reject their position.

(7) It is my conviction that mental predicates (like 'is in pain', or 'is thinking of Vienna') require a subject. In the case of any particular episode of thought or sensation, there must be a thing, one thing, that is doing the thinking and feeling. In order to suppose that the historian who writes "The Paston family was in the ascendancy throughout the sixteenth century" thereby asserts a truth, one need not (though one may) regard 'the Paston family' as the name of a certain object—as it may be, the mereological sum of all the Pastons. One may, and this seems to be an eminently reasonable position, say instead that our historian's assertion is best understood (by one who shares the preoccupations of the metaphysician) as a thesis about the interconnected and cooperative, but ultimately individual, activities and adventures of the several Pastons. Thus—one may say—although the predicate 'was (a family that was) in the ascendancy throughout the sixteenth century' is grammati-

cally singular, one need not take this feature of its grammar as a guide in serious studies of what there is. My position is that matters are quite otherwise with predicates like 'is thinking of Vienna' and 'is in pain'. The facts expressed by concatenating such predicates with singular terms—and the sentences so constructed often do express facts—must be taken at face value: their grammatically singular subject and grammatically singular predicate get the ontology of thought and sensation right. When I say to my students, "Descartes invented analytical geometry," what I have told them cannot be true unless 'Descartes' denotes an object (the same object that Descartes called 'moi' and 'ego') and that object had the property of having invented analytical geometry. What I have told them, moreover, *is* true, is as strictly and literally true as any assertion that has ever been made.

(8) I suppose that such objects—Descartes, you, I—are material objects, in the sense that they are ultimately composed entirely of quarks and electrons. They are, moreover, a very special sort of material object. They are not brains or cerebral hemispheres. They are living animals; being *human* animals, they are things shaped roughly like statues of human beings. (When Descartes used the words 'moi' and 'ego' he was referring *malgré lui* to a living animal, a biological organism. When Hume looked within himself and failed to find himself, he was looking in the wrong place: like everyone else, he could see himself with his eyes open.) It follows from this, and from well-known facts about animals, that it is possible for a material object to be composed of different elementary particles at different times. "Mereological essentialism" is therefore false.

Descartes and his fellow human beings are not immaterial things, as he and Plato imagined. And they are certainly not, as some philosophers seem to think (but I have a hard time believing that this can really be what they mean), wholly abstract objects like computer programs. While there are, or so I believe, immaterial persons—God, say, or the Archangel Michael—that is just not what we human persons are. And there are *no* abstract, program-like persons. That idea makes no more sense than the idea of an abstract, program-like waterfall or hydraulic jack.

(9) I suppose that what there is, is never a matter of stipulation or convention. (This conviction would seem to entail that I am a "realist" in at least one sense of that versatile word.) I do not, of course, deny that one can appropriate or invent a word or phrase and stipulate a meaning for it—thereby establishing a convention among those who agree to use that word or phrase in the sense one has stipulated, a convention that will have the consequence that certain existential sentences express truths. I can stipulate that, or adopt the convention that, I shall call something a "dwod" if it is either a dog or a squid. And I can go on to say

(correctly) that there are dwods; but this thing that I can go on to say is correct only because there are animals of at least one of the kinds *dog* and *squid. Whether* there are dogs or squid, however, is not a matter that can be settled by establishing conventions: the conventions governing the use of 'dog' and 'squid' were established by our ancestors and we are more or less stuck with them; more to the point, if our ancestors had, for some reason, not established these conventions, there would still be dogs and squid.

Convention regulates behavior, including linguistic behavior, and regulating behavior has no ontological implications beyond implying the existence of regularities in behavior. By establishing a convention, I bring it about that there exists a convention having certain features, and there's an end on't. But many able philosophers do not see matters this way. Consider, for example, the following passage from a paper by Carl Ginet:

> But is it incoherent to suppose a type of *material* thing whose constitutive matter could completely change from one time to another in a nonpiecemeal fashion? Could I not introduce such a type of material thing by definition? I might stipulate that a *monewment* is a material object performing the same sort of function as a monument (commemorating something) and such that monewment x at t_2 is the same monewment as monewment y at t_1, *if* the matter constituting y at t_1 were subsequently destroyed all at once and thereafter new matter of pretty much the same sort and shape were put in the same place in order to restore the commemorating in the same fashion of whatever it was that monewment y at t_1 commemorated.[1]

Perhaps Ginet has a coherent idea here and I have failed to understand it; but it seems to me that the thesis of this passage is at best extremely elusive, and that the locus of the trouble is the words 'introduce such a type of material thing by definition'. One can, of course, stipulate that the word 'monewment' is to apply to objects having features A, B, and C. But that stipulation will not ensure that the neologism actually applies to anything; that, by definition, will occur just in the case that something has the properties A, B, and C—and making a stipulation does not normally ensure that anything has the properties that one mentions in the course of making it. (Not normally: one could, of course, stipulate that a 'stipulaytion' will be any stipulation that contains the quotation-name of a neologism that is pronounced the same as some already-existing word.) Let us always remember Abraham Lincoln's undeservedly neglected riddle: How many legs has a dog got if you call a tail a leg? The answer, said Lincoln, and he was right, is *four*, because calling a tail a leg doesn't make it one.

Ginet's "monewment" example and the argument in which it figures have been carefully analyzed by Alvin Plantinga (in the "Replies" section of the book in which Ginet's paper is printed), and Plantinga's analysis is, in my view, correct. I have nothing to add to what he says about the "monewment" example, but I want to make some general remarks about the "stipulationist" point of view that Ginet's use of this example illustrates.

Suppose that the world consists of certain mereological atoms (things without proper parts) and such other things as have these as their ultimate parts. "Such other things"—but what other things? Could there be any room for stipulation or convention here? Suppose that X, Y, and Z are three atoms. Can we *stipulate that* or *establish a convention that* or *make it true by definition that* there is an object that has X, Y, and Z (and no other atoms) as parts? Let us ask what one might actually *say* in order to accomplish something along these lines.

Let us begin with the most straightforward candidate. One might say, "I hereby stipulate that there exists an object that has X, Y, Z, and no other atoms as parts." But then one might say, "I hereby stipulate that a rich aunt has died and left me ten million dollars." Neither of these sentences makes any sense. One stipulates not facts but meanings for words. Of course, one could ignore the dictionary meanings of individual words like 'rich' and 'aunt' and stipulate that the complex predicate 'has been left ten million dollars by a rich aunt' is to have the same meaning as some predicate that one satisfies. And one could stipulate that the predicate 'is a thing that has X, Y, Z, and no other atoms as parts' is to have the same meaning as some predicate that is satisfied; for good measure, some predicate that is satisfied uniquely if and only if X, Y, and Z exist, and is otherwise not satisfied—perhaps 'is identical with X, and such that Y and Z exist'. The trouble with this strategy is that the individual words 'parts' and 'has' (like 'rich' and 'aunt') already have meanings, and these meanings have sufficient content to ensure that anything that has X, Y, and Z, and no other atoms as parts will have a certain rather comprehensive set of properties. If it happens that *nothing* has that set of properties, then any stipulation to the effect that 'is a thing that has X, Y, Z and no other atoms as parts' is to have the same meaning as some specified predicate (a predicate that is satisfied) will have the following consequence: 'is a thing that has X, Y, Z, and no other atoms as parts' will be satisfied by something that has properties that would not belong to a thing that had X, Y, Z, and no other atoms as parts. Suppose, for example, that the antecedent meanings of 'parts' and 'has' are such as to ensure that whatever satisfies the complex predicate 'is a thing that . . .' will have the properties A, B, and C. (To take a wholly uncontroversial example, A might be "has X, Y, and Z as parts.") And suppose that nothing has A, B, and C. Suppose we make the stipulation suggested above: our predicate is to mean 'is identical with X, and such that Y and Z exist'. Then 'is a thing that has X, Y, Z, and no other atoms as parts' will apply to an object of which Y and Z are not parts. Our first attempt to imagine what one might say in order to "stipulate that there is an object that has X, Y, Z, and no other atoms as parts" would therefore seem to be a failure.

Let us make a second attempt. One might say, "I hereby stipulate that 'Alfred' will name the object that has X, Y, Z, and no other atoms as parts." And one might say, "I hereby stipulate that 'Bertha' will name the rich aunt who has died and left me ten million dollars."

Let us make a third attempt. One might say, "Without prejudice to the question whether there really is an object that has X, Y, Z, and no other atoms as parts, I propose to talk and act as if there were: I will talk and act as if, for any time at which X, Y, and Z all exist, there were then an object which individually occupied the region of space these three atoms jointly occupied, and which then had as its mass the sum of the masses they had; and I will talk and act as if, for any t_1 and t_2 at which X, Y, and Z all exist, the object whose spatial extent and mass at t_1 were, in the way I have described, determined by the spatial extents and masses of X, Y, and Z at t_1 was the same object as the one whose spatial extent and mass at t_2 were determined by the spatial extents and masses of X, Y, and Z at t_2." (In saying these words, one would be making a resolution, and not stating a definition or making a stipulation. But I suppose one could be said to be establishing a convention.) And one might say, "Without prejudice to the question whether I really have inherited ten million dollars from a rich aunt, I propose to talk and act as if I had: I will write checks for vast amounts. . . ."

It may be that stipulations about parts and wholes are, in some way that undermines my materteral analogies, unlike stipulations about aunts and legacies. But I confess that I don't see what the difference might be.

I can think of nothing else that one might say if it were one's intention to "stipulate that" or "establish a convention that" or "make it true by definition that" there was an object that had X, Y, Z, and no other atoms as parts. But if these phrases make sense, then, one would suppose, there would be something one could say to effect the ends these phrases are supposed by their users to describe. I tentatively conclude that there are no such ends and that these phrases do not make sense.

Before leaving the topic of "defining things into existence" (a phrase which one usually encounters in dismissive accounts of the ontological argument, but which seems at least equally appropriate in the present context), I want to describe a procedure that is *not* a case of "introducing a type of material thing by definition" (or "by stipulation" or "by establishing a convention"). I think that some philosophers may have had something like this procedure in mind when they have used phrases like the ones I have put in scare-quotes.

Suppose there is a philosopher—call him Q—who believes that every "filled region of space-time" is occupied by a material object and that every material object occupies a filled region of space-time. (Q may, or may not, hold the further view that in this setting 'is occupied by' and 'occupies' means 'is identical with'.) These "material objects" are, of course, four-dimensional objects of the kind deprecated in (2) above. *Three*-dimensional material objects, insofar as there are such things, are instantaneous "slices" of four-dimensional material objects. It is obvious that Q believes in a great many material things. Most of them will be too complex for any finite being to be aware of or to describe. Of the infinitesimal residue that people like us could perceive or form a conception of, most will be too widely scattered and too involuted to be of any practical, or even theoretical, interest to us. But changes in our practical and theoretical interests might compel us to pay attention to objects that we had previously not even thought about. One way to pay attention to an object is to name it. One way to pay attention to a class of objects is to devise a general term that has that class as its extension. Names and general terms come to exist (sounds or marks become names or general terms) by means of definition, stipulation, or the establishment of convention. If Ginet subscribed to Q's ontology of the material world, he could introduce the word 'monewment' into his discourse in words not entirely unlike the words of the passage I have quoted. 'Monewment' would then be a general term whose extension was a certain class of filled regions of space-time (or a certain class of occupants of filled regions of space-time). But this would not be a case of "introducing a type of material thing by definition," whatever exactly that means. It is, if Q is right, simply a case of providing a general term to cover a class of material objects whose members are "already there." But suppose Q is *not* right. Suppose they are *not* already there. Suppose Q's general ontology of the material world is wrong. Or, in order to avoid large ontological questions, let us simply consider the fact that there are those who don't accept Q's ontology. Suppose a philosopher called Carl-prime attempts to introduce the word 'monewment' into a conversation he is having with me—for I am one of those philosophers who do not accept Q's general ontology of the material world—as a general term covering a certain class of items belonging to Q's ontology. I shall have to interrupt him and say something like "Hold on—I don't think that there *are* any objects having the right properties to fall under the general term 'monewment' as you have explained it." At this point, if Carl-prime wants the conversation (eventually) to proceed on the course he has anticipated, he will have to digress and attempt to get me to accept Q's general ontology of the material world. And this, I believe, brings the distinction between Ginet and Carl-prime into high relief. I would not expect *Ginet* to reply to my interruption by defending a *general* thesis about what there is, Q's or any other. I would expect Ginet to reply by saying something along the lines of "You don't understand—I'm introducing such objects by *definition*." And this I certainly *don't* understand. It is only when one has some sort of grip on what exists independently of convention that one can establish conventions that regulate one's conceptual dealings with what exists. Lines and meridians are "drawn" on the globe by convention to enable navigators and cartographers to deal with the globe. But the globe itself is there, antecedently to any convention; if it weren't, there'd be nothing to draw the lines on.

This point applies a fortiori to the philosopher who proposes to introduce by definition not merely a type of object but a general theory of what there is. Suppose, for example, that someone were to say that he was "introducing" Q's ontology of the material world "by definition" or that he was adopting a convention to the effect that things are as Q says. I should regard this as a perfectly maddening statement. I think I should reply by saying that I had adopted a convention to the effect that one couldn't introduce Q's ontology by adopting a convention, and let it go at that. But, really, no such retaliatory convention is needed, for it makes no sense to talk of "introducing" Q's ontology or any other by adopting a convention. Q's ontology is a substantive philosophical theory; it entails comprehensive and intransigent theses about what exists. If, moreover, we propose to identify cows (say) with certain of the items in Q's universe, it entails comprehensive and intransigent theses about cows. The business of this book is to investigate competing ontologies of this comprehensive sort and to try to decide which of them to accept.

Before leaving this topic, I will note that my use of Q's theory has been merely illustrative. Many theories of the material world are like Q's theory in that they endorse some very general and very powerful principles about what material things there are. Any such theory will assert the existence of material objects that, at any given moment, we have no "use" for. And it is generally imaginable that we should come to recognize a need to refer to sorts of objects that we have not hitherto had any use for. If our ontology tells us that there are no objects of kinds that would satisfy our newly recognized needs, we have a prima facie reason for trying to devise a new ontology. If, however, our ontology tells us that there are indeed objects that meet our needs (or if it allows us to construct them, as the unfortunate idiom has it), we can establish conventions that enable us to recognize them—in the sense of enabling us to refer to them by short, handy terms like 'monewment', as opposed to predicates that take half a page to write out. This, I believe, is the only coherently specifiable procedure that could possibly be referred to by phrases like 'introduce objects of such-and-such a kind by definition' or 'establish a convention that there exist objects of such-and-such a kind'. But these phrases are not correct descriptions of that procedure, or, at best, they are very misleading descriptions of it. We should therefore avoid them. (After reading the foregoing, Carl Ginet has informed me that his own view is that of "Carl-prime" and not that of "Ginet." Such are the hazards of interpreting the writings of a living philosopher! Unfortunately, I learned of my mistake too late to do anything more about it than add this brief acknowledgment of its existence. Let the reader regard the "Ginet" of the preceding pages as an imaginary philosopher who wrote the same words as Ginet and who meant by them what I thought Ginet meant.)

(10) Whether certain objects add up to or compose some larger object does not depend on anything besides the spatial and causal relations they bear to one another. If, for example, someone wants to know whether the bricks in a certain brickyard make up a composite object, he need not attend to anything outside the brickyard, for no information gathered from that quarter could possibly be relevant to his question. An important special case of this general principle is the following: he need not attend to the beliefs, attitudes, or interests of any person outside the brickyard. (Or inside it, for that matter. The brickyard is meant to define an easily visualizable region of space that contains certain bricks, but the essential point I want to make is that nothing outside *any* region of space that contains the bricks is relevant to the question whether they compose anything. Every person will, of course, be outside *some* region that includes the bricks.) A similar point, but it is harder to state, applies to identity across time. If object A is at place x at t_1, and if object B is at place y at t_2, then nothing besides the causal processes or chains of events that connect what is going on at x at t_1 with what is going on at y at t_2 is relevant to the question whether A and B are the same object. "Closest Continuer" or "Best Candidate" theories of identity across time provide examples of theories that violate this principle. Closest Continuer theories permit cases of the following description: (1) the man at x at t_1 and the man at y at t_2 are the same man, but (2) there is a possible world w in

which the man at x at t_1 is the man who is actually at x at t_1; and the man at y at t_2 in w is descriptively identical with the man who is actually at y at t_2; and the causal processes or chains of events that link what is going on at x at t_1 in w with what is going on at y at t_2 in w are the actual ones; and the man at x at t_1 in w is *not* the man at y at t_2 in w. Such a case could arise if in w (and not in the actual world) there is a man—perhaps on another continent—who is a better candidate for being the "continuer" of the man at x at t_1 than is the man at y at t_2. The idea of a "better candidate" is, moreover, to be spelled out partly in terms of the *interests* of certain citizens of w: as it may be, the man who is at y at t_2, his "rival," and the friends, relations, and creditors of the man who was at x at t_1. The essential idea is that the "continuer" of a given person at a given future time will be the best candidate (or perhaps the best candidate on some slate that contains candidates that satisfy some minimal set of requirements) for that office. In the actual world the man at y at t_2 is the best candidate for "continuer of the man at x at t_1" and thus *is* his continuer, is *he*; but the descriptively identical man at y at t_2 in w is not chosen for that office since there is, in w, a better man for the job.

We should note that the principle I am now describing is not equivalent to the denial of the "conventionalism" that was rejected in (9). If someone holds that "external" factors are relevant to the identity of an object through time, or to its existence at a time, this position would not seem to commit him to the position that it is a matter of convention whether this is so, or to the position that the "external" factors affecting the identity of an object through time, or its existence at a time, might be modified by a change in the prevailing conventions.

We should also note that the principle I am endorsing does not entail that "internal" spatial or causal factors *are* relevant to the identity of an object across time or its existence at a time. The principle entails only that *if* any spatial or causal factors are relevant to these things, then these factors must be "internal." Consider, for example, the position that the members of any set of atoms whatever must compose an object—and must always compose the *same* object—no matter how widely those atoms may be separated and no matter what causal relations (even none at all) they may bear to one another. This position entails that spatial and causal factors are irrelevant to questions of existence and identity. It is therefore consistent with our "internalist" principle, since it entails that *external* spatial and causal factors are irrelevant to questions of existence and identity.

This completes the promised list of constraints. The body of this book consists of an attempt to construct a theory of material objects that is consistent with these ten constraints. (Cutting the list off at this point is somewhat arbitrary. I have recently read a paper by a philosopher who believes that many objects can be identical with one object—for example, that one forest can be identical with many trees. This idea makes no sense to me, and I might add its rejection to my list of constraints. But one must make an end somewhere.) If my ten constraints are considered individually, it will be seen that each of them has its adherents. But no other philosopher, I believe, subscribes to all ten of them. It is for this reason that the argument of the book makes only incidental reference to the writings of many philosophers who have written about material objects and their parts. I very much admire the work on the ontology of the material world that has been produced by such philosophers as Richard Cartwright, Roderick Chisholm, Mark Heller, Eli Hirsch, Mark Johnston, Derek Parfit, W. V. Quine, Nathan Salmon, Peter Simons, Ernest Sosa, Judith Jarvis Thomson, James Van Cleve, Samuel C. Wheeler III, and David Wiggins.[2] Their thinking on these matters has been (and continues to be) serious, imaginative, and able. But none of them has accepted the same system of constraints as I, and their work has, as a consequence, taken them in directions in which I cannot follow. In almost every case, in fact, if you set a paper or book by one of these philosophers alongside the present book, you will see that the two works diverge almost immediately. Each of the works goes in a direction permitted by the constraints the author accepts, and my constraints, at least, allow me little latitude. (Of course, many of the authors I have mentioned operate under constraints that I am free from: "mereological essentialism," for example. From their point of view, therefore, *I* almost immediately set off in a direction in which *they* cannot follow.) One's theorizing about material objects seems to be extraordinarily sensitive to the system of constraints one adopts: differing systems of constraints almost always lead to immediate divergence. As a result, most of what is said in this book can be of little use to someone who accepts different constraints. And, sadly, the reverse is true. Most of what is said on the topic of material objects by a philosopher who believes that objects are extended in time as well as in space, or that the same atoms can simultaneously compose two material objects, or that human persons do not strictly persist through time, or that human persons are immaterial substances, can be of no use to me in my theorizing—not unless it converts me; but then I must scrap almost all of my work and start over. A philosopher who accepts a different system of constraints will see no problems where I see only problems and will see only problems where I see no problems. He will regard my book as a sustained attempt to solve problems that do not exist and will charge it with failing to consider the real problems or with "solving" them by theft where he has toiled honestly. And I, sadly, will regard his book the same way.

Nevertheless, his book and mine are in competition. Each of us lays his work before the same philosophical public, who must make their own judgments about who has the better theory.

What I have said does not apply only to living philosophers. The philosopher who comes closest to sharing my constraints is Aristotle. The only one of them he clearly rejects is (5)—that matter is ultimately particulate. But it is difficult to translate Aristotle's thought into the idiom of twentieth-century analytical philosophy, and one risks anachronism if one tries. I will point out, however, that the theory of individual substances that Montgomery Furth finds in *Metaphysics* (see his "Transtemporal Stability in Aristotelian Substances," *Journal of Philosophy* 75 [1978]: 624–46) seems to me to be extraordinarily like the theory of material objects presented in this book—and this despite Aristotle's rejection, and my espousal, of atomism.

There are certain points of contact between what John Locke says about living organisms and what I say about them. I discuss these points of contact in Section 14. Jonathan Bennett has pointed out to me that the questions I have raised concerning the factors that bind parts together to form a whole had been raised by Leibniz in his correspondence with Arnauld. (See Leibniz's letter of 28 November–8 December 1686, and particularly his discussion of the first five of the seven objections that Arnauld had raised against the idea that the soul is the "substantial form" of the body.)[3] I cannot accept Leibniz's answer to the question, What are the factors that bind parts together to form a whole? but his way of posing this question is characteristically clear and beautiful. If it were not so readily available, I would include it in this book as an appendix.

Three of the nineteen sections of this book (4, 5, and 7) contain some rather difficult material that is not necessary to the main thread of the argument. Readers who wish to do so may skip them without fear of losing their way. I have marked these sections with asterisks.

Very little of the material in the book has appeared in any other form. Parts of Sections 1 through 8 are contained in "When Are Objects Parts?" (*Philosophical Perspectives* 1 [1987]: 21–47). A part of Section 18 has appeared as "How to Reason about Vague Objects," *Philosophical Topics* 16, no. 1 (1988): 255–84. I thank the editors of these journals for the permission to reprint this material.

The first draft of the book was written while I held a Research Fellowship from the National Endowment for the Humanities in 1983–84. I am very grateful to the Endowment for its generous support.

Many philosophers have given me the benefit of their criticism. I want to single out five people for special thanks. Jonathan Bennett convinced me that my discussion of physical bonding in Section 6 was incomplete because it did not consider the possibility that I now examine in Section 7. Frances Howard, an assiduous reader of drafts of this book, has brought to my attention more invalid arguments, unclear transitions of thought, and puzzling statements than I care to dwell on. David Lewis made me see clearly that if the theory presented in this book is correct, then existence and identity must be vague. Nathan Salmon gave me the benefit of extensive comments on the paper ("How to Reason about Vague Objects") on which Section 18 is based. Peter Unger's "nihilistic" arguments (and my correspondence and conversation with him) have had a deep influence on almost every section of the book. If this is a good book, it would have been much less good without their help; if it is a bad book, it would have been far worse.

PETER VAN INWAGEN

Syracuse, New York

1. Introduction

The topic of this book is material objects. Like most interesting concepts, the concept of a material object is one without precise boundaries. A thing is a material object if it occupies space and endures through time and can move about in space (literally move about, unlike a shadow or a wave or a reflection) and has a surface and has a mass and is made of a certain stuff or stuffs. Or, at any rate, to the extent that one was reluctant to say of something that it had various of these features, to that extent one would be reluctant to describe it as a material object. Few philosophers would be perfectly happy about calling a quark or a proton or even a large organic molecule a material object, for one has to be very careful in ascribing any of the features in the above list to such things; and talk about the surfaces of submicroscopic objects, or about the stuffs they are made of, tends to verge on nonsense. (But there can be controversy about such matters. A physicist once told me that *of course* a gold atom was a piece of gold, and a physical chemist has assured me that the smallest possible piece of gold would have to be composed of sixteen or seventeen atoms. I once heard a Nobel-prize-winning physicist shout, in reaction to a philosopher's incautious statement that what elementary-particle physicists studied was "abstract," "A proton is a *thing*! Like a *rock*!") Some philosophers are happy to call clouds and forests and galaxies material objects and others are not. But virtually all philosophers believe that there are central, perfectly clear cases of things that fall under the concept *material object*, and that the extensions of many English count-nouns—'ship', 'house', 'cat'—comprise such "paradigmatic" material objects.

That there are deep and intractable metaphysical problems about material objects—even paradigmatic ones—is evident from the antinomies and paradoxes involving material objects. The best known of these are about artifacts, the puzzle of the Ship of Theseus being the best known of all. Others, at least as worthy of remark, involve living organisms. If a cat's tail is cut off, for example, it seems natural to describe this episode in words that appear to imply that the cat becomes identical with a former proper part of itself—a violation of the attractive modal principle that a thing and another thing cannot become a thing and itself. Or, talking of cats, consider a cat that is composed at t of certain atoms arranged in a certain way; it is at least logically possible for those very same atoms to be arranged in the same way at some later time and then to compose a different cat; but that apparently implies that certain things can compose a material object at t, and, even though arranged in precisely the same way, compose a distinct material object later. How could that be?

In this book, I shall present and defend a theory about the nature of material things that takes seriously the apparently paradoxical features of their unity and persistence. If this theory is correct, the nature of material things is radically unlike what most philosophers suppose it to be. I shall try to make the radical thesis about material things that I advocate seem as plausible as I can make it seem. I shall do this in a variety of ways. I shall try to draw out what I believe to be incoherencies in competing theories. I shall try to show that the "deep and intractable" metaphysical problems about the unity and persistence of material things have simple and intellectually satisfying solutions if my proposals are correct. I shall even argue directly for some of these proposals. But it will not be easy to make these proposals seem plausible, for they are radical indeed. They entail, among other things, that there are no visible objects but men and women and cats and other living organisms, that there are no tables or books or rocks or hands or legs. Many philosophers will regard any position that has such a consequence as not a "live option." But even these philosophers may find something of value in this book, for one can learn something from arguments one regards as perverse by examining them to see just where they go wrong. One needn't, for example, accept McTaggart's conclusions about time in order to learn something about time from him.

It is evident that all three of the "unresolved paradoxes and antinomies involving material objects" that I mentioned above involve not only material objects but the *parts* of those material objects: no such paradoxes could be raised in connection with material objects that were not composed of parts. And this fact is not an accidental consequence of my choice of illustrative examples of metaphysical problems raised by material objects. The metaphysically puzzling features of material objects are connected in deep and essential ways with metaphysically puzzling features of the constitution of material objects by their parts. Parthood will occupy a central place in the present study of material objects. It is therefore worth noting that the word 'part' is applied to many things besides material objects. We have already noted that submicroscopic objects like quarks and protons are at least not clear cases of material objects; nevertheless, every material object would seem pretty clearly to have quarks and protons as *parts*, and, it would seem, in exactly the same sense of *part* as that in which one paradigmatic material object might have another paradigmatic material object as a part. A "part," therefore, need not be a thing that is clearly a material object. Moreover, the word 'part' is applied to things that are clearly *not* material objects—or at least it is on the assumption that these things really exist and that apparent reference to them is not a mere manner of speaking. A stanza is a part of a poem; Botvinnik was in trouble for part of the game; the part of the curve that lies below the x-axis contains two minima; parts of his story are hard to believe . . . such examples can be multiplied indefinitely. Does the word 'part' mean the same thing when we speak of parts of cats, parts of poems, parts of games, parts of curves, and parts of stories?

I do not know how to answer this question, any more than I know how to answer the question, Does the word 'rising' mean the same thing when we speak of balloons rising, temperatures rising, and the average age of death rising? But I do think, as Ryle did, that it would be odd to maintain that there is something called 'rising' that balloons and temperatures and average ages can all do—although, of course, each can do it only in a manner appropriate to the kind of thing it is. Rather, it seems to me, there is something called 'rising' that a balloon can do, something else called by that name that a temperature can do, and so on.[4] It seems to me, moreover, that we use the same word for all of these things on the basis of some sort of analogical resemblance they bear to one another— whatever, exactly, that may mean.

I want to say more or less the same thing about 'parthood'. There is one relation called 'parthood' whose field comprises material objects and those things like elementary particles which are not clear cases of material objects but which share many of their salient features (they are substances or continuants; they can move about and collide with and rebound from one another; they have masses). There is another relation called 'parthood' defined on events, another still defined on stories, yet another defined on curves, and so on, through an indefinitely large class of cases. And yet it is no accident—as it is with the pitch of a roof and the pitch of a whistle—that we apply the same word in each case, for these applications are bound together by a "unity of analogy." (The analogy is, no doubt, as etymology would suggest, grounded in the idea of "cutting" a thing, but this explains little, for cutting *in re* and cutting *in intellectu* are themselves only analogically united.)

Many philosophers, if I understand them, do not see parthood like that. They see 'part of' as a transcendental or "high-category" predi-

cate—like 'is identical with' or 'three in number', and unlike 'rising'—
which can be applied to any sort of object and which always expresses
the same *very* abstract relation. They may go so far as to insist that there
are objects of which you and I and the number two are all three of us
parts. I do not know how to argue against this thesis. In this book I shall
simply presuppose my own understanding of 'part of'. I am not sure to
what degree the things I shall say about material objects and their parts
will depend on my assumption that the relation called 'parthood' that
electrons and cells bear to cats is not, strictly, the relation called 'parthood' that—for example—words and stanzas bear to poems, but only a
relation that is, in a sense I am unable to explain, analogous to it. In any
case, the reader is to understand me in the sequel as employing 'part of'
to express a relation whose field is the set of material objects and those
things that share with material objects the features I have listed above. In
any sentence of the sequel containing both 'part of' and variables, the
range of those variables is to be understood as comprising just that set.

The theory of material objects that I shall present in this book grew out
of a sustained attempt to find a satisfactory answer to a certain question
about parts: In what circumstances is a thing a (proper) part of something?[5] (This is one formulation of what I shall call the Special Composition Question—"special" because I shall have occasion to distinguish it
from a question I shall call the General Composition Question.) I think
that this fact about how the theory grew is of more than autobiographical
interest. I have discovered that the various components of the theory
arise and fall into place quite naturally in the course of an attempt to
answer the Special Composition Question, and I have let that discovery
dictate the organization of the book. I shall begin (once some rather
extensive logical preliminaries are out of the way) by examining six
possible answers to the Special Composition Question. I shall argue that
each of these answers is wrong. I shall go on to discuss certain variants
on these six answers. I shall then present and defend my own answer
and apply this answer to two problems about mereological change, one
involving artifacts (the Ship of Theseus) and one involving human beings
(the Brain Transplant). I shall finally discuss certain problems about
vagueness, for my answer to the Special Composition Question will
entail that parthood is a vague relation, and this will in turn entail that
identity and existence are vague.

A great many topics will turn up in one way or another in the course of
this discussion: paraphrase, common-sense beliefs, thinking, the nature
of living organisms, artifacts, memory, identity, and existence, to name a
few of the more important ones. And, running like a thread through the
discussion, there will be a developing theory of the nature of material
objects.

2. The Special Composition Question

In this section I will present a precise formulation of the Special Composition Question. This formulation will require some logical apparatus and some remarks about the theory on which that apparatus rests.

I have said that the Special Composition Question is the question, In what circumstances is a thing a (proper) part of something? But this is a misleading formulation of the question we shall be addressing under that name. This formulation suggests that our question is, In what circumstances does a pair of objects satisfy the predicate 'x is a proper part of y'? But to ask that question at the outset of our inquiry would be to begin *in medias res*. The relation expressed by 'x is a proper part of y' is antisymmetrical, and a pair of objects related by it will in typical cases—in my view, in *all* cases—be very unlike each other. For example: A plank is very unlike a ship; a cell is very unlike a whale. I have found it to be of great heuristic value to let one of these objects (the larger and more complicated) drop out of the picture and to concentrate on the other (the smaller and simpler) and its fellows—the other planks or the other cells. For example, I have found it helpful to ask not 'In what circumstances is a plank a part of a ship?' but, rather, 'In what circumstances do planks compose (add up to, form) something?' When we ask a question of this sort, we are asking a question about the mutual relations that—at least in typical cases—hold among various objects of the same type (among atoms, among planks, among cells, among bricks), relations in virtue of which they are bound together into a whole. If we ever find an answer to a question of this sort, we can go on to ask various questions about what comes to be when atoms or cells or planks or whatever become in this way bound together: We can ask whether its properties supervene upon the properties of and arrangement of its parts; we can ask whether it could survive being taken apart and put together again; we can ask whether it is properly called a ship or a whale. But initially we do not have to talk about it at all, and, I would argue, it is better not to, if only because the fewer the questions a philosopher is attempting to answer simultaneously the better off he is.

Instead of asking about the conditions a pair of objects must satisfy if one is to be a part of the other, therefore, we shall ask about the conditions a plurality (or aggregate, array, group, collection, or multiplicity) of objects must satisfy if they are to compose or add up to something. But I am not entirely satisfied with this formulation of the Special Composition Question either, for I do not like substantives like 'aggregate' and 'plurality'. I do not like them because they are, after all, substantives— and substantives, as it has often been observed, represent themselves as naming substances. Even 'plurality' sounds rather as if, like 'lion' or 'number', it were a name for a kind of object. If we use nouns like 'plurality', 'aggregate', and 'multiplicity', we shall be tempted to ask what the properties of pluralities or aggregates or multiplicities are and how these things achieve their perhaps rather minimal degree of unity and what their identity conditions are. We may even be tempted to ask questions like these: Consider the aggregate of particles that are currently parts of this oak: What is the relationship between the aggregate and the tree? What properties has the one got that the other lacks? Is the tree a temporal succession of aggregates? I think these are bad questions, and I want to avoid them. But even if they were good questions, it would be well to avoid them at the outset of our inquiry, on the principle that recommends dealing with as few questions as possible at any one time. Let us, therefore, place ourselves out of temptation's way.

One way to avoid being tempted by these questions would be to use no collective noun but 'set' in our investigations. It is at least fairly clear that a set is an abstract thing (but many philosophers are puzzled about what that means), and that the existence of a set in no way depends on the relations that hold among its members. Moreover, the laws governing sets are embodied in a much-studied theory of which extremely careful and explicit statements are available. But I think that if we were to conduct our investigation in terms of sets, we should soon discover that the sets played no essential part in our investigation. Suppose we were to ask, In what circumstances does a set of objects compose or add up to something? Unless we take it to be the case that any objects that are metaphysically capable of being parts of something just automatically and of necessity add up to something, we shall, presumably, say that a set of objects adds up to something just in the case that its members bear certain relations (as it may be, causal or spatial) to one another. But then the set itself, as opposed to its members, has dropped out of the picture. If we say, for example, 'The set of blocks on the table adds up to something owing to the fact that the blocks are stacked', the set (as opposed to its members) seems to play no role in our answer beyond that of picking out or enabling us to refer to certain blocks—the ones on the table. But we do not need to appeal to any set to do that. We can call them 'the blocks on the table'. Names of sets are singular terms. Phrases like 'the blocks on the table' are "plural referring expressions." I believe that we can achieve all the powers of plural or collective reference we shall need for our discussion of composition without using singular terms that purport to refer to pluralities or aggregates or sets. We shall need only plural referring expressions.[6]

The idea of a "plural referring expression" has sufficient currency that I need not devote a great deal of space to an explanation of it.[7] 'The members of the college', 'my closest friends', and 'Tom, Dick, and Harry' are plural referring expressions. In my usage, at least, plural referring expressions will not contain quantifier words.[8] (I shall explain this restriction later in the present section.) Thus, in my usage, 'all the king's men' and 'the Mortons and some of the Hanrahans' are not plural referring expressions, though 'the king's men' and 'the Mortons and the Hanrahans' are. I shall assume that we understand "open" plural referring expressions ('Tom, x, and Harry', 'z's men') and the sentences formed by quantifying into them. For example: $\forall x$ (x is a king $\rightarrow \exists y\, y$ and the sons of x are conspiring).

We should note that the word 'and' in 'Tom, Dick, and Harry' and 'the Mortons and the Hanrahans' is not the familiar sentential connective, but a special operator that "takes" singular terms and plural referring expressions and "builds" complex plural referring expressions. The syntax and semantics of this operator (and everything else about it) are so obvious that I shall not bother to discuss it further, nor shall I bother to introduce a notational distinction between 'and' the operator and 'and' the sentential connective.

One may form sentences containing plural referring expressions by combining these expressions with so-called variably polyadic or indefinitely polyadic predicates: 'are in a minority', 'are quarreling', 'are carrying a beam', 'outnumber', 'run the risk of alienating', and so on. We have, for example, such sentences as 'Tom, Dick, and Harry are carrying a beam' and 'The Democrats run the risk of alienating those voters who live on a fixed income'. Each of the predicates 'outnumber' and 'run the risk of alienating' requires both a subject and a direct object, and each is thus in an obvious sense structurally analogous to an ordinary dyadic predicate. The logical structure of variably polyadic predicates is a topic of considerable intrinsic interest, but we shall not need to pursue it.

Some variably polyadic predicates "express" a state or activity that an object can be in or engage in "all by itself." There can be a minority of one, and a man observing two men carrying a beam might say, "I could do that all by myself." (On the other hand, it takes at least two to make a quarrel.) A plural referring expression refers to the objects that satisfy a certain condition, and sometimes this will be a condition that could be satisfied by a single object. Thus, 'my allies' refers to those people who satisfy the condition 'being an ally of mine', and I might have only one ally. Now consider the sentence 'My allies are in a minority'. Suppose I have one ally and six adversaries. I shall count this sentence as expressing, in that circumstance, a truth. In other words, we stipulate that, while the use of a plural referring expression doubtless normally carries the "conversational implicature" that that expression refers to more than one thing, the proposition expressed by a sentence containing a plural referring expression may nevertheless be *true* if that expression refers to only one thing. In consequence of this stipulation, the following sentences express truths: 'Tully and Cicero were Roman orators'; 'The even primes are fewer than the odd primes'; 'The people identical with Frege were all born in the same year'.

We can speak generally about objects without speaking of them collectively. We do this by using the quantifier-variable idiom. Syntactically speaking, variables behave like singular referring expressions (or, to employ the more usual expression, "singular terms"). Is there any linguistic device that stands to plural referring expressions as quantifiers and variables stand to singular terms? Or if there is not, can we invent such a device? The existence of sentences like 'There are some men in the street who are carrying a beam' suggests that there is indeed such a device. In fact, the resources of ordinary English include many such devices, all of them sources of potential confusion and ambiguity. (There are many English adverbs and adverbial phrases whose sole function is to ameliorate this ambiguity. For example: 'individually', 'collectively', 'as a group'. They do not work very well.) We shall need a clear way of writing sentences that stand to sentences like 'Tom, Dick, and Harry are carrying a beam' and 'The Democrats run the risk of alienating those voters who live on a fixed income' as quantificational sentences stand to 'Tom is carrying a beam' and 'The governor runs the risk of alienating my uncle'. I shall not attempt to refine or standardize any of the devices that are used for this purpose in idiomatic English. I shall construct a device for this use out of rather more basic semantical materials.

How are ordinary or "singular" or "individual" variables, the familiar 'x', 'y', and 'z' of the logic texts, introduced? There are many ways of introducing variables. The most satisfactory pedagogically is probably the Berlitz-style method of total immersion favored by mathematics departments. The next-best way stresses the identical syntactical properties of variables and singular terms. The worst way depends on drawing an analogy, or even asserting an identity, between variables and the third-person-singular pronouns of ordinary English. But if one is interested not in introducing variables to beginners in logic or mathematics but in giving an adequate theoretical account of variables to people who already know how to manipulate them, the order is reversed. "Total immersion" is no account at all. Explanations in terms of syntax do not satisfactorily distinguish true variables from dummy or schematic letters. Identifying variables with pronouns, however, provides a genuine explanation of what variables are.

Let us look at the pronominal method, since our interests are theoretical. The *locus classicus* is Quine's *Mathematical Logic.*[9] What follows is inspired by Quine's explanation of variables but does not reproduce it. Imagine a language that is exactly like English except that it has been supplied with an indefinite stock of third-person-singular pronouns, phonetically diverse but semantically indistinguishable. Suppose they are 'it$_x$', 'it$_y$', 'it$_z$', and so on. Call phrases of the form 'it is true of at least one thing that it$_x$ is such that' existential-quantifier phrases. Then introduce the familiar variables and existential quantifier of formal logic by means of the obvious scheme of abbreviation. For example, '$\exists x \exists y\, x$ loves y' will be an abbreviation for

it is true of at least one thing that it$_x$ is such that it is true of at least one thing that it$_y$ is such that it$_x$ loves it$_y$.

(A similar account, of course, can be given of the universal quantifier.)

We may follow an exactly parallel route in combining generality with collective reference. Imagine a language that is exactly like English except that it has been supplied with an indefinite stock of third-person-plural pronouns: 'they$_x$', 'they$_y$', 'they$_z$', and so on. (For obvious reasons we shall also need a corresponding stock of objective-case pronouns.) Now abbreviate 'they (them)$_x$' by 'the xs', 'they (them)$_y$' by 'the ys', and so on. Call these phrases *plural variables*. (We shall sometimes find 'those xs' to be stylistically preferable to 'the xs', and we shall therefore count phrases of this form as plural variables.) Phrases of the form

it is true of certain things that they$_x$ are such that

will be called *existential plural-quantifier* phrases. We shall abbreviate them in a way congruous with our abbreviations of plural variables. For example, the displayed phrase may be abbreviated as 'there are xs such that' or 'there exist xs such that' or 'for some xs'. A worked example:

For some xs and for some ys, those xs run the risk of alienating those ys

abbreviates

It is true of certain things that they$_x$ are such that it is true of certain things that they$_y$ are such that they$_x$ run the risk of alienating them$_y$.

A truth-conditional semantics for the plural existential quantifier would be an elaboration of the following statement: A sentence of the form 'For some xs, those xs F' expresses a truth just in the case that there is some (nonempty) set such that the members of that set F.

Universal plural quantification can be introduced in an exactly parallel fashion. Phrases of the form

it is true of any things whatever that they$_x$ are such that

will be called *universal plural-quantifier* phrases and may be abbreviated by phrases of the form 'for any xs'. (For some reason that I can't grasp, it does not seem to be possible to construct plural-quantifier phrases around the words 'all' or 'every'.) The reader may find it instructive to write out the sentence

For any xs, if those xs are finite in number, then there are ys such that those ys are finite in number and there are more of the ys than there are of the xs

in unabbreviated form. A sentence of the form 'For any xs, those xs F' will, of course, express a truth just in the case that every nonempty set is such that its members F.[10]

It is important to realize that 'for some xs' and 'for any xs' do not bind—or interact in any way with—the singular variable 'x'. By the same token, '$\exists x$' and '$\forall x$' do not bind, or otherwise interact with, the plural variable 'the xs'. 'The xs' and 'x' are two distinct variables, just as 'x' and 'y' are two distinct variables. 'The xs' is, officially at least, a symbol that has no meaningful parts: 'the . . . s' is not a *context* within which a singular variable occurs. (As an aid to clarity, however, I shall not use, for example, 'x' and 'the xs' in the same sentence.)

The expressive power of a language containing both singular and plural variables and quantifiers is greatly increased by the addition of a variably polyadic operator analogous to the '$\in$' of set theory. I shall use the English words 'is one of' for this operator. (I hope that these words convey its meaning, for no explanation of its meaning is possible.) If everything that is one of the xs is one of the ys, then we say that the xs *are among* the ys. Let us write this definition out formally, just to illustrate the syntax of 'is one of':

the xs are among the ys = df

$\forall z$ (z is one of the xs $\rightarrow$ z is one of the ys).

If the xs are among the ys and the ys are among the xs—if something is one of the xs if and only if it is one of the ys—then we say that the xs *are identical with* the ys. If the xs are among the ys but are not identical with the ys, then we say that the xs *are properly among* the ys.

I said earlier that I should not count as a plural referring expression any expression that contained a quantifier word like 'some' or 'all'. We can now appreciate the reason for this restriction. We obviously want to count as plural referring expressions only those expressions that can replace plural variables in syntactically correct sentences without yielding syntactically incorrect sentences; and 'James is one of some of the Hanrahans' and 'The conspirators are among all of the members of the Senate' are syntactically incorrect. Our official reading of, for example, 'The Mortons and some of the Hanrahans are having a picnic' is 'For some xs, the xs are among the Hanrahans, and the Mortons and the xs are having a picnic'.

Certain plural referring expressions, expressions like 'the Democrats' and 'my closest friends', are in an obvious way analogous to definite descriptions. Having 'is one of' at our disposal, we may, if we wish, provide a "Russellian" treatment of these expressions. For example, we may treat 'The dinosaurs are extinct' as an informal abbreviation for 'For some xs [$\forall y$(y is one of the xs $\leftrightarrow$ y is a dinosaur) & the xs are extinct]'.

I shall feel free—even when writing out formal definitions—to use English idioms that do the same work as 'is one of' when their meaning is clear. For example, a formal definition that we shall come to shortly contains the clause 'the xs are all parts of y'; this is clear and idiomatic and there would be no point in replacing it with an "official" sentence like 'for all z, if z is one of the xs, then z is a part of y' or 'the xs are among the parts of y'.

We have, then, open sentences containing both free singular and free plural variables. It is important to distinguish in theory—although not always terribly important to distinguish in practice—between open sentences and *predicates*. The three distinct open sentences 'x loves y', 'y

loves x', and 'z loves z ', are all instances of a single (dyadic) predicate; and the third, 'z loves z ', is *also* an instance of a distinct monadic predicate of which 'x loves y' and 'y loves x' are *not* instances. (But 'x loves x' and 'y loves y' are instances of that predicate.) The same point applies, *mutatis mutandis*, to variably polyadic predicates. I shall not bother to introduce a special notation—involving Greek letters or circled numerals—for predicates. Instead, I shall talk as if predicates contained variables. The reader will always be able to tell whether, when I mention an open sentence in the course of making some point, I mean my point to apply only to *that* sentence—the one containing *those* variables in *those* places—or whether I mean my point to apply to the predicate of which that sentence is a typical instance.

Just as ordinary predicates—predicates containing free singular and no free plural variables—express relations, so variably polyadic predicates—predicates containing free plural variables—express relations. ('Variably polyadic predicate' is not always an appropriate description of a predicate containing a free plural variable; there is nothing "variable" about 'the xs are three in number'. I do not think that this will cause any confusion, however.) An n-adic predicate (a predicate containing n free singular variables and no plural variables) expresses an n-ary relation: the dyadic predicate 'x likes x better than x likes y' expresses a binary relation. Variably polyadic predicates express so-called multigrade relations. For example, 'the xs belong to the same political party' expresses a multigrade relation. ('Multigrade relation' is not always an appropriate description of a relation expressed by a predicate containing free plural variables; there is nothing "multigrade" about the relation expressed by 'the xs are three in number'. Indeed, it could be plausibly argued that this relation is just the ternary relation expressed by 'x is not identical with y and y is not identical with z and x is not identical with z'. If this is so, 'multigrade' and, for instance, 'ternary' are compatible descriptions. But even if this is so, there will be some multigrade relations—such as the one expressed by 'the xs belong to the same political party'—that cannot be identified with any n-ary relation. Again, I do not think that the traditional terminology will cause any confusion.) If we wished seriously to study multigrade relations, we should have to develop a system of classification analogous to the classification of ordinary relations into unary, binary, ternary (and so on) relations. (Consider, for example, the relation expressed by 'the xs and y are conspiring against the zs, the father of y, and the former leader of the xs'.) Fortunately, we shall be concerned only with very simple multigrade relations, and we shall be able to get along without a systematic classification of them.

Let us now return to the Special Composition Question. We shall use the expression the xs compose y

as an abbreviation for

the xs are all parts of y and no two of the xs overlap and every part of
y overlaps at least one of the xs.

(Remember that we are using 'part' in such a way that everything is a part
of itself. A thing *overlaps* a thing—or: they overlap—if they have a
common part. If no two of the xs overlap, we shall sometimes say that the
xs are *disjoint*.) For example, if there is a house made entirely of bricks,
then the bricks compose the house. If, as some philosophers believe,
there are such things as the north half and the south half of the house,
then the north half and the south half compose the house—and, of
course, there is no inconsistency in saying both that the bricks compose
the house and that the two halves compose the house.[11] On the other
hand, the north half of the house and the south two-thirds of the house
do not compose the house, owing to the fact that they have parts in
common.

It follows from our definition that, for any x, the things identical with x
compose x. If the xs compose y and the xs are two or more, then we shall
say that the xs *properly* compose y.

The verb 'compose' in the predicate 'the xs compose y' is to be understood as being in the present tense, and the same point applies to 'are' in
'are parts of' and to all other verbs that occur in the *definiens* of 'the xs
compose y'. Thus, 'are parts of' and 'compose' should be read 'are *now*
parts of' and '*now* compose'. Strictly speaking (given the use we shall
make of it), our *definiendum* should have been 'the xs compose y at t',
and our "primitive" mereological predicate should have been 'x is a part
of y at t'. But I do not think that any confusion will result from our not
speaking that strictly.

In addition to the notion of composition, it will be useful to have the
weaker notion of summation, summation being just composition without the "no overlap" requirement:

y is a sum of the xs = df

the xs are all parts of y and every part of y overlaps at least one of the
xs.

For example, the north half and the south two-thirds of our house of
bricks have the house as a sum; the house is a sum of the house, the
north half of the house, and any seven of the bricks. (It will be noted that

we say 'a sum' rather than '*the* sum'. Although *I* think that, for any xs, there is at any given time at most one object such that the xs are all parts of that object and every part of that object overlaps at least one of the xs, I am willing to argue with anyone who thinks otherwise, and I see no reason to define 'sum' in such a way as to unfit it for use in such an argument. And there *are* those who think otherwise. Some philosophers believe that a gold statue and the lump of gold from which it is formed are numerically distinct objects. Such philosophers presumably believe that there are xs—certain gold atoms, for example—such that the statue is one sum of the xs and the lump is another sum of the xs. We shall touch on the question of the lump and the statue in Sections 5 and 13.)

Having defined 'sum', we are in a position to examine the sentence 'A whole is the sum of its parts'. I want to take a moment to do this because many philosophers misuse this sentence. Is it true that "a whole is the sum of its parts"? We have decided not to legislate about the question whether, in general, the xs can have more than one sum (at a time). Let us, therefore, examine the thesis that a whole is *a* sum of its parts. If we take a whole to be something that has parts—and what else could a whole be?—this thesis may be formally expressed as follows: If x has parts, then x is a sum of the parts of x'. Now, in our inclusive sense of 'part', according to which x is itself one of the parts of x, this thesis is obviously a trivial truth. But even the thesis 'if x has proper parts, x is a sum of the proper parts of x' is a trivial truth. This may be seen by substituting 'the proper parts of y' for 'the xs' in the above definition of 'sum'. Why, then, do some philosophers (philosophers unconcerned with the question whether there could be objects that had more than one sum) persist in treating the sentence 'A whole is the sum of its parts' as if it expressed a substantive metaphysical thesis? The answer is, I think, that they use this sentence to express the proposition that, if y is the (or a) sum of the xs, then the intrinsic properties of the xs, and the relations in which they stand to one another, determine the intrinsic properties of y; that the intrinsic properties of a whole *supervene upon* the intrinsic properties and arrangement and causal interactions of its proper parts.[12] This is indeed a substantive metaphysical thesis, but (unless it were made to do so as the consequence of an arbitrary stipulation, a stipulation having no basis in the meanings of the words that make up the sentence) the sentence 'A whole is the sum of its parts' does not express that thesis.[13]

We now have the equipment necessary for a reasonably precise discussion of the Special Composition Question. Our official formulation of the Special Composition Question is this: When is it true that

$\exists y$ the xs compose y?

More formally, can we find a sentence which contains no mereological terms and in which no variable but 'the xs' is free and which is necessarily extensionally equivalent to '$\exists y$ the xs compose y'? (Two sentences are "necessarily extensionally equivalent" if the universal closure of their biconditional is a necessary truth. A "mereological term" is a word or phrase that can be given a trivial definition in terms of 'part'. For example, 'sum' and 'compose' are mereological terms.) Less formally, in what circumstances do things add up to or compose something? When does unity arise out of plurality?[14]

It will be instructive to approach the Special Composition Question as if it were a practical rather than a theoretical question. Here is a "practical" version of the Special Composition Question:

> Suppose one had certain (nonoverlapping) objects, the xs, at one's disposal; what would one have to do—what *could* one do—to get the xs to compose something?

For example: Suppose that one has a lot of wooden blocks that one may do with as one wills; what must one do to get the blocks to add up to something? Asking the Special Composition Question in this "practical" form has the virtue of concentrating our attention on the xs and on the question, What multigrade relation must the xs (be made to) bear to one another in order for them to form a whole? (I am going to assume that for no *two* relations is it true in every possible world that just the same objects enter into each of those relations in that world. Hence, necessarily extensionally equivalent sentences express the same relation. Nothing substantive hangs on this assumption, which could be dispensed with at the cost of some verbal complication in the sequel.) The question 'In virtue of what do these n blocks compose this house of blocks?' is a question about $n + 1$ objects, one of them radically different from the others. But the question 'What could we do to get these n blocks to compose something?' is a question about n rather similar objects. To adapt what I said about parthood at the beginning of this section to the case of composition, questions of the former sort turn our minds to various metaphysical and linguistic questions about the "special" $n + 1$st object and our words for it: What are the identity conditions for houses of blocks? Is 'house of blocks' a phase-sortal? And so on. It may be that our inquiries will eventually force us to attend to such questions, but we can make a good beginning without raising them.

The present section has been devoted to various logical points about plurality and composition. There are certain other logical points related to these notions that will need to be made explicit. But, although these points are very general and are no more closely tied to one answer to the

Special Composition Question than to another, they will be more easily grasped if they are presented in connection with a fairly detailed exposition of a theory about the conditions under which composition occurs that they would be if they were presented in the abstract. I therefore postpone discussion of them till we have examined an answer to the Special Composition Question.[15]

3. *Contact,* a Representative Answer
to the Special Composition Question

To get the xs to compose something, one need only bring them into contact; if the xs are in contact, they compose something; and if they are not in contact, they do not compose anything.

The xs are "in contact" if they do not overlap spatially and are "clumped together." That is, the xs are in contact if (1) no two of them overlap spatially, and (2) if y and z are among the xs, then y is in contact with z, or y is in contact with w, which is one of the xs, and w is in contact with z—and so on. (We stipulate that everything is in contact with itself. Thus Tully is in contact with Cicero, Tully and Cicero are in contact, and the men identical with Frege are in contact. We make this stipulation because of our adherence to the convention that a thing is a part of itself. It is easy to see that if x is not in contact with x, then the principle labeled *Contact* above entails that x is not a part of x.) For example consider six blocks arranged like this and surrounded by empty space:

3	5	7	9

The odd-numbered blocks are in contact. The square, odd-numbered blocks—of which there is only one—are in contact. The even-numbered blocks are in contact. Blocks 3, 5, and 7 are in contact. The six blocks are not in contact. The square blocks are not in contact. The oblong blocks are not in contact. (Block 3 is in contact with a block that is in contact with Block 7, but that "intermediate" block is not one of the oblong blocks.)

Suppose that blocks 5 and 7 compose just one thing. Call it 57. Suppose it occupies (exactly fills) the region of space jointly occupied by 5 and 7, which it certainly appears to do. Suppose it is in contact with 3, as it certainly appears to be. Then 57 is in contact with 3, which is in contact with 5. Nevertheless, 3, 5, and 57 are not in contact, since two of them overlap spatially.

Here is a formal definition of 'are in contact'. For any xs, there is a binary relation that holds between y and z just in the case that y and z are among the xs and are in contact: the contact relation on the xs, so to call it. The xs are in contact if no two of them overlap spatially and if, for any y and z that are among the xs, the ancestral of the contact relation on the xs holds between y and z.

It is to 'contact' in this sense that the answer to the Special Composition Question *Contact* refers. If *Contact* is correct, then in the situation pictured above there are, in addition to our six blocks, certain other objects. (I assume that part of what is represented in the figure is that no two of the blocks have a common part. *Contact* entails that, for example, 2 and 4 compose something; but nothing that 2 and 4 compose can be one of the blocks, for no block has both 2 and 4 as parts.) How *many* other objects? Well, there might be a great many if the blocks have proper parts, but let us assume that none of them does. This assumption, however, is not enough to give us a count of the nonblocks in the picture. Various further assumptions could give us various counts. Assume that, for any blocks, those blocks compose at most one thing (at a time). Assume that, if certain blocks compose x and x alone, and certain blocks compose y, and if the former blocks are among the latter blocks, then x is a part of y. On these two assumptions, the count of nonblocks in the illustration is seven.

How plausible is *Contact*? If we confine our attention to objects of the sorts we are in the habit of attending to in everyday life, *Contact* has a certain intuitive appeal. But it is evident on scientific grounds that *Contact* cannot be right. The concept of contact applies only to objects whose dimensions differ from ours by no more than (say) ten orders of magnitude. But it is undeniably true that, if there are any composite material objects at all, they are composed of elementary particles and that the elementary particles that compose a given material object are not in contact. (It is in fact probably meaningless to say of two electrons that they are in contact.) This consideration by itself is sufficient to refute *Contact*. But *Contact* faces other problems, and it is these that I shall be mainly concerned with. Suppose we lay aside the picture of the fine structure of matter that twentieth-century physics has provided us with and imagine ourselves in a comfortable seventeenth-century physical world, a world that consists entirely of material objects of various sizes— solid objects having surfaces and made of stuffs.

If we so restrict our imaginations, *Contact* has, as I said, a certain intuitive appeal. It seems plausible to say that if one has ten thousand wooden blocks none of which touches any of the others, then there is nothing that these blocks compose. It seems plausible to say that if one proceeds to build a model of Salisbury Cathedral out of them (laying them dry, as it were), then one has brought into existence something that they compose: a model of Salisbury Cathedral. But this answer seems less plausible in simpler cases. If I bring two cubes into contact so that a face of one is conterminous with a face of the other, have I thereby brought into existence a solid that is twice as long as it is wide? Or have I merely rearranged the furniture of earth without adding to it? If I cause the cue ball to rebound from the eight ball, do I thereby create a short-lived object shaped like two slightly flattened spheres in contact? (In these two examples, I assume that the spatial properties of a whole are determined in the obvious way by the spatial properties of its parts.) One might suspect that there is no answer to these questions laid up in heaven, and that how we answer them—assuming they're worth answering—is going to be simply a matter of which of various alternative conventions we adopt. But I think that we can see that there are at least some cases in which mere contact is not sufficient for the production of a new object.

Suppose you and I shake hands. Does a new thing at that moment come into existence, a thing shaped like a statue of two people shaking hands, a thing which has you and me as parts and which will perish when we cease to be in contact? Is there an object that fits just exactly into the region of space that you and I jointly occupy? Not in my view. But, surely, if you and I composed something when we were shaking hands, it would have all of these features. Despite our being in contact, therefore, nothing is such that you and I compose it. Or, at least, if you and I compose something, this is not *in virtue of* our being in contact. Some philosophers think that any two things necessarily have a sum (and hence think that any two nonoverlapping things compose some-thing), and these philosophers would say that when you and I are shaking hands, there is a thing, a sum of you and me, that (presumably) occupies the sum of the regions of space that we occupy individually. But, according to the theory these philosophers advocate, that sum of you and me did not come into existence at the moment you and I came into contact; rather, it already existed and had existed at every moment at which you and I both existed. (It would, I suppose, be logically possible to hold that you and I had one sum before we were in contact and another afterward, this second sum being generated at just the moment we came into contact. But this thesis would have little to recommend it, and I am sure no one in fact holds it. We shall discuss this issue further in Section 8.) All that happened to this sum at the moment you and I touched, say these philosophers, is that it changed from being a scattered to being a connected object. (A connected object is an object that is "all in one piece," an object such that any two points within it can be joined by a continuous path that nowhere emerges from it. A scattered object is a nonconnected object. It might be thought that *Contact* ruled out scattered objects, at least given the reasonable assumption that if the xs compose y, then y occupies the space the xs occupy jointly. It is not absolutely clear that it does, however, for there might be scattered objects without proper parts; and if a scattered object without proper parts could be in contact with another object, then *Contact* fails to rule out the existence even of composite scattered objects.) That is not the theory we are currently considering. We shall examine *that* theory in Section 8. The theory we are considering entails that you and I have a sum when *and only when* we are in contact.

It is a basic conviction of mine that this theory is wrong and that its being wrong is in no sense a matter of convention. I cannot prove this thesis, for I know of no propositions more plausible than itself from which it could be derived. I can only say that I shall try to display in this book the fruits of agreeing with me about this and various similar theses. I will content myself for the present by pointing out that if you disagree with me about *Contact*, you face a host of metaphysical problems that I avoid. For example, suppose that I were to touch your knee with my elbow. Would the object that came into existence when this happened be the same one that came into existence when we shook hands or a different one? For that matter, does the same object come into (or resume) existence every time we shake hands? One would like to believe that these questions had answers. (The philosophers I alluded to in the preceding paragraph will of course say that the thing you and I compose when we are shaking hands is the thing that you and I compose when my elbow is touching your knee. But if you believe, as they do not, that the existence at a given time of a thing that is then our sum depends upon our being in contact at that time, then it is far from obvious whether this statement is available to you. We shall return to this point in Section 8.) I am happy to have a position that enables me to avoid these difficult questions. Nevertheless, it is not in order to avoid difficulties that I have adopted the position that the coming into contact of two human beings is without metaphysical issue. I have adopted it because it seems to me, on reflection, to be true.

We have talked so far only about the case of *two* human beings coming into contact. Reflection on more complicated cases of human contact (ring-dances, say) convinces me that, however many people we may consider, those people do not begin to compose something at the moment at which they begin to be in contact. Therefore, the relation *the xs come into contact at t* is not (for it is not even coextensive with) the relation *the xs begin at t to compose something.* This is not to say, however, that there are no cases in which certain things come to compose something at the moment at which they come into contact. It is to say that the mere fact that they come into contact cannot be a complete explanation of the generation of a new thing that is their sum.

4. *The General Composition Question

Let us now turn to those logical points a discussion of which was promised at the end of Section 2. (The reader whose interest in finical points of logic is small will miss nothing essential to the main plan of this book by proceeding to Section 6.) These points have mainly to do with the following two closely related topics: why it is that an answer to the Special Composition Question tells us nothing about the nature of composite objects; why it is that an answer to this question tells us nothing about the nature of composition. Let us suppose, just for the sake of illustration, that *Contact* is the correct answer to the Special Composition Question. *Contact* is formally suitable for this role because 'the xs are in contact' contains one free plural variable and no other free variables. If one maintains that *Contact* is the correct answer to the Special Composition Question, then one is maintaining that the sentences

$\exists y$ the xs compose y

and

The xs are in contact

are necessarily equivalent, that the multigrade relations they express are the same. But this is not everything one might want to know about composition. If '$\exists y$ the xs compose y' makes sense, then 'the xs compose y' makes sense. And singular variables can take singular terms as substituends. What singular terms might be appropriate substituends for 'y' in 'the xs compose y', given that *Contact* is the correct answer to the Special Composition Question? There is no way of answering this question, for neither *Contact* nor any other answer to the Special Composition Question tells us anything about the identity, or even the qualitative properties, of any composite object. Moreover, no answer to the Special Composition Question will tell us what composition *is*.[16] To say what composition *was* would be to say what multigrade relation was expressed by the sentence 'the xs compose y', and an answer to the Special Composition Question tells us only what multigrade relation is expressed by the (singular) existential generalization of this sentence.

Let us look at an example. Suppose we have some bricks. Call them 'the bricks'. Suppose we arrange them in a way that would normally be described as "building a house out of them." Suppose that so arranging them causes them to be in contact. It follows from *Contact* that there is something the bricks compose. Can we then say that if *Contact* is correct, we have built a house and the bricks compose the house we have built? Well, these things are consistent with *Contact* and they may be true, but *Contact* gives us no license to say them.

In the first place, *Contact* tells us nothing about things called 'houses'. But this may seem to some to be an overly nice point. What about the *thing* we have built (or the largest thing—the thing composed of *all* the bricks—for some might want to say that in building the house we have also built various proper parts of the house)? Doesn't *Contact* show us the nature of that thing, and doesn't *Contact* show us what multigrade relation it is that the bricks bear to that thing? These questions raise several important points. The most obvious is a point about number. What makes us think that we haven't built *several* things, *each* of them composed of all the bricks? *Contact* tells us that the bricks, being in contact, compose at least one thing. It does not tell us that they also compose at most one thing.

Suppose we explicitly made a uniqueness assumption about the products of composition (or, more generally, of summation):

Uniqueness   For any xs, the xs have at most one sum at any given time.

Would *Contact* and *Uniqueness* together "tell us what composition was"? No. Not, at any rate, in the sense of enabling us to find a sentence containing no mereological terms that was necessarily extensionally equivalent to 'the xs compose y'. (Let us say that such a sentence would constitute an answer to the *General Composition Question*. As the Special Composition Question may be identified with the question, Under what conditions does composition occur? so the General Composition Question may be identified with the question, What *is* composition?) One cannot deduce from the two sentences

(There is a y such that the xs bear F to y) if and only if the xs are G

There is at most one y such that the xs bear F to y

any sentence of the form

The xs bear F to y if and only if ϕ

unless ϕ contains both 'F' and the free variable 'y'. For example, it has sometimes been suggested that the biological concept of "membership in a genus" can be reduced to or explained in terms of "mutual fertility"—where x and y are mutually fertile if they are of different sexes and one can impregnate the other, or they can both impregnate the same females, or they can both be impregnated by the same males; and the xs are mutually fertile if every pair of them are mutually fertile. (We ignore the immature and the impaired.) There is at least one sense in which this is not true. From the two sentences

(A)   (There is a y such that y is a genus and the xs are members of y) if and only if the xs are mutually fertile

(B)   There is at most one y such that y is a genus and the xs are members of y

we cannot deduce any sentence of the form

(y is a genus and the xs are members of y) if and only if ϕ

unless ϕ contains the free variable 'y' and the predicates 'is a genus' and 'are members of'. Thus, (A) and (B) do not enable us to "reduce membership in a genus to mutual fertility, and, by the same token, *Contact* and *Uniqueness* do not enable us to reduce composition to contact. The logical reasons for this have nothing in particular to do with plural variables. It is a fact about ordinary logic that one cannot deduce from the sentences

$\exists y \, Fxy. \leftrightarrow Gx$
$Fxy \,\&\, Fxz. \rightarrow y = z$

any sentence of the form

$Fxy \leftrightarrow \phi$

unless ϕ contains both the predicate 'F' and the free variable 'y'. For example, one obviously cannot deduce anything of the form 'y is a successor of $x \leftrightarrow \phi$' from '$\exists y \, y$ is a successor of $x. \leftrightarrow x$ is a natural number' and 'y is a successor of x & z is a successor of x. → y = z' unless φ contains both the free variable 'y' and the successor predicate. Thus, one cannot specify the binary relation *is a successor of* simply by pointing out that x has this relation borne to it by something or other if and only if x is a natural number, and that nothing has this relation borne to it by more than one thing. After all, many relations satisfy that condition: *is two more than*, for example.

Here is a second mathematical example, one that is especially helpful in clarifying the distinction between the Special and the General Composition Questions. Suppose you have heard mathematicians talk of numbers' "having reciprocals" and are curious about what such talk might mean. If I were to tell you *which* numbers had reciprocals (that is, tell you that 0 had no reciprocal and that all other numbers had at least one), this would not enable you to grasp the concept "having a reciprocal." More formally, if I were to tell you that the sentence '∃y y is a reciprocal of x' was equivalent to—could always replace *salva extensione*—the sentence 'x is a number other than 0', this would not tell you what binary relation was expressed by the sentence 'y is a reciprocal of x'. Moreover, if I were to go on to tell you that a number has at most one reciprocal, this would not help; you would *still* not know what relation was expressed by 'y is a reciprocal of x'. What I should have to do to get you to know *that* would be to present you with an appropriate sentence in which 'y' was free ('y is a result of dividing 1 by x' is, of course, what is needed). To provide an answer to the Special Composition Question (to say when composition occurs) is analogous to disclosing the information that '∃y y is a reciprocal of x' is equivalent to 'x is a number other than 0'. To provide an answer to the General Composition Question (to say what composition *is*) is analogous to disclosing the information that 'y is a reciprocal of x' is equivalent to 'y is a result of dividing 1 by x'.

What was said in the preceding two paragraphs about specifying binary relations is easily adapted to the case of multigrade relations. Just as there are many binary relations that satisfy the condition 'an object x has R borne to it by something if and only if x is a natural number, and nothing has R borne to it by two or more things', so there are many multigrade relations that satisfy the condition 'any objects enter into R with something if and only if those objects are mutually fertile, and no objects enter into R with more than one thing'; and many multigrade relations satisfy the condition 'any objects enter into R with something if and only if those objects are in contact, and no objects enter into R with more than one thing'. This last condition, for example, is satisfied by the relation expressed by 'the xs are in contact and y is the number of the xs'—a relation that, for example, the books now stacked on my table enter into with the number seven. (The phrase "enter into with" represents an impressionistic attempt to convey something an adequate articulation of which would require the detailed taxonomy of multigrade relations that I have avoided giving. But I think my meaning should be tolerably clear; remember, we are talking about multigrade relations of the type expressed by sentences containing one free plural variable and one free singular variable.) If anyone protests that objects in mutual contact enter into the relation we have specified only with numbers—whereas objects of the sort that can be in mutual contact enter into composition only with material objects—we can specify a second relation as follows. Let W be a well-ordering of material objects. Consider the relation expressed by 'the xs are in contact, and y is the W-least of the xs'.

Contact, therefore, even when conjoined with Uniqueness, does not provide an explanation of composition. It tells us an important thing about composition—the circumstances in which it occurs—but it does not tell us what composition is. It is perhaps worth pointing out that since Contact does not tell us what it is for the xs to compose y, it therefore does not tell us what it is for x to be a part of y. If we knew what composition was, we could easily explain parthood, via the equivalence

x is a part of y if and only if there are zs such that x and the zs compose y.

But since Contact (even when conjoined with Uniqueness) does not explain composition, it does not enable us to understand parthood. Of course, if Contact is right, we can do as well with parthood as we can with composition: We can say when it occurs. Or, rather, since improper parthood, in a manner of speaking, always occurs, we can say when proper parthood occurs: There is something of which x is a proper part if and only if x is in contact with something besides itself. (But the converse does not hold. We cannot deduce Contact from the premise that there is something of which x is a proper part if and only if x is in contact with something besides itself. The premise entails that if x and y are in contact, then x is part of something and y is a part of something; unlike Contact, it does not entail that there is something of which x and y are both parts.)

Perhaps the reader has been experiencing a vague sense of unease. Perhaps it could be articulated in these words. "Look, maybe Contact (even when conjoined with Uniqueness) doesn't tell us what composition is. But it certainly looks as if it does. Suppose we have thirty-five blocks that are arranged like this:

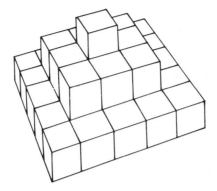

If we know that *Contact* and *Uniqueness* both hold, then we know that the thirty-five blocks compose one and only one object. And don't we know a lot *about* that object? We know that it has each of the blocks as a part; we know that it is step-pyramidal in shape; we know that each point on its surface is a point on the surface of one of the blocks; we know that its mass is the sum of the masses of the thirty-five blocks; we know that it fits exactly into the region of space that is collectively occupied by the thirty-five blocks. And if we know all these things, then, surely, we know *what object it is* that the blocks compose. We know about the blocks individually; we know how they are arranged; we know that in virtue of this arrangement the blocks compose exactly one thing; and we know what thing it is. And, really, there isn't anything more to know about the composition of a certain object by the blocks. If we are allowed to assume the correctness of *Contact* and *Uniqueness*, then looking carefully at the blocks and the step-pyramidal thing, we see *what* relation it is that holds between the blocks and the pyramid in virtue of the fact that the blocks are in contact."

I would reply by asking another question. "Why do you suppose that, if the blocks compose a unique object in virtue of their being arranged as they are in the figure, then this object has the properties you have listed? Why do you suppose that it is step-pyramidal in shape and so on?" And, I expect, the answer would be that one who has been supposing these things has been supposing them on the basis of certain rather obvious "principles of composition," principles, that is, that govern the ways in which the properties of a composite object are determined by the properties of and the relations that hold among its parts. Here are three plausible principles of composition; there are obviously many more. We should note that these principles do not presuppose *Uniqueness*, and presuppose neither *Contact* nor any other answer to the Special Composition Question.

If each of the xs has a surface and the xs compose y, then y has a surface and the surface area of y is less than or equal to the sum of the surface areas of the xs.

If each of the xs has a mass and the xs compose y, then y has a mass and the mass of y is the sum of the masses of the xs.

If each of the xs occupies a region of space and the xs compose y, then y occupies the sum of the regions occupied by the xs.[17]

Now, the "vague sense of unease" I have attempted to articulate is one I myself felt at one time; I have reproduced it to the best of my ability because I suspect it may strike a responsive chord in some readers. It now seems to me to be based partly on insight and partly on a red herring. The insight is this: An answer to the General Composition Question must have a great deal to do with "principles of composition," with the ways in which the properties of a composite object are determined by the properties of and the relations among its parts. The red herring is this: the assumption that the General Composition Question would somehow be easier if *Uniqueness* were true.

In order to appreciate both the insight and the herring, let us try to say something systematic and general about how a knowledge of the correct principles of composition might help us to answer the General Composition Question. We want to find a sentence (one containing no mereological vocabulary) that is equivalent to 'the xs compose y', a sentence, of course, in which both 'the xs' and 'y' are free. Suppose a careful study of certain principles of composition enabled us to discover a "composition function," that is, a multigrade function f which took properties as values and which could be specified without employing any mereological concepts and which was such that, for any xs, y had f(the xs) if and only if the xs composed y. A composition function f would immediately provide us with an answer to the General Composition Question, an answer of the form

The xs compose y if and only if y has f(the xs).

If there is no other strategy than this for approaching the General Composition Question—and *I* can certainly think of no other—then *Uniqueness* is a red herring for students of the General Composition Question. It will either be possible for there to be xs such that f(the xs) is had by two or more things at the same time, or it won't. In the former case *Uniqueness* will be false, and in the latter case, true. But we need not suppose that it is true in order to attempt to discover a general way of determining, for any xs, a property that an object has if and only if the xs compose it, and it is hard to see why adopting *Uniqueness* as a working assumption at the outset of our attempt would be even a promising stratagem.

Do the principles of composition listed above help us to discover a way of determining, for any xs, a property had by y if and only if the xs compose y? It is very doubtful whether the first two of them could be of much help in this endeavor. Suppose that the xs compose y; it will probably be true, and certainly *could* be true, that there will be many objects wholly unrelated to y and the xs that have the same surface area as y or the same mass as y. The first two principles, therefore, will not enable us to find, for any xs, a property had by y *only if* the xs compose y.

The third principle—call it *Summation*—is more promising, since it is at least plausible to suppose that an object that occupies the same space as y will not be "wholly unrelated" to y and its parts. (Of course, we shall certainly not be able to make any use of *Summation* if anything has parts that do not occupy space. Let us assume for the sake of argument that every part of everything occupies, at any moment, a certian region of space.) But *Summation* is not by itself sufficient to enable us to find, for any xs, a composition property on those xs. It may be "plausible to suppose" that an object that occupies the same space as y will not be wholly unrelated to y—that is, will bear some interesting relations to y besides spatial relations—but it is not a truth of logic. If *Summation* is to help us to find an answer to the General Composition Question, *Summation* will have to be supplemented with some principle that specifies some mereological connection between spatially coincident objects. The following principle seems to me to be the most promising:

> If each of the xs occupies a region of space and no two of the xs occupy overlapping regions of space, then the xs compose any object that occupies the sum of the regions of space occupied by the xs.

Let us call this principle *Exclusion*, since it entails that objects behave rather exclusively toward any object they do not compose: The xs prevent any object they do not compose from occupying the region they occupy jointly. *Exclusion* and *Summation* (together with the trivial premise that if y occupies the sum of the regions of space occupied by the xs, then each of the xs occupies a region of space) entail the following answer to the General Composition Question:

> *Composition*   The xs compose y if and only if no two of the xs occupy overlapping regions of space and y occupies the sum of the regions of space occupied by the xs.

The first thing to note about *Composition* is that it seems to have nothing to do with *Contact*, which we have been supposing to be the correct answer to the Special Composition Question. *Composition* could be true if *Contact* were false, and it in no way involves the concept "being in contact." (*Composition*, incidentally, is essentially equivalent to the thesis that x is a part of y if and only if x occupies a part of the region of space occupied by y.)

Now, an adherent of *Contact* who insists on having an answer to the General Composition Question that involves the concept "being in contact" can deduce one from *Composition* and *Contact*:

> The xs compose y if and only if y occupies the sum of the regions of space occupied by the xs and the xs are in contact.

(The right-hand constituent of this biconditional need not contain 'no two of the xs occupy overlapping regions of space', since this sentence follows by definition from 'the xs are in contact'.)

To regard this proposition, which I shall label *Composition/Contact*, as a better answer than *Composition* to the General Composition Question is analogous to regarding 'y is a reciprocal of $x \leftrightarrow .y$ is a result of dividing 1 by x & x is a number other than 0' as a better answer than 'y is a reciprocal of $x \leftrightarrow y$ is a result of dividing 1 by x' to the question, What is it for something to be a reciprocal of a given number? It is not clear to me in what sense, if any, either of the more elaborate answers is "better" than the corresponding simpler answer.

However this may be, we have a biconditional that satisfies the formal requirements for being an answer to the General Composition Question, and we have a second biconditional which also satisfies these requirements and which can be deduced from the first and our illustrative answer to the Special Composition Question, *Contact*. (By the same device, we could obviously deduce an answer to the General Composition Question from *Composition* and any given answer to the Special Composition Question; and just as *Composition/Contact* involves the concept "being in contact," so the answer to the General Composition Question that we thereby arrived at would involve the "central" concept of that answer to the Special Composition Question.) It is obvious that any answer to the General Composition Question will "automatically" yield an answer to the Special Composition Question—by existential generalization, as it were. (More exactly, by an analogue in the logic of plural quantification of the valid inference form, $Fxy \leftrightarrow Gxy \vdash \exists yFxy. \leftrightarrow \exists yGxy$.) Corresponding to *Composition* and *Composition/Contact*, we have two answers to the Special Composition Question:

($\exists y$ the xs compose y) if and only if $\exists y$ y occupies the sum of the regions of space occupied by the xs and no two of the xs occupy overlapping regions of space.

($\exists y$ the xs compose y) if and only if $\exists y$ y occupies the sum of the regions of space occupied by the xs and the xs are in contact.

It is interesting to note that the second of these answers is not *Contact*; moreover, *Contact* can be deduced from it only with the aid of a non-trivial premise, to wit, that if the xs are in contact, then something occupies the sum of the regions of space they occupy individually. (*Contact* itself, of course, is not of the right logical form to be derivable "by existential generalization" from any answer to the General Composition Question.) The lesson is: Although any answer to the General Composition Question automatically provides an answer to the Special Composition Question, the answer it provides will not necessarily be the best or most interesting or most informative answer to the Special Composition Question—not even if that answer to the General Composition Question is the best and most interesting and most informative answer to the General Composition Question. And that should not be too surprising. 'y is a reciprocal of $x \leftrightarrow y$ is a result of dividing 1 by x' entails '$\exists y$ y is a reciprocal of $x. \leftrightarrow \exists y$ y is a result of dividing 1 by x'; but this is in an obvious sense a less interesting answer to the question, Which numbers have reciprocals? than is '$\exists y$ y is a reciprocal of $x. \leftrightarrow x$ is a number other than 0'.

Is there any particular reason to want an answer to the General Composition Question that involves the central, essential concepts of the best and most interesting and most informative answer to the Special Composition Question (in the sense in which "being in contact" is the "central and essential" concept of *Contact*; and in the sense in which *Contact* would be—if only it were true—a better, more interesting, and more informative answer to the Special Composition Question than the answer to that question formed by supplying both sides of *Composition* with existential quantifiers)? I think not. But the names '*General* Composition Question' and '*Special* Composition Question' may suggest that there is such a reason. They may suggest that the best answer to the question, When does composition occur? should somehow be a special case of or should somehow "fall out of" the best answer to the question, What is composition? (No one is denying, of course, that the best answer to the Special Composition Question might be deductible from the best answer to the General Composition Question *and* certain nontrivial and intuitive supplementary premises. Here is a model for such a deduction:

Contact can be derived from *Composition* and the premise 'Something occupies the sum of the regions of space occupied by the xs if and only if the xs are in contact'. Perhaps, in the case of some answers to the two questions, the corresponding premise will be an interesting one—as 'Something is a result of dividing 1 by x if and only if x is a number other than 0' is an interesting mathematical statement.)

The appeal of this suggestion can be undermined by reflection on the implications of the fact that 'the xs compose y' contains not one but two bindable variables. This means that the General Composition Question may be thought of as "general" in relation to not one but two questions about "when composition occurs." One, of course, is the Special Composition Question, which, for present purposes, we might informally paraphrase like this: In which cases is it true of *certain objects* that *they* compose something? But there is also the question, In which cases is it true of *an object* that there are objects that compose *it*? (More exactly: '. . . there are objects that *properly* compose it?' Even if an object has no proper parts, it is true of that object that the things identical with that object compose it.) That is to say, Which objects are composite? We may call this question the Inverse Special Composition Question. To answer the Special Composition Question would be to find a suitable replacement for '∃y the xs compose y', a sentence containing a free plural variable. To answer the Inverse Special Composition Question would be to find a suitable replacement for 'For some xs, the xs properly compose y', a sentence containing a free singular variable. (Without the qualification 'properly', the sentence '$y = y$' would be a "suitable replacement.")

An answer to the Special Composition Question would not automatically supply us with an answer to the Inverse Special Composition Question. One cannot deduce from

$$\exists y\ Fxy. \leftrightarrow Gx$$

anything of the form

$$\exists x\ Fxy. \leftrightarrow \phi$$

unless ϕ contains 'F' and an existentially bound variable in the 'x'-place. And the corresponding logical fact (the one expressed by replacing 'x' by 'the xs' and '∃x' by 'For some xs' in this schema) holds for the logic of plural quantification.

Now suppose, for the sake of illustration, that *Contact* is a right (and the best) answer to the Special Composition Question. Does this provide us with any reason to think that the best answer to the Inverse Special

Composition Question must involve the concept "being in contact"? The logical fact cited in the preceding paragraph strongly hints that that supposition provides us with no such reason. One can without too much difficulty propose an answer to the Inverse Special Composition Question that involves contact. In fact, such an answer—call it *Inverse Contact*—follows by plural existential generalization (an inexact characterization), and a little fiddling to deal with the need to introduce a reference to *proper* composition, from the answer to the General Composition Question that we have called *Composition/Contact*:

(For some xs, the xs properly compose y) if and only if, for some xs, the xs are two or more and are in contact and y occupies the sum of the regions of space occupied by the xs.

But *Inverse Contact* does not follow from *Contact*. (Suppose that there are two spatially coincident objects, one of which is simple and the other of which is composite, that have no parts in common. This supposition is consistent with *Contact* but inconsistent with *Inverse Contact*.)

There would seem, therefore, to be no reason to suppose that the "best" answer to the Inverse Special Composition Question must involve any of the concepts that play a central role in the "best" answer to the Special Composition Question. But the General Composition Question is no more intimately related to one of the two special questions than to the other. (If we wished to have a terminology that was wholly devoid of a tendency to suggest otherwise, we might call the two special questions the Plural Special Composition Question and the Singular Special Composition Question.) *Composition* is *an* answer to the General Composition Question. Suppose, for the sake of illustration, that *Contact* is the best answer to the Special Composition Question. This would seem to provide us with no particular reason for doubting that *Composition* is as good an answer to the General Composition Question as there is, despite the fact that it does not involve the concept "being in contact"; after all, the General Composition Question is "general" in relation to the Inverse Special Composition Question in the same sense as that in which it is "general" in relation to the Special Composition Question. And, for all we know, the best answer to the Inverse Special Composition does *not* involve contact. (Exercise for the reader: Show that having answers to both of the special questions would not provide an answer to the General Composition Question.)

Composition, therefore, for all we have said, may be a correct, and even the best, answer to the General Composition Question. Unfortunately, it is not at all clear that *Composition* is *true*. A counterexample to *Composi-*

tion is suggested by the sort of case that was used above to show that *Inverse Contact* does not follow from *Contact*, the case of spatially coincident objects. Let us say a bit to flesh out this notion and make it plausible. Suppose that there are two types of matter, A and B, that interact only very weakly. They interact so weakly that an object made of matter of type A can occupy exactly the same region of space as a "duplicate" object made of matter of type B. (The weakness of the interaction accounts for the fact that we, who are made of B, haven't noticed any of the objects of type A.) If this much is possible, then, surely, it is possible for there to be two spatially coincident composite objects, *a* and *b*, made, respectively, entirely of A and entirely of B. But this possibility is inconsistent with *Composition* (and with *Exclusion*, from which, together with the very plausible principle *Summation, Composition* was derived.) In showing this, we shall assume that if an object is entirely made of a certain stuff (butter, steel, matter of type A), then each of its parts is made of that stuff. But that's all right, for that principle is pretty evidently true. (At any rate, it's pretty evidently true if we count as 'parts' only objects large enough to be made of that stuff. A vase may be made entirely of clay and have a part—an atom, say—that is not made of clay. But we may assume that our quantification over parts *is* so restricted, and that *a* and *b* are not only composite, but that each is composed of certain objects large enough to be made of matter of type A and matter of type B.) *Composition* entails that if the xs compose *a*, then, since *b* occupies the same region of space as *a*, they also compose *b*. But, since there *are* xs that compose *a*, *b* has parts—any of those xs—that are made of A. And hence *b* is not made entirely of B, *contra hyp*. (Exercise: Show that both *Exclusion* and *Composition* entail that *a* is a part of *b* and *b* is a part of *a*. Hint: *b* occupies the sum of the regions of space occupied by the things identical with *a*. Note that it is generally taken to be a formal truth about parthood that if x is a part of y and y is a part of x, then x and y are identical. Hence, if *Exclusion* or *Composition* were true, there could not be distinct, spatially coincident objects. But the force of this argument can be evaded by tinkering with *Exclusion* and *Composition*, so I do not appeal to it.)

It may, of course, be that spatially coincident objects are metaphysically impossible. But that they are impossible is a substantive metaphysical thesis and should not, therefore, be "built into" what is essentially an explanation of parthood. We have, therefore, failed to find an answer to the General Composition Question. I see *no* way of approaching this question other than the way we have followed and which has proved to be a cul-de-sac (that is, by working from the assumption that any object that occupies the region of space jointly occupied by the xs is such that, if the xs do not overlap spatially, the xs compose it). I am inclined to think that there is no way of answering the General Composition Question. I am inclined to think that the concepts "part," "sum," and "compose" form what (by analogy to "the modal circle" or "the moral circle") one might call 'the mereological circle', a closed family of concepts. Although we have employed only one sort of concept—spatial—in the course of our attempt to answer the General Composition Question, we may risk a general conclusion. The problem we have come up against is strongly analogous to the problems one comes up against if one tries to give an "external" account of modal or moral (or existential or spatial or temporal) concepts. Suppose someone claims to have found what we earlier called a composition function, f. Couldn't a skeptic meet any such claim with a version of the "open-question argument"? Couldn't the skeptic say, "Yes, I admit that, for any xs, whatever the xs compose will have f(the xs). But I think I can imagine an object which is *not* one of the things the xs compose and which also has f(the xs)"? (Compare: Yes, I admit that, for any xs, whatever the xs compose will have the property *occupying the sum of the regions of space the xs occupy.* But I think I can imagine an object which is *not* one of the things the xs compose and which also has that property.)

This, however, is speculation. What I am sure of is that *I* know of no way to answer, or even to approach, the General Composition Question.

5. *What We Shall Not Presuppose

In this section I will list several very general theses about composition that we shall not presuppose in our investigations (and a few that we shall). By saying that we shall not presuppose these theses, I mean that we shall not regard them as self-evident truths, and that any appeal to them must be justified, or, at least, not allowed to pass unnoticed. (And it is easy for an appeal to these theses to pass unnoticed in a discussion of parts and wholes.)

Although this is evident from what has already been said, I mention for the sake of completeness that we shall not presuppose that for just any xs those xs have a sum. In fact, in Section 8, I shall attempt to show that there are xs that have no sum. Certain formal systems (descended either from Lesniewski's "mereology" or the Leonard-Goodman "Calculus of Individuals") include among their axioms something very much like 'For any xs, those xs have a sum'.[18] These formal systems express, on their intended interpretations, substantive metaphysical theories. If the central theses of this book are correct, these theories are false.

We shall not presuppose that any material object has noncomposite parts ("simples" or "mereological atoms"), nor shall we presuppose the denial of this thesis.

We shall not presuppose *Uniqueness*. This thesis is controversial. According to some philosophers it is possible for certain objects simultaneously to compose two or more distinct objects. Such a position was briefly mentioned in Section 2. The advocates of that position maintain that certain gold atoms might simultaneously compose a golden statue and a statue-shaped lump of gold, these two things being numerically distinct in virtue of the fact that the statue could not survive certain radical changes in the arrangement of its constituent atoms that the lump of gold could survive.

Uniqueness follows from the Principle of the Identity of Indiscernibles, together with the principle that the properties of a composite object are completely determined by the properties of its parts. More exactly, *Uniqueness* follows from (1) the principle that numerically distinct objects must differ either in their intrinsic or their relational properties, and (2) the principle that, for any xs, if the xs compose an object, then both the intrinsic and the relational properties of that object are completely determined by the intrinsic and relational properties of the xs. Anyone who denies *Uniqueness*, therefore, must deny one or the other of these principles. It is easy to see that those philosophers who hold that certain gold atoms simultaneously compose the statue and the lump must deny (2): Although the same atoms compose both the statue and the lump, the lump has the (intrinsic) property *can survive radical deformation* and the statue lacks this property.

Uniqueness also follows from two theorems of the Calculus of Individuals (CI), theorems embodying theses about parthood that one might be inclined to accept even if one rejected the very strong "automatic summation" principle that is such a salient feature of CI:

T1 $\forall z(z$ overlaps $x \rightarrow z$ overlaps $y) \rightarrow x$ is a part of y

T2 x is a part of y & y is a part of $x. \rightarrow x = y$

For let x and y each be a sum of the zs. Suppose w overlaps x; then w overlaps one of the zs; but then w overlaps y. Similarly, whatever overlaps y overlaps x. Hence, by T1, x is a part of y and y is a part of x. Hence, by T2, x and y are identical, and *Uniqueness* is proved. The enemies of *Uniqueness* must, therefore, reject T1 or T2. T1 is the one for them to reject. For example, those who believe that the statue is distinct from the lump should concede that whatever shares a part with the statue shares a part with the lump but deny that the statue is a part of the lump. The proposal to "reject" T1 is complicated by the fact that, in developments of CI in which 'overlaps' is the mereological primitive—normally, either 'overlaps' or 'is discrete from' is the primitive—the biconditional corresponding to T1 is given as the *definition* of 'part of', and the sentence 'x overlaps $y \leftrightarrow \exists z$ (z is a part of x & z is a part of y)', or something equivalent to it, is included among the axioms of the system. But consider CI*, which is like CI except that 'part of' is the mereological primitive, and the definition and the axiom "change places." CI and CI* are obviously equivalent systems. (CI* seems to me to be much more "natural" than CI, for, although one can acquire the concept of parthood without first acquiring the concept of overlapping, one can acquire the concept of overlapping only via the concept of parthood. In fact, I think something stronger is true: In Chisholm's terminology,[19] one can "conceive" parthood without conceiving overlapping, but one cannot conceive overlapping with conceiving parthood.) The enemies of *Uniqueness* can make their proposal—to reject T1—in relation to CI* without appearing to be in the position of "rejecting" a mere stipulative definition.

We shall not presuppose that if the xs compose y at some time, then the xs compose y at all times at which y exists. That is, we shall not presuppose that an object cannot change some of its parts—or even all of its proper parts—with the passage of time.

We shall not presuppose that if the xs compose y at some time, then the xs compose y at any time at which the xs compose anything. We shall not presuppose that it is impossible for certain objects to compose one thing at one time and another at another time. (This thesis should not be confused with *Uniqueness*, which is the thesis that it is impossible for any objects to compose two things at the *same* time.) Nor shall we presuppose that if the xs compose y at t, then they compose y at any time at which they are arranged just as they are at t. Nor shall we presuppose that if the xs compose *something* at t, then they compose *something* at any time at which they are arranged just as they are at t.

We shall not presuppose that if the xs compose a material object, then any of the xs is a material object. My cat, perhaps, is composed of electrons, quarks, photons, and gluons. And perhaps none of these things can be described as a material object "without some risk of terminological inexactitude."

We shall not presuppose that if the xs compose y at some time, then the xs compose y at some time (or even that some of the xs and various other objects compose y at some time) in every possible world in which y exists. Thus, we do not rule out a priori the possibility that in some possible worlds the cup on my table have been composed of entirely different atoms from the atoms that in fact compose it.

There are, however, a *few* theses about parthood and composition which, in my view, we may take to be self-evident and which we can justifiably allow to function as suppressed premises in our arguments. For example, I think that we are justified in taking the three principles of composition listed on p. 44 to be self-evident. And I would suppose it to be self-evident that if x is a part of y at a given moment, then x and y both exist at that moment.

In addition to these theses about the metaphysics of parthood and composition—theses, that is, that involve not only logical and mereological concepts but also concepts belonging to neither of these categories—we shall presuppose some theses about the logic or the formal features of parthood and composition—theses which involve only logical and mereological concepts, and which, or so I contend, ought to be common to all metaphysical theories about parthood and composition:

—Parthood is transitive.
(This principle entails the converse of T1 but does not entail T1.)

—No two things are parts of each other.
(It is, of course, true by definition that everything is a part of itself.)

—If x is a proper part of y, there are zs (none of which is x) such that x and the zs compose y.
(But we shall *not* suppose that if x is a proper part of y, then there is a z such that x and z compose y.)

—If the xs have a sum and the xs are among the ys, then every sum of the ys has a sum of the xs as a part.

(Some of these we have already appealed to.) If, in these four sentences, we replace 'is a part of' with 'is a subset of' and 'sum' with 'union' (and replace 'compose' appropriately), we obtain four truths of set theory. Therefore, these four sentences are logically consistent if set theory is— in fact, if the Boolean theory of classes is. I believe, but I have not tried to prove, that none of the four can be deduced from the other three. I have no idea whether some or all of the four could be deduced from some more fundamental statements that (unlike 'For any xs, those xs have a sum') I should be willing to endorse. I do not claim that these four statements suffice for the deduction of the whole set of formal truths about parthood and composition. Indeed, I am far from clear about what those truths are. Here, for example, is a statement I regard as problematic: 'if y and z are both sums of the xs and are not identical, then there is nothing of which y and z are both parts'. I conjecture that this statement cannot be deduced from the four statements listed above. It is a theorem of the Calculus of Individuals, since the falsity of its antecedent is deducible in CI. I am inclined to think that it should be accepted even by one who rejected *Uniqueness*. (If the statue and the lump are distinct sums of the same gold atoms, could there be something that had both the statue and the lump as parts—have *they* a sum, for example? Is the top half of the lump a part of the statue?) But I have no firm convictions about what is true if *Uniqueness* is false.

However this may be, the arguments of this book will not require any formal truths about parthood besides the four listed above.

In the next two sections we shall return to the Special Composition Question and examine four answers to it, answers I believe to be incorrect.

6. Answers to the Special Composition Question According to Which Composition Occurs When Some Type of Physical Bonding Occurs

Answer (ii) *Fastening*

To get the χs to compose something, one need only cause them to be fastened to one another.

To separate two normal, middle-sized material objects that are in contact, one need often do no more than apply to one of them a force that would have sufficed to move it if it had not been in contact with the other. Contact is therefore typically a highly unstable relation, a fact that may lead one who reflects on it to the conclusion that objects that have simply been brought into contact have not really been *joined*. More generally and abstractly, one may be led to the conclusion that if the χs are to compose an object, then the arrangement of the χs should be one of the more stable among the possible arrangements of the χs. If a rather small force could radically change the positions of the χs relative to one another, then one might be inclined to say that the χs did not compose anything; if the *direction* in which an impulse of a given magnitude was applied to one of the χs were largely immaterial to whether that impulse would radically change the disposition of the χs, then one might be inclined to say that the χs did not compose anything.

Suppose that two objects are in contact and suppose that they are so arranged that, among all the many sequences in which forces of arbitrary directions and magnitudes might be applied to either or both of them, *at most only a few* would be capable of separating them without breaking or permanently deforming or otherwise damaging either of them. Then let us say that these two objects are *fastened to each other* or simply *fastened*. (If we know what it is for two objects to be fastened to each other, then we can easily give a general explanation of what it is for the χs to be fastened to one another. We need only employ the device that was used in Section 3 to define 'the xs are in contact'.) For example, if a nut is threaded onto a bolt, then the nut and bolt are fastened, since most ways of applying force to the nut or to the bolt or to both would not suffice to remove the nut from the bolt; most ways of applying force would produce no movement of either, or else would cause them to move as a unit. A house, a structure built of Tinkertoy parts, and a watch are examples of things that are built up largely by successively fastening things to one another—at least, assuming that there are such objects as these things and their parts. A watch is unlike a house of blocks in that an arbitrarily applied force will almost certainly not cause the watch to come apart (unless, of course, the force is great enough actually to cause something to break), whereas a force great enough to move any of the blocks composing a house of blocks "separately" will quite possibly cause the house of blocks to disintegrate. One can toss a watch about, but one cannot toss a house of blocks about.

Now the concept of "fastening" is pretty vague, and my attempts to explain it could probably be improved upon. One source of this vagueness and unsatisfactoriness is the notion of "only a few among all the possible ways of applying forces to a thing." It would not be difficult to devise some set-theoretical constructions to play the parts of "ways of applying forces" to a thing. And if these objects were constructed in any standard or obvious way, the cardinality of, for example, the set of ways of applying forces to a nut and a bolt that would unthread the nut from the bolt would be just the cardinality of the whole set of ways of applying forces to the nut and the bolt.[20] (Still, there seems to be something to this idea. Consider the ill-named notion of a "child-proof cap." Isn't what differentiates a child-proof cap from a garden-variety cap the fact that comparatively few of the ways of applying force to a child-proof cap will suffice to remove it from its bottle?) But there would be no point in trying to provide a better account of fastening, for it does not seem to be true that if two things become fastened there must at that moment come into existence a new object which has them both as parts, an object which occupies all the space that they individually occupy and which wouldn't have existed if they had merely come into contact. I think we can find perfectly clear cases of two objects' becoming fastened, cases that ought to be allowed by any reasonable way of spelling out the concept of fastening, that are simply not cases of anything's coming to be. Suppose again that you and I shake hands. We have already agreed that it would be wrong to suppose that our coming into contact in this way would result in the existence of a new object, one that you and I compose. Now, suppose that the fingers of our hands were suddenly to become paralyzed, with the embarrassing consequence that we were unable to let go of each other. Suppose that, in fact, because of the paralysis of our entwined fingers, it had become impossible for anyone to pull us apart by main force, short of doing us damage. On any reasonable account, then, we have suddenly become fastened to each other. But it is certainly not true that an object composed of you and me comes into existence at the instant our fingers became paralyzed. Our paralysis has not added to the furniture of earth; it has merely diminished its capacity to be re-arranged. Therefore, composition is not, primarily, a matter of things being fastened to one another. This is not to say that there may not be some cases in which certain things come to compose something at the moment they become fastened to one another; it is to say that the mere fact that they have become fastened is not a complete explanation of the generation of a new thing that is their sum.

Answer (iii) *Cohesion*

. . . one need only cause them to cohere.

Objects that are merely fastened to one another can often be separated by one who knows how without breaking anything. It is, of course, possible to join objects so that they can't be pulled apart, or even moved in relation to one another, without breaking some of them. One might, for example, glue two blocks of wood together, using a glue the particles of which attract particles of wood more strongly than particles of wood attract one another. (Perhaps the layer of dried glue is a third object. In that case we have three objects joined in this fashion.) Or one might weld two pieces of metal together. We might say that in such cases one causes objects to *cohere*. If one causes two things to cohere, does one thereby cause a new object to come into being, an object which they compose and which would not have existed if they had merely been in contact or had merely been fastened to each other? It would seem not. Suppose once more that you and I shake hands, this time after I have smeared my hand with one of those glues whose manufacturers warn us that they "bond skin instantly." No new thing comes to be in the course of our consequent painful adventure.

Answer (iv) *Fusion*

. . . one need only cause them to fuse.

Between objects that have been caused merely to cohere, there is a discernible boundary: a welding seam, say, or a layer of dried glue. It is possible to cause objects to be joined more intimately than this, so that they melt into each other in a way that leaves no discoverable boundary. If two very smooth pieces of chemically pure metal are brought together, for example, they become attached to each other in just this intimate way. (Such an event could scarcely occur outside a laboratory. Under normal conditions, each of the pieces of metal would almost immediately acquire a coating of its oxide, and these coatings would be thick and irregular enough to prevent the pieces' being brought into effective contact.) Let us say that if two things are caused to "merge" in this way, they become *fused* or that they *fuse*. (N.B.: in some discussions of parts and wholes, 'y is a fusion of the xs' is used to mean what I mean by 'y is a sum of the xs'.) Is the fusion of two or more objects a sufficient condition for their beginning to compose something? No. Consider Alice and Beatrice, who are identical twins. A mad surgeon cuts off Alice's left hand and Beatrice's right hand and joins their stumps together, so that they look rather as if they were part of a chain of paper dolls. The surgeon thus produces what might be described as a case of artificial Siamese twins. It is at least theoretically possible that the anatomy of Alice's wrist be so nearly an exact match to the anatomy of Beatrice's wrist, and the healing of one to the other be so nearly perfect, that no boundary between Alice and Beatrice be discoverable; it may be that there is a region such that there is simply no answer to the question whether the cells in that region are Alice's cells or Beatrice's cells. And yet, it seems to me, it is quite unreasonable to say that our mad surgeon has, like Dr. Frankenstein, created a new being by causing parts of existing beings to fuse. (Perhaps Dr. Frankenstein's success was due to his using only *proper* parts of existing beings.) Despite the fact that they are fused and separable only by surgery or sheer brutality, there is nothing but Alice and Beatrice (and such undetached parts as they may have) *there*: If R_A is the region of space that Alice fits just exactly into and R_B is the region of space that Beatrice fits just exactly into, there is no *one* thing that fits just exactly into the region of space that is the sum of R_A and R_B. That is, despite their fusion, nothing is such that Alice and Beatrice compose it. Or, at least, if Alice and Beatrice compose something, this is not *in virtue of* their fusion. It may, of course, be, as we noted in our discussion of *Contact*, that any two nonoverlapping objects "automatically" compose something. We shall consider that possibility in Section 8. But if Alice and Beatrice of necessity compose some object at every moment at which they exist, then, surely, they always compose the same object. (Though this seems evident enough, it is formally possible to deny it. An analogous possibility was briefly noted in our discussion of *Contact*. We shall discuss this matter more fully in Section 8.) And if, necessarily, Alice and Beatrice always compose the same object, then one could not bring the object they compose into existence by surgically fusing them. *Fusion*, therefore, is not the right answer to the Special Composition Question.

7. *Answers to the Special Composition Question According to Which Composition Occurs When Combinations of Various Types of Physical Bonding Occur

We have so far failed to find an answer to the Special Composition Question. We have been looking for an answer along one dimension, as it were. Each of our answers has been a sort of strengthening of the previous one. We seem to have gone as far as we can in this direction. No answer to the Special Composition Question could be a strengthening of *Fusion*, for that answer is a limit point. The right answer must be of another sort. (There is another consideration that can be brought against our four answers. The concepts they involve—contact, fastening, cohesion, and fusion—can be distinguished from one another only in application to "moderate-sized specimens of dry goods" and objects not much larger or smaller than these, such as small planetoids and large molecules. It would make no sense to appeal to this fourfold distinction in discussions of stars or nucleons.)

We may describe the four answers to the Special Composition Question that we have considered and rejected as *Simple Bonding* answers, owing to the fact that each of them entails that there is *one* multigrade bonding relation such that, for any objects, those objects compose something when and only when they instantiate that bonding relation. (To put things this way, we have to count mere contact as a sort of degenerate case of bonding, bonding of degree 0, as it might be.) All Simple Bonding answers have the consequence that it is possible for there to be objects that compose something and also possible for there to be objects that compose nothing; or, more exactly, that it is possible for there to be objects that *properly* compose something and also possible for there to be *disjoint* objects that compose nothing. We may call any answer to the Special Composition Question that has this feature *Moderate*. In addition to whatever Moderate answers there may be, there are two other possible answers, which I shall label *Extreme*: (1) it is not possible for there to be objects that properly compose something, and (2) it is not possible for there to be disjoint objects that compose nothing. The Extreme answers are obviously radically different from Simple Bonding answers, since if either Extreme answer is right, composition has nothing whatever to do with physical bonding, or, indeed, with any causal relation. We shall examine the two Extreme answers in Section 8. In Section 9 I shall propose my own answer to the Special Composition Question, which, despite the fact that it is Moderate, is also radically different from any Simple Bonding answer.

Before we leave the subject of bonding, however, let us ask what possibilities this concept may suggest for an answer to the Special Composition Question beyond the four we have considered. There are, of course, other bonding relations than those I have discussed. But I think it should be reasonably clear that any answer to the Special Composition Question that is of the form

($\exists y$ the χs compose y) if and only if the χs stand in R,

where R is a multigrade bonding relation, will have counterexamples involving human beings. Any bonding relation that can hold between any two moderate-sized specimens of dry goods can (I should think) hold between two human beings, and it is pretty clear that one cannot bring a composite object into existence by bonding two human beings— or two living organisms of any sort[21]—to each other. And the corresponding thesis about any number of human beings would also seem to be true.

But it does not follow that a correct answer to the Special Composition Question cannot be constructed around some notion of bonding. Consider the possibility of an answer of this form:

($\exists y$ the χs compose y) if and only if

the χs are all Fs and the χs stand in R.

Here is a thesis of this sort, one that was perhaps held by the Greek atomists:

Democ   ($\exists y$ the χs compose y) if and only if

the χs are immutable and indestructible objects ("atoms") and the χs are maximally fastened (or there is only one of the χs).

By 'the xs are maximally fastened', we mean that the xs are fastened and there are no ys such that the ys are fastened and the xs are properly among the ys. Thus, if the atom y is fastened to the atom x and the atom z is fastened to y, then x and y are fastened but not maximally fastened. If we had said only 'the xs are fastened', *Democ* would have entailed that an object composed of three atoms had exactly four parts—itself and those three atoms—and also that that object had at least two parts that were composed of two atoms. (The proof is left as an exercise.)[22]

One cannot show that *Democ* is false by pointing out that to fasten two living organisms to each other is not to bring into existence an object that they compose, for living organisms, being mutable and destructible, are not atoms. But I suppose that few philosophers would be willing to accept a thesis that entailed that visible objects had no parts but atoms— even if those "atoms" were not the quaint hook-and-eye affairs of Democritus. Take you, for example. (I mean you *qua* object, not you *qua* philosopher.) Most philosophers, at least if they are materialists, think that you have lots of parts that are not atoms: cells, organs, bones, limbs, genitalia, a head, a brain. . . . Even I, who (it will transpire) do not believe in most of the items in this list, think that you have cells as parts—millions of millions of them.

The quaint Democritean atoms featured in *Democ* could no doubt be replaced with something more up to date, and "fastening" could (no doubt) be dispensed with in favor of some bonding relation that will not become quaint in the near future. But an up-to-date version of *Democ* that had the consequence that visible material objects had no proper parts but, say, quarks and leptons and bosons would be no more acceptable to the generality of philosophers than *Democ*, and considerably less charming to boot. But perhaps we can avoid this consequence and yet preserve the two "nice" features of *Democ*: (1) its immunity to counterexamples that turn on the bonding of living organisms, and (2) its nonarbitrariness—that is, its avoidance of ad hoc clauses excluding living organisms from the field of the multigrade bonding relation to which it appeals.

We might try to do this by postulating a sequence or hierarchy of multigrade bonding relations, $R_1, R_2, \ldots R_n$, each of which can, for certain relata, but not all relata, be the relation that binds those relata together to form a composite object. More formally, we could try to do this by constructing an answer to the Special Composition Question that is of this form:

Series: ($\exists y$ the xs compose y) if and only if

the xs are F_1 and stand in R_1, or the xs are F_2 and stand in R_2, or . . . , or the xs are F_n and stand in R_n.

Consider, for example, a simple universe that contains just three kinds of material object: "particles," which have no proper parts, "atoms," which are composed of particles, and "molecules," which are composed of atoms and which are not themselves proper parts of anything. This simple universe has a feature, we may note, that is incompatible with the truth of any answer to the Special Composition Question that has a logical structure like that of *Democ*: It contains objects some of whose proper parts have proper parts. Let us further suppose that particles compose something when and only when they are maximally "P-bonded," and that atoms compose something when and only when they are maximally "A-bonded," where P-bonding and A-bonding are some multigrade relations of physical bonding. (The xs are *maximally* P-bonded if they are P-bonded and there are no ys such that the xs are properly among the ys and the ys are P-bonded; and similarly for maximal A-bonding.)

One would initially be inclined to suppose that it would be easy to write out a *Series*-style answer to the Special Composition Question that holds in this simple universe. One might propose something like this:

($\exists y$ the xs compose y) if and only if

the xs are particles and are maximally P-bonded or the xs are atoms and are maximally A-bonded (or there is only one of the xs).

But this proposal would face two grave logical difficulties, which I shall call the circularity difficulty and the transitivity difficulty.

First, the circularity difficulty. The right-hand constituent of our proposal contains the word 'atom'. And what does 'atom' mean (in respect of our imaginary universe) if not 'object composed of particles'—and what does 'particle' mean if not 'object without proper parts'? And the right-hand constituent of an answer to the Special Composition Question may not contain 'part' or 'compose' or any other mereological term.

Now, we might be lucky with our simple universe. It might be that it is in some very strong sense impossible for anything but particles to be P-bonded and impossible for anything but atoms to be A-bonded. Then we could replace the right-hand constituent of the above proposal with

the xs are maximally P-bonded or the xs are maximally A-bonded (or there is only one of the xs).

But *this* proposal is not really an instance of *Series*. We might just as well call the logical sum of the two bonding relations 'bonding' and write

the xs are maximally bonded (or there is only one of the xs).

We should remember why the prospect of a *Series*-style answer to the Special Composition Question is attractive. It is attractive because it is plausible to suppose, for example, that Tinkertoy parts may compose something in virtue of their being fastened, but that human beings cannot compose anything in virtue of being fastened—although they can be fastened. More generally, a *Series*-style answer to the Special Composition Question is interesting only if it is "irreducible": only if it cannot be reduced to a Simple Bonding answer by taking the logical sum of all the bonding relations it involves. And a *Series*-style answer *will* be reducible unless some of the bonding relations it involves have this feature: it is possible for them to relate things that, despite their being so related, do not compose anything. Our problem, then, is this: An answer of the *Series*-type must either involve words that function as 'atom' does in the above example, or else not. In the former case, mereological concepts are present in the right-hand constituent, and they ought not to be; in the latter case, the answer is not really of the *Series* type after all. I do not know how to solve this problem.

Now, the transitivity difficulty. Suppose the above biconditional is true. Then parthood is not transitive, for no molecule has a particle as a part. Suppose our simple universe is in fact so simple that it contains just four particles A, B, C, and D. Suppose that A and B are P-bonded and that C and D are P-bonded and that that is all the P-bonding there is. Suppose that A and B thereby compose one atom and that C and D likewise compose one atom and that these two atoms are A-bonded, thereby forming one molecule. Diagrammatically:

Our proposal has the consequence that A is a part of the atom A—B, and that A—B is a part of the molecule, but A is not a part of the molecule. For A to be a proper part of x is for there to be ys other than A such that A and the ys compose x. And for that to be the case (our proposal says), A and those ys must be P-bonded. But A is P-bonded only with B, and, hence, A is a proper part of nothing but the atom A—B.

Perhaps it would be possible to rewrite our proposal so as to save the transitivity of parthood—which is, of course, a nonnegotiable feature of parthood. The major problem to be solved would be the following (or, rather, a generalization of it): In the case displayed in the above diagram, describe a multigrade relation of physical bonding such that A, B, C, and D stand in that relation in virtue of the fact that A and B are P-bonded and C and D are P-bonded and A—B and C—D are A-bonded—*and* describe this relation without using any mereological vocabulary. I do not know whether this can be done. I certainly do not see how to do it.

Because I am unable to solve either the circularity problem or the transitivity problem, I am unable to write out an answer of the *Series* type. Or, better, I am unable to write out an answer to the Special Composition Question that would satisfy the expectations aroused by our rather vague description of what would count as a *Series*-style answer to the Special Composition Question.

Now, my inability to write out an answer of the *Series* type does not constitute a very strong argument against the thesis that the right answer *is* of that type. It may just be that composition is such a complex phenomenon that finding the right answer to the Special Composition Question would require the solution of some very difficult logical problems, ones too difficult for me. Still, it would be *nice* if we could find a "one-tiered" answer to the Special Composition Question—that is, an answer that did not involve the generation of certain composite objects in one way, and the generation of "the rest" out of these in other ways. A one-tiered answer would be nice because it would enable its proponents to avoid all those difficult logical problems. The answer I shall propose in Section 9 is one-tiered.

In addition to the logical problems I have described, there are certain considerations that can be urged against the idea that the right answer to the Special Composition Question is of the *Series* type. I present them in the form of four "remarks."

Remark One

No one has actually provided any answer of this form. Therefore, the thesis that the correct answer to the Special Composition Question may be of the type *Series* is hard to evaluate.

Remark Two

How shall we decide which multigrade bonding relations are to figure in our *Series*-style answer to the Special Composition Question? I can think of only one way. We must first decide what objects we think there are and then try to devise an answer that will generate them. Our answer will therefore be somewhat ad hoc. It would be nice if we had an answer that had something to *tell* us about what objects there were. Moreover, a *Series*-style answer will almost certainly be disgracefully messy, since there are many ways in which the relatively noncomposite objects that make up larger objects are related to each other to compose those larger objects—provided the larger objects exist at all. Suppose we have decided that, among other things, there are atomic nuclei, grains of salt, and stars. Grains of salt, if there *are* really grains of salt—if sodium and chlorine ions bunched together in a certain sort of crystalline structure really *compose* anything—are held together by ionic bonding, which is something entirely unlike what holds many other small, solid objects (diamonds, for example) together. A clause in a *Series*-style answer that generated grains of salt out of sodium and chlorine ions would be easy to write. One could use *Democ* as a model, substituting ionic bonding for fastening. A clause in a *Series*-style answer that generated atomic nuclei would be a more complicated undertaking. It would have to take account of the fact that nuclei are held together by a *balance* between electromagnetic forces—which operate only between the protons—that are trying to push the nucleus apart, and strong nuclear forces—operating both between protons and neutrons—that oppose this tendency. And this leaves out the fact that the strong nuclear force is a residual effect of the forces operating inside the nucleons and holding *their* constituents together, and it leaves out the fact that the strong force doesn't always pull nucleons together, but pushes them apart if they get too close, and it leaves out the fact that neutrons contribute to the holding together of the nucleus in two ways, both by contributing their bit of attractive nuclear force while not contributing any electromagnetic repulsive force, *and* by interposing themselves between the protons, thus keeping the protons at some distance from each other and thereby reducing the repulsive force the protons exert on one another, and it leaves out the weak interactions that are responsible for nuclear decay. . . . What is the point of all this? The point is to underscore the fact that the *logical* structure of nuclear bonding is very complicated indeed: It isn't as if there were some sticky stuff on the protons and neutrons that held them together like a clump of peas coated with honey. (I didn't mention that all these things are in constant motion in quantized orbits and that they exert forces on each other by exchanging little force-carrying particles.) What holds a grain of salt together is relatively simple. We *can* almost think of a grain of salt on the model of a clump of peas and honey (though not quite). Stars, however, are complicated. They are just as complicated as nuclei and their complexity—their *structural* complexity; I am not talking about the content of particular physical laws—is of a different type. A star, like a nucleus, is held together by a balance between repulsion and attraction. The attraction is gravitational. A full explanation of the repulsive force, however, would take us right back into the nucleus. (For I think that it is part of the *essence* of a star—if stars there are—that the radiation pressure that opposes the star's tendency to gravitational collapse has its source in the release of no-longer-needed nuclear binding energy when colliding nuclei fuse in the star's hot core.) Thus, what collectively holds together the atoms, free electrons, and stripped nuclei that make up a star essentially involves what holds those nuclei together individually: If its parts weren't held together in the way *they* were, *it* couldn't be held together in the way it was. More logical complexity.

Would any of this complexity actually have to turn up in the statement of a *Series* answer to the Special Composition Question that allowed the existence of nuclei and stars? Couldn't an answer to the Special Composition Question simply quantify over multigrade bonding relations without actually mentioning any of them, as Davidson's account of causation quantifies over causal laws without mentioning any of them? Perhaps. I don't know. Again, I am hampered by not having an actual proposal of the *Series* type to examine. But even if such an answer could not be devised, this fact would not constitute a refutation of the thesis that the right answer to the Special Composition Question was of the *Series* type—although (if that answer generated all the sorts of material object that common philosophical opinion would put on a list of all the sorts of material object there are), it would probably have the consequence that this answer was so complex that only God could know it. Still, perhaps composition just *is* so complex that only God could write out a necessary truth of the form '$\exists y$ the xs compose y. $\leftrightarrow \phi$', where ϕ contains no mereological vocabulary. It would be nice, however, if someone could actually propose a humanly accessible "Moderate" answer to the Special Composition Question that was not subject to counterexamples involving bonded organisms. The answer I shall propose in Section 9 has this feature.

Remark Three

There is a second way in which *Series*-style answers to the Special Composition Question are ad hoc—or so it seems to me. Let R be a multigrade bonding relation that figures in a certain *Series*-style answer. We have already touched on the point that if this answer is at all interesting, it will entail (together with a few uncontroversial facts) the following two statements:

There are xs which stand in R and which (thereby) compose something.

There are xs which stand in R and which (despite this fact) do not compose anything.

For example, one *Series*-style answer might entail that if inanimate objects are fastened to one another, they thereby compose something, but that if living organisms are fastened to one another, they nevertheless do not compose anything. But what could justify such discrimination? If the operation *fastening* has the power to turn inanimate objects into the parts of a whole, why doesn't this operation have the same power with respect to living organisms? (Living organisms, after all, are material objects and can be fastened in the same sense as that in which inanimate objects can be fastened.) Isn't there a great deal of plausibility in this principle: If there are xs that compose something just in virtue of the fact that they stand in R, then, for any ys, if the ys stand in R, the ys compose something?

Remark Four

Why does a philosopher study material objects? One reason, surely, is this: He sees paradoxes in the homely world of everyday objects. He tells a friend proudly that he still rides the bicycle he was given for Christmas when he was thirteen. But, he reflects, the bicycle has had new wheels and handlebars and pedals . . . in fact, the only part of the bicycle he was given in 1954 that remains is the frame, and that has been straightened after being badly bent. Is it the same bicycle? He certainly doesn't doubt that he would have been right at any given moment in the past quarter-century to say, "This is the same bicycle I had last week," and identity is transitive, isn't it? And these thoughts, since he is a philosopher, lead him to the Ship of Theseus and perhaps create a vertiginous sense of inhabiting a world to which the laws of logic do not apply. And if, like many philosophers, he believes that human beings are material objects, he will be faced with graver questions: Is a severed head kept alive and cheerily chattering now the person whose head it used to be? What about a brain? How do people (if they are material objects) manage to retain their identities through a complete replacement of the atoms that compose them?

What a philosopher would *like* is an answer to the Special Composition Question that would at least shed some light on these ancient puzzles. I do not think he will get much light from any *Series* answer. While I must concede that, since we have no *Series* answer to examine, all such judgments can be little more than prejudices, it seems to me that *Series* answers—this criticism also applies to *Contact, Fastening, Cohesion, Fusion,* and *Democ*—will simply generate certain objects out of others and, as one might put it, leave them there. Consider *Contact,* for example. Suppose A, B, and C are material objects in connection with which we perceive no puzzles about identity. (Perhaps they are Democritean atoms or something else without parts.) A, B, and C come into contact and thus, according to *Contact,* come to compose at least one object. Suppose, to make things simple, that they come to compose exactly one object, ABC. Given our plausible "principles of composition" (Section 4), we can infer various things about ABC from our knowledge of the properties of A, B, and C: its mass and shape and so on. But we can infer nothing about the properties of ABC that we should really like to know: whether it could have been composed of other objects than A, B, and C; whether it is the same object that A, B, and C composed the last time they were in contact; whether it will continue to exist as long as A, B, and C are in contact (perhaps they compose different objects at different times?); whether it would exist if A, B, and C were in contact but arranged differently. . . . And not only can we not *infer* answers to these questions from *Contact,* but *Contact* does not seem even to suggest answers to them, or to provide some sort of minimal support for one answer rather than another. A "mereological essentialist" who believes that this table exists and that certain planks compose it and that no other planks could have composed it can be perfectly comfortable with *Contact,* and so can the mereological inessentialist who thinks that other planks could have composed the table. Each of them can be fully committed to the thesis that if planks ever compose a table (or anything else), they do this only when they are in contact. And *Contact* says nothing more than this. What is true of *Contact* will, I think, be true of answers of the *Series* type. No such answer will even suggest or lend any plausibility to any purported solution to any of the great, intractable paradoxes or the great philosophical puzzles about the existence and identities of material objects.

Still, the universe may be disinclined to make things easy for philosophers. Perhaps it is simply a feature of composition that an answer to the Special Composition Question, or even an answer to the Special and the General Composition Questions supplemented by every plausible principle of composition we can discover, will simply not tell us what we need to know to adjudicate hard cases like Reconstructed Ship versus Continuous Ship or Doe's Brain in Roe's Body versus Roe's Brain in Doe's Body.

But it would be *nice* if we had an answer to the Special Composition Question that suggested ways of adjudicating these hard cases. The answer that I shall propose in Section 9 will provide us with some guidance in hard cases.

This completes our discussion of real and imaginary answers to the Special Composition Question that involve physical bonding. Before turning to my own answer, which, like these answers, is Moderate, we must examine the two possible immoderate or Extreme answers.

8. Extreme Answers to the Special Composition Question: Nihilism and Universalism

Answer (v) *Nihilism*

It is impossible for one to bring it about that something is such that the xs compose it, because, necessarily (if the xs are two or more), nothing is such that the xs compose it.

If this answer is correct, then (if current physics is to be believed) the physical world consists entirely of quarks, leptons, and bosons—there is just nothing else in it, for these particles have no parts and they never add up to anything bigger. Where one might have thought there was a hydrogen atom (the Nihilist holds) there are just two up-quarks, a down-quark, an electron, and assorted photons and gluons; these minute objects, it is true, instantiate a very complicated multigrade physical bonding relation, but their instantiating this relation has no mereological consequences. And what goes for hydrogen atoms (the Nihilist holds) goes for cats and stars: any region of space that one might have thought contained a cat or a star in fact contains only elementary particles.

The Nihilist who wished to describe the consequences of his theory without employing the categories of current physics might say this: There are no composite material objects; there are only *physical simples*. A *simple* or mereological atom is an object without proper parts, and a *physical* simple is a simple that, unlike mathematical objects or God or Cartesian egos, belongs to the subject matter of physics. (We said in Section 5 that we should not presuppose that there were mereological atoms. It is evident, however, that the Nihilist must suppose that there are mereological atoms—at least if he is to suppose that there are any physical or material objects at all.)

Here is a precise statement of Nihilism:

($\exists y$ the xs compose y) if and only if
there is only one of the xs.

An examination of this statement reveals that Nihilism has an interesting
and unique logical property. We said in Section 4 that no answer to the
Special Composition Question entailed an answer to the General Composition Question. This is not quite true. There is one exception. Nihilism entails an answer to the General Composition Question:

The xs compose y if and only if
each of the xs is y.

(*Left to Right:* The xs compose y. Hence, the xs compose something.
Hence, by Nihilism, for some z, the xs are the things identical with z.
Hence, the things identical with z compose y. Hence, z is a part of y. But
Nihilism entails that y has no proper parts. Hence, y is identical with z.
Hence, each of the things identical with z is y. Hence, each of the xs is y.
Right to Left: Each of the xs is y. Hence, each of the xs is a part of y and
every part of y overlaps one of the xs. And no two of the xs overlap, there
being only one of them. Hence, the xs compose y.)

It is easy to see intuitively why Nihilism is the *only* answer to the
Special Composition Question that entails an answer to the General
Composition Question. Nihilism is the only answer that, for any xs that
compose something, "ties down" the identity of the thing they compose:
they compose the thing that is identical with all of them.

Unfortunately for the student of the General Composition Question,
Nihilism would appear to be false, for you and I exist and we are composite objects.

Some readers will find this argument rather too brief. They may be
inclined to say, with Plato and Descartes, that you and I are simples—
though not, of course, *physical* simples. Or they may be inclined to say,
with Spinoza and Hume and Peter Unger, that you and I do not really
exist. These inclinations will be discussed at various points in the sequel.
It is, however, unlikely that very many philosophers will be willing to
accept Nihilism. Some of *their* arguments—"Here is a hand and here is
another hand"—strike *me* as rather too brief. These arguments, too, will
be discussed in the sequel. (A terminological note: Peter Unger calls
himself a nihilist,[23] but his sense of the word is different from mine.
Unger apparently concedes the existence of composite objects; *his* nihilism consists in a denial that any of these composites is the right sort of
thing to belong to the extension of 'woman' or 'cat' or 'chair' or any of the
other count-nouns of ordinary language.)

Answer (vi) *Universalism*

It is impossible for one to bring it about that something is such that
the xs compose it, because, necessarily (if the xs are disjoint), something is such that the xs compose it.

According to this answer, one can't bring it about that the xs compose
something because they already do; they do so "automatically." Just as,
according to the theory of sets, there has to be associated with the xs a
certain abstract object, a set that contains just the xs, so, according to the
theory we are considering, there has to be associated with the xs a
certain concrete object, a sum of the xs. Universalism corresponds to a
position about sets that almost everyone holds: In every possible world
in which, for instance, Tom, Dick, and Harry exist, there also exists a set
that contains just them. Nihilism corresponds to nominalism (about
sets): In no possible worlds are there any sets. Some philosophers who
accept Universalism accept it because it is entailed by a certain stronger
thesis, which they accept on grounds that are, in theory, independent of
their views about material things. This stronger thesis, which we may
call Super-universalism, is the thesis that any objects whatever have a
sum. According to Super-universalism, for example, if there are such
things as the color blue and the key of C-sharp and I, then there is an
object that has the color blue and the key of C-sharp and me as parts. I do
not understand Super-universalism because, though I think that the
color blue and the key of C-sharp and I all exist, I am unable to form a
sufficiently general conception of parthood to be able to conceive of an
object that has these three rather diverse things as parts.[24]

Whatever problems Super-universalism may face, however, it is Universalism *simpliciter* that is our present concern. In my view, Universalism is false, since there are disjoint objects that compose nothing whatever. My conviction that Universalism is false rests on two theses that, on
reflection, seem to me to be correct. First, Universalism does not seem to
force itself upon the mind as true. A theory that denies Universalism is
not in prima facie trouble, like a theory that denies the reality of time.
(There is, however, a difficulty facing the denial of Universalism that we
are not in a position to discuss at this point, a difficulty that may seem to
many to constitute a knock-down objection to that thesis. In Sections 18
and 19 we shall see that if we reject Universalism, then—unless we
embrace Nihilism—we shall be forced to conclude that there is vagueness "in the world," that there are cases of vagueness that do not derive
from language.) Secondly, Universalism is in conflict with certain plausible theses (which I shall presently lay out). Now these two judgments are

highly subjective ones. Many philosophers for whom I have the highest respect not only accept Universalism but, apparently, regard it as just obviously true. And these philosophers will (I suppose) say that some of the "plausible theses" I shall lay out are obviously, or at least demonstrably, false. Well, I shall have to do the best I can. Here are the theses I regard as plausible and which entail the falsity of Universalism.

(A)   I exist now and I existed ten years ago.

(B)   I am an organism (in biological sense), and I have always been an organism.

(C)   Every organism is composed of (some) atoms (or other) at every moment of its existence.[25]

(D)   Consider any organism that existed ten years ago; all of the atoms that composed it ten years ago still exist.

(E)   Consider any organism that exists now and existed ten years ago; none of the atoms that now compose that organism is among those that composed it ten years ago.

(F)   If Universalism is true, then the xs cannot ever compose two objects. That is, the xs cannot compose two objects either simultaneously or successively. More formally, if Universalism is true, then it is not possible that $\exists y\, \exists z\, \exists w\, \exists v$ (the xs compose y at the moment w, and the xs compose z at the moment v, and y is not identical with z).

Of these propositions, (C), (D), and (E) would appear to express empirical facts.[26] Propositions (A) and (B), however, entail theses that have been denied on various philosophical grounds. As we noted in our discussion of Nihilism, various philosophers would deny that I exist. Many philosophers deny that, in the strict, philosophical sense, objects persist through time, and others find special reasons to doubt that persons—I suppose I am a "person," though what philosophers mean by this word is not always clear—persist through time. And, of course, all manner of philosophers have argued that personal pronouns do not refer to material things and would therefore reject (B).

I will later defend against various objections the thesis that such things as you and I exist and strictly persist through time. But to defend a thesis against particular objections is not to prove it, and in any case these defenses will presuppose an answer to the Special Composition Question that is inconsistent with Universalism, the refutation of which is our present concern. I have, therefore, nothing to say in defense of (A).

In view of the history of Western philosophy, (B) deserves an extended and careful defense. I have a lot to say that is relevant to the contention that we human beings are organisms—a lot of remarks to make about the ontology of human beings—though I am not sure that what I have to say adds up to a "defense" of premise (B). In any case, most of what I have to say about the ontology of human beings is only very obliquely relevant to our present concerns. But because this topic is a very important one, and because (B) is essential to my argument against Universalism, I will make one remark (more autobiography than argument) now. Perhaps this remark will explain a certain otherwise puzzling lacuna in my vocabulary.

Many philosophers, I believe, will concede that there is a biological organism, which, though it is not identical with me, stands in a relationship to me that is far more intimate than the relationships in which it stands to anyone else. These philosophers will say that this organism to which I am so intimately related (they will differ among themselves about my intrinsic nature and about the nature of my relation to it) is properly referred to as 'my body'. I do not understand them. I believe that 'body', as such philosophers use it, has no clear meaning. It has neither a sense that is supplied by ordinary speech nor a sense that has been supplied by explicit definition. But I have argued for these conclusions elsewhere, and I will not repeat my arguments here.[27] Given that I think this, however, it is not surprising that the word 'body' will not appear in the sequel. (It should go without saying that I am unwilling to accept the thesis that we "are our bodies." I don't know what that means. I do think that we are material objects, things made of flesh and blood and bone, and that we are shaped roughly like statues of human beings. If this constitutes a belief that we "are our bodies," then I believe that we are our bodies; but I don't know why those words are an expression of my belief.)

Anyone who rejects either (A) or (B) should ask himself at this point whether he thinks that there are *any* living organisms (human bodies, cats, bacteria . . .) that, strictly and literally, persist through time—or, more generally, whether he thinks that there are any objects of any sort that are composed of different parts at different times. In my view human beings, you and I, provide the clearest examples of objects that are composed of different parts at different times. But what is essentially the same argument as the one we are considering would obviously "go through" if there were any objects whatever that changed their parts with the passage of time.

Let us turn to (F). All the Universalists I am aware of do accept the consequent of (F). (Generally this acceptance consists simply in using expressions of the form 'the sum of x and y' and in treating them as unproblematical proper definite descriptions, ones that no more demand the addition of 'at t' than does 'the set that contains just x and y'). And I think they are right to. Here is the reason why. The consequent of (F) might reasonably be denied by adherents of certain of the answers to the Special Composition Question that we have considered. Take, for example, those who accept *Contact*. If someone thinks that in building a model of Salisbury Cathedral out of a set of blocks I thereby bring a certain object (the model) into existence—that is, that I do not merely change an already existing scattered object into a model—and if he also thinks that in building a model of the Colosseum out of the very same blocks I thereby bring (the object that is) that model of the Colosseum into existence, then perhaps it would be reasonable for him to suppose that the model of the cathedral and the model of the arena are two distinct objects, and that, therefore, the same blocks can compose two distinct objects at different times. But suppose someone thinks (as Universalists do) that the arrangement of the blocks is quite irrelevant to the question whether they compose an object: suppose he thinks that the blocks must at any moment at which they all exist compose an object, even if at that moment each of them is thousands of miles from the others, and even if they are moving at high velocities relative to one another, and even if they exert no causal influence to speak of on one another. If the arrangement of the blocks is irrelevant to the question whether they compose anything, why should it be supposed to be relevant to the identity of the thing they compose? Consider an object that is composed of the blocks at t, when they are widely scattered and moving rapidly in relation to one another. How long does it last? Only two answers seem possible. (1) It doesn't last at all; it exists only at t. (2) It lasts as long as its constituent blocks do. Any compromise between these two answers would be intolerably arbitrary: If the blocks "automatically" compose an object, then either any rearrangement of the blocks must destroy that object, or else no rearrangement could destroy it. And the former answer seems intolerably severe: It implies a doctrine beside which mereological essentialism pales: *positional* essentialism, according to which not only the identities of the parts of a whole are essential to that whole but their relative positions and attitudes as well. It is bad enough to suppose that the replacement of a rusty bolt leaves me with what is, "in the strict and philosophical sense," a new car. It is infinitely worse, and never has the phrase 'infinitely worse' been used more appropriately, to suppose that when I sit in my car and turn the wheel, what I am occupying is, "in the strict and philosophical sense," a compact series of infinitesimally differing cars. Or let us consider a simpler case, easily visualized because it involves only two objects. According to Universalism, this pencil and this cup always (when they both exist) compose an object, one that fits exactly into the nonconnected region of space they jointly occupy. Assuming we can make sense of this thesis, can we make sense of the thesis that at different times they compose different objects? I think not: If they always compose an object, then they always compose the same object. Universalism, therefore, cannot countenance the supposition that at two different times—or at one time—the xs compose two different objects. For the Universalist, 'the sum of those blocks' must be a proper definite description—assuming "those blocks" to exist—one that needs no temporal qualification. In this respect it is like 'the product of those numbers' or 'the set containing just exactly those blocks and those numbers'.

It is pretty evident that propositions (A) through (F) entail the denial of Universalism. Here is the argument in outline: assume the truth of Universalism; consider the atoms that composed me ten years ago; if (F) is true, those atoms compose me now; but those atoms obviously do not compose me now, and Universalism is therefore false. But let us set out the argument in pedantic detail to make sure that nothing has been overlooked.

It follows from (A) and (B) that I existed ten years ago and was then a biological organism. It follows from (C) that ten years ago that organism—I—was composed of certain atoms. Let us use 'T' as an abbreviation for 'the atoms that composed me ten years ago'. By (D), all of T still exist.

Now assume that Universalism is true. Then T now compose something. Call it 'the thing that is at present the sum of T' or '+T'. From Universalism and (F) it follows that T composed +T ten years ago. But, by definition, T composed me ten years ago. Therefore, by (F), I was +T ten years ago. But then I am +T now. If ten years ago a certain object and I were such that there was only one of us, then there is only one of us still: A thing and itself cannot go their separate ways. But I am not now +T. At present, +T, if it exists at all, is (I would suppose) a rarefied spherical shell of atoms, about eight thousand miles in diameter and a few miles thick; in any case, +T is now composed of atoms none of which are now parts of me. Our assumption of Universalism has, therefore, led us to a falsehood, and Universalism must be rejected.[28]

We must conclude that Answer (vi), Universalism, is incorrect: disjoint objects do not necessarily and automatically compose anything. (The lesson of the above argument, I would argue, is that T do not now compose anything, though they did once.) Alternatively, it does not follow from the mere existence of certain objects that there is any object that has them all as parts; not every set of objects has a sum.

Before leaving the topic of Universalism, we should take note of a fact that our informal, "practical" statement of Universalism has disguised. Universalism is not, strictly speaking, an answer to the Special Composition Question, for it is a principle about *summation*, not composition. Universalism tells us that, for any xs, those xs have a sum. It does not tell us that, for any xs, those xs compose something, for that would not be true by anyone's lights. (By definition, distinct overlapping objects compose nothing.) Of course, if Universalism is true, it follows that any xs that do not overlap compose something. But that does not count as an answer to the Special Composition Question, since 'overlap' is a mereological term. Our "practical" statement of Universalism disguised this difficulty by encouraging us to think of "the xs" as objects capable of independent motion and, therefore, to think of them as nonoverlapping objects.

The other answers to the Special Composition Question that we have examined do not face this problem. It is obvious that Nihilism does not face it, for, if Nihilism is true, then summation and composition coincide—for if Nihilism is true, no two objects overlap. Nor do Simple Bonding answers face this problem, for the multigrade bonding relations that they involve can hold only among disjoint objects. Consider, for example, *Contact*. Suppose the xs are in contact. It follows that the xs all occupy space, and that no two of them occupy overlapping regions of space. It is obvious that if y and z both occupy space and y is a part of z, then the region occupied by y is a part of the region occupied by z (an object, we might say, must be partly located where any of its parts is located); this is, in fact, a consequence of *Summation*. (But the converse is not obvious. The converse is equivalent to *Composition*.) Therefore, no two of the xs have a common part.

Nevertheless, if Universalism is not, strictly speaking, an answer to the Special Composition Question, the student of the Special Composition Question cannot ignore Universalism, for Universalism is incompatible with all Moderate answers to the Special Composition Question. (Each Moderate answer entails that there could be disjoint objects that do not compose anything and, therefore, entails that there could be objects that have no sum.) Indeed, since Universalism is also incompatible with Nihilism and is not itself (strictly speaking) an answer to the Special Composition Question, it is doubtful whether, if Universalism is true, there is (strictly speaking) any right answer to the Special Composition Question. If there were a condition which could be specified without the use of mereological concepts and which, necessarily, the xs satisfied if they were disjoint, then Universalism would entail an answer to the Special Composition Question. Suppose, for example, that it is necessary that if the xs are mereologically disjoint, then they are spatially discrete (that is, no point in space falls inside more than one of them). It is not hard to show that, on that supposition, Universalism entails the equivalence of '$\exists y$ the xs compose y' and 'the xs are spatially discrete'. But we saw in Section 4 that this supposition can easily be doubted. How do we know that there could not be two objects with no parts in common that occupied overlapping regions of space? (In fact, doesn't current physics endorse the possibility of two particles' occupying the same space at the same time?) I am inclined to think that there is no such condition, whether spatial or of some other sort, and therefore that Universalism entails that, for every sentence of the form

$$(\exists y \text{ the } x\text{s compose } y) \leftrightarrow \phi,$$

either the universal closure of that sentence fails to express a necessary truth, or else ϕ contains 'overlap' or 'part' or some other mereological term.

I offer the following conjecture. If Nihilism is true, there is a right answer to both the Special and the General Composition Question; if some Moderate thesis about composition is true, there is (of course) a right answer to the Special but no right answer to the General Composition Question (see the speculations at the end of Section 4); if Universalism is true, there is a right answer neither to the Special nor to the General Composition Question.

9. The Proposed Answer

What, then, *is* the answer to the Special Composition Question? When do we have a case of parthood? What must, or could, be done to cause objects to compose something?

I believe that the correct answers to these questions are radically different from what most philosophers have supposed. To begin with—though this is not so very radical—parthood essentially involves causation. Too many philosophers have supposed that objects compose something when and only when they stand in some (more or less stable) spatial relationship to one another. Very roughly speaking, this is the single error that underlies our four Simple Bonding answers to the Special Composition Question. It is true that these four answers involve more than the relative positions of the xs and that this additional element is a causal element. (It might be thought that being in contact requires only spatial juxtaposition and that there is therefore no causal element in *Contact*. But contact is in fact a causal relation. Suppose, for example, that a man and a ghost can overlap spatially without interacting causally. Suppose that John and James are shaking hands and are therefore in contact. If a ghost happens to occupy the same region of space as James, the ghost is not in contact with John, despite the fact that James and the ghost bear exactly the same spatial relations to John.) But even this additional causal element is in a way subordinate to spatial considerations, for what is it in each case but a requirement that the xs possess some sort of disposition to retain their relative positions?

Simply to say that parthood involves causation, however, is to say something that, if it is not wholly vacuous, is at any rate too abstract to be of much interest. *What* causal relations are involved in parthood? *What* multigrade causal relations must hold among the xs if they are to compose something? Here is the answer I propose:

$(\exists y$ the χs compose $y)$ if and only if

the activity of the χs constitutes a life (or there is only one of the χs).[29]

I shall devote the present section to an exposition of this answer. The remainder of the book will be largely devoted to its defense. To understand this answer, it is necessary to understand what it is for the activity of certain objects to constitute a certain event, and it is necessary to understand what it is for an event to be a life.

I haven't too much to say about what it is for the activities of objects to constitute an event. I must leave this notion at a more less intuitive level and proceed by giving examples: the activities of the Household Cavalry and the Life Guards constituted the parade; the activities of the members of the Household Cavalry and the members of the Life Guards constituted the parade (thus the activities of the χs may constitute a certain event and the activities of the ys constitute that same event, even though nothing is both one of the χs and one of the ys); the activities of the candidates, the Board of Elections, and the electorate constituted the election; the activities of the cattle constituted the stampede; the activities of the water molecules in the pan constituted the cooling of the water in the pan. (The last example shows that I am using 'activity' in a sense that does not simply mean action: talking of the "activities" of things in this sense is no more than a way of talking about the changes they undergo.)

I will have little to say about the ontology of events. (We are of course talking of "events" that are individuals or particulars, like the fall of the Alamo, and not about "events" in any sense in which an event is something that can recur.) It is certainly no part of my purpose either to contend or to deny that events are "irreducible entities" or "ultimately real." If a philosopher wishes to maintain that sentences that are apparently about events are misleading expressions of facts that in reality involve only substances or continuants, I will not protest. I will simply ask him to understand those of my sentences that are apparently about events in the same way he understands any other sentences that are apparently about events.

There are three points about the constitution of events by the activities of objects that are perhaps worth making.

First, I do not presuppose that every event is constituted by the activities of objects. Perhaps there are "pure" events, changes that occur without anything to undergo them. But some events, at least, are constituted by the activities of objects.

Secondly, I do not presuppose that if the activities of the xs constitute a certain event at t, then that event is the only event they constitute at t. Perhaps the rotation of a certain sphere and the gradual cooling of that sphere are two distinct events, and perhaps the activity of the molecules that compose the cooling, rotating sphere constitutes both events.

Thirdly, I do not presuppose that, if the activities of the xs constitute a certain event, then just any change in the properties of some or all of the xs, or in the relations among some or all of the xs, is in any sense a part of, or contributes to, or is in any way relevant to, the occurrence of that event. A soldier marching in a parade may simultaneously be swinging his arms and becoming bored. The former change in the soldier is a "part of" the parade in a way in which his becoming bored is not. Or at least this seems a very reasonable thing to say, and the use I shall make of the notion of the constitution of an event by the activities of certain objects does not require me to deny it.

Let us now turn to the question of what is meant by a "life." I mean the word "life" to denote the individual life of a concrete biological organism. (But I use these words only to give the reader an intuitive sense of the extension that I am giving to the term 'life'. Ultimately, I shall have to explain what I mean by 'life' without making reference to composite objects like organisms.) Thus 'life', in my usage, will be a count-noun. Pope used this term in this sense (though fancifully) when he wrote of birds shot on the wing that they "leave their little lives in the air." Locke was probably using the word in this way when he wrote that the identity of a man consists "in nothing but a participation of the same continued life by constantly fleeting particles of matter."[30] (But the count-noun 'life' and the mass term 'life' are not clearly distinguished by Locke.) The Greeks sometimes meant by *psuche* what I mean by 'life', though I do not suppose, as some Greeks did, that a *psuche* can detach itself from the material whose activity had constituted it, after that material has become quiescent. (Insofar as I can make sense of the vitalism-versus-mechanism controversy, I am a mechanist.) It *should* go without saying that I am using 'life' in its most narrow, biological sense. But I have been asked questions about my position that indicate that this does not go without saying, so I shall say it. The word 'life' can certainly be used in such a way that, for example, the phrase 'Bertrand Russell's life' denotes something like the totality of Lord Russell's adventures or that event the course of which is narrated in his autobiography. But the word also has a perfectly legitimate sense according to which 'Russell's life' denotes a purely biological event, an event which took place entirely inside Russell's skin and which went on for ninety-seven years. It is in this sense that I use the word 'life'.

But what is a life? What features distinguish lives from other sorts of event? In the last analysis, it is the business of biology to answer this question, just as it is the business of chemistry to answer the questions 'What is a metal?' and 'What is an acid?', or the business of physics to answer the question 'What is matter?' (The ultimate answer of the biologists to the question 'What is a life?' will, I suspect, involve abstract thermodynamic concepts like entropy. I should not be surprised if it also involved much less abstract chemical concepts like "enzyme" or even "carbon atom.") But I think that I can say something useful in response to this question, though what I say must be rather abstract. I shall approach the question 'What is a life?' by constructing what I fear is a rather lengthy and elaborate analogy.

Imagine a club the new members of which are always shanghaied. When a new member is wanted, a press-gang is sent to find a suitable candidate. When one is found, he is dragged to the club's premises and forcibly inducted. The induction ceremony (we may imagine) is so impressive that members are fiercely loyal to the club as long as they remain members. But few if any members remain members long. When a member is exhausted by his efforts on the club's behalf, and after his resources have been appropriated and placed in the club's treasury, he is ruthlessly expelled. The membership of the club is therefore in constant flux. The one stable thing about the club is its constitution (which, of course, is not an identifiable object but rather a complex set of dispositions and intentions that is maintained by the assiduous indoctrination of new members). One important feature of this constitution is its prescription that whenever anyone ceases to be a member, a press-gang is to be sent out to capture a replacement for him, someone who is as much like the way he was when he was inducted as is possible. As a consequence, the club "looks" much the same from one year to the next, despite the continual replacement of its members. It is important to note that the relatively unchanging aspect of our club is due to what might be called "internal causation," to the causal relations its members bear to one another, and is not due to the actions of any external "policing" or monitoring or maintenance agency. The population of a jail may likewise present an unchanging aspect as the years pass, even if the average prisoner stays in the jail for only a few days. But the unchanging appearance of the population of the jail is not due to the causal relations the prisoners bear to one another—if those relations alone influenced the location of the individual prisoners, they would disperse very rapidly indeed—but on a plan or *telos* which exists independently of the prisoners and which controls the admission, organization, and discharge of the prisoners by the application of external forces. The stability of our club is therefore unlike the stability of the population of a jail. The stability of a typical social organization, whether it is an organization like the jail or like the club or something intermediate between these two rather unusual extremes, is a dynamic stability. Some groups of people—one would not call them organizations—display a purely static stability. One might cite passengers trapped in a bus buried by a landslide (a case of stability imposed upon the members of a group by boundary conditions), or the inhabitants of a village that has lost its economic raison d'être, who stay on out of a disinclination to move, despite the fact that they do not much care for one another and are wholly lacking in civic esprit de corps (a case of stability due to the inertia of the individual members of the group). The stability of our club in no way resembles the stability of the trapped passengers or the apathetic villagers.

In describing our imaginary club, I have talked as if there really *were* (in the story) such a thing as the club, a thing that persists through all its changes of membership. But it is arguable that I need not have talked that way. One might suspect that I could have laid out the same imaginary state of affairs by talking only of individual people and the causal relations they bear to one another and their common resolution that this set of relations shall continue in a more or less stable way, shall at any given future time be instantiated by *some* suitable set of people. Should I have left anything out if I had described matters with such ontological caution? That is a good question. In Section 12, I shall take up the corresponding question about lives and living organisms.

Let us now modify slightly the story of our club. The members of the club are, of course, human beings and are conscious and the possessors of intentional states. Let us replace them with unconscious automata, machines that never, literally speaking, intend anything. But let us suppose that in order effectively to predict the behavior of these machines, one would have to adopt toward them what Daniel Dennett calls the "intentional stance" and treat them as if they were members of a club and were cooperating in the endeavor to carry out the prescriptions of a constitution like the one I have imagined. In order to suppose this, we must suppose that there are many automata which are not "members of the club" and which are suitable for forcible induction. But let us change one feature of our story that pertains to this. Let us replace our press-gangs with hunting parties: parties of automata that are sent out not to find new members (for we now imagine that the ambient free automata are physically unsuited for membership) but to obtain parts—nuts and bolts and diodes and so on.[31] When such a hunting party returns with a captured "wild" automaton, the club does not attempt to induct it. Rather, it is taken apart and various of its components and subassemblies are used to construct an automaton that is physically suited for membership. (We may also suppose that worn-out "members" are not expelled as in our original story. Rather, they are taken apart and various of their components and subassemblies are thrown out, while others are used in the construction of new members.) Let us also imagine that all the automata in our imaginary world are made ultimately of certain indestructible and immutable "standard components." There are, we may imagine, sixteen types of these, each token of each type being absolutely interchangeable with the others of its type. (But our automata do not build new members "from scratch," for standard components are far too small for them to manipulate individually. Instead, they break their victims down into subassemblies that are composed of thousands of standard components and then reassemble these in a different order to produce new members.)

Perhaps there is no need to add further details to this story. (The reader will, of course, have seen that I have been adumbrating a mechanical analogue of a living organism. The analogue is still far from adequate, but it is getting there.) We can understand our "club" well enough in a way by adopting the intentional stance. In a way. But let us not forget that we have stipulated that none of our automata literally possesses intentional states. What can we make of our club—but we must no longer call it a club—if we refuse to allow ourselves to pretend that the automata that compose it have intentions? Let us ask the question this way: What could a rational being who did not possess the concept of social organization say about our pseudo-club? Suppose none of the brute, physical facts of the situation was hidden from this being: Suppose he knew all about the standard components and such things. I think that if he wanted to say anything at all, he would have to resort to metaphor. He might use the metaphor of a storm:

What I am observing is an unimaginably complex self-maintaining storm of standard components. I would compare it with the Great Red Spot on Jupiter, which has been in existence for hundreds of years. (Or I might compare it with a wave, or the propagation of a wave, which is a sort of self-maintaining event that involves different particles of fluid at different times.) The surface of the world is littered with standard components assembled in various ways. This storm that I am observing moves across the surface of the world drawing swirls and clots of standard components into it and expelling others, always maintaining its overall structure. One might call it a homeodynamic event.

Now the events and processes that collectively constitute an organism's being alive might be described in similar terms by some disembodied intellect that knew its physics and chemistry but which had never heard of organic life and which was observing its first living organism:

> What I am observing is an unimaginably complex self-maintaining storm of atoms. This storm moves across the surface of the world, drawing swirls and clots of atoms into it and expelling others, always maintaining its overall structure. One might call it a homeo-dynamic event.

This observation is an acute one. There are such events as these. They are what I call lives. (As I have said, I am not making any abstract, ontological point when I say that there are lives. I mean that there are lives if there are individual, concrete events at all.)

Lives, as seen by the innocent and immaterial eye of our disembodied intellect, are self-maintaining events. But not just any self-maintaining event is a life. A flame or a wave is a self-maintaining event, but flames and waves are not lives. It is, as I have said, the business of biology to tell us what lives are. But we may add a few notes to the abstract picture of what a life is that I have tried to draw by means of the analogy of a self-maintaining club of automata.

First, a life is a reasonably well-individuated event. There is often a reasonably clear answer to the question whether a life that is observed at one time (or observed in part at one place: imagine observing two waving tendrils that may or may not emanate from the same organism) is the same life as a life that is observed at another time (or place). This is because a life is a self-directing event. If a life is at present constituted by the activities of the xs and was ten years ago constituted by the activities of the ys, then it seems natural to identify the two events if there is a continuous path in space-time from the earlier to the present space-time location, along which the life of ten years ago has propagated itself. It is this feature of lives, their seeming to be well individuated, that made it possible for Locke to explain the identity of a man in terms of the identity of a life and thereby to offer something that we can at least take seriously as a possible explanation of human identity. If lives did not at least appear to be well-individuated events, Locke's explanation would not even be worth considering; we should all regard it as an explanation of the obscure through the no less obscure. A flame, though it is a self-maintaining event, does not seem to be nearly so well individuated as a life. For sentimental reasons we may want to say that the "eternal flame" in some shrine has been kept burning for many centuries. But the content of such judgments is doubtful, if we think of cases in which a flame is allowed to go its own way. Was the flame constituted by the combustion of elements in the careless smoker's match the same flame as that constituted by the combustion of all the trees in the forest? If I light seven candles from one taper, has a spatially connected flame become a scattered flame, or have seven new flames come into existence? Presumably, there are no answers to these questions. (Suppose someone maintained that in addition to flames there were *fires*, substances or continuants that stand to flames as organisms stand to lives. Suppose he were asked for the principle of identity for fires. Suppose that, inspired by Locke, he answered, "Same flame, same fire." This would be an unhelpful explanation in a way in which Locke's explanation of the identity of a man is not unhelpful.) We should note in this connection that not every event that involves the spread of a type of life (in the mass-term sense of 'life') is a life. Some such events are more like flames. I am not thinking only of events like the growth of a certain population of multicellular organisms; there are events that involve at most one multicellular organism and are spreadings out of a certain type of life but are not lives. The growth of a tumor, for example. A tumor is not an organism (it is not a parasite), and there is no self-regulating event that is its life. The space occupied by a tumor is not filled by some one thing that fits exactly into it; it is a locus within which a certain sort of thing is happening: the spreading of a certain sort of (mass-term) life. This spreading may be a self-maintaining event, but it is not well individuated, and, despite its entirely biological nature, it is not a life.

There are self-maintaining events which are not lives but which might be described as reasonably well individuated. A wave, for example, can often be "followed" through various episodes of reflection, superposition, and refraction. (There are of course problem cases about waves; a wave, for example, can be split into parts that go their separate ways. But then there are also problem cases about lives.) I think that lives are much *better* individuated than waves, but there is an interesting and important feature of lives that is not shared by waves. Consider two waves (in water, say) which are moving in opposite directions and which pass through each other. A still photograph taken at the moment the waves coincide spatially will show what seems to be one wave whose amplitude is the sum of the amplitudes of the two coincident waves. I think we must say (always assuming that there are waves at all) that both the waves exist at the moment of superposition and that each is at that moment constituted by the activities of the same water molecules. We may describe this possibility—the possibility of two waves' being simultaneously constituted by the activities of the same objects—by saying that a wave is not a *jealous* event. Lives, however, are jealous. It cannot be that the activities of the xs constitute at one and the same time two lives. Lives are, in fact, so jealous that only in certain special cases can two lives overlap: Only in certain special cases can there be xs and ys such that the activity of the xs constitutes a life and the activity of the ys constitutes a life and the xs are not identical with the ys and, for some zs, the zs are among both the xs and the ys. The only clear case, in fact, is the case in which one of the lives is subordinate to the other, as the life of one of my cells is subordinate to my life. (A case, that is, in which the activity of the xs constitutes a life and the activity of the ys constitutes a life and the ys are properly among the xs. And the only possible case of *this* kind, I think, would be the case in which the activity of the ys constitutes the life of a cell and the activity of the xs constitutes the life of a multicellular organism. I doubt whether there could possibly be xs and ys such that the activity of the xs constitutes a life, the ys are properly among the xs, and the activity of the ys constitutes the life of, say, a hamster.) The case of Alice and Beatrice that figured in our discussion of *Fusion* in Section 6 might be thought to show that it is possible for two lives to overlap without one's being subordinate to the other, but I think that this shows only that it is possible for the vague haloes of influence that surround lives to overlap. We shall return to this matter in Section 19.

If we think about the kind of activity that a life—as opposed to, say, a wave—imposes on the particles of matter whose activities constitute it, it is not surprising that lives are jealous events. When two waves impinge upon the same water molecules, the activities that each demands of those molecules, in order to secure its passage through the region the molecules occupy, sum neatly according to the rules of vector addition. No such automatic tolerance of one another's activities is possible for lives, however. A wave contributes energy to the particles of a fluid and then collects that same energy once more as it passes. (All this is metaphor, of course. A wave is a moving agent only in the sense in which the locus of disturbance in a row of falling dominoes is a moving agent. And energy is not a stuff.) A life, on the other hand, does not simply deposit and withdraw sequentially an invariant sum of energy from a series of "banks," like a nervous traveler making his way in stages across dangerous country. A life takes the energy it finds and turns it to its own purposes. If a wave is a nervous but law-abiding traveler, a life is a brigand. (This is obviously metaphor, but the metaphorical features of this comparison go deeper than its colorful surface: A life is no more a moving agent than a wave is. When our disembodied intellect sees a life as a moving storm, what it is seeing is the motion of the locus of a kind of activity.) If this metaphor is apt, then it should be obvious why lives are jealous and waves are not. Two nervous, law-abiding travelers can simultaneously use the same bank; two bank robbers cannot.

Now that we have some sort of grasp of what is meant by a life, let us recall our proposed answer to the Special Composition Question:

($\exists y$ the xs compose y) if and only if

the activity of the xs constitutes a life.

Suppose that something is such that certain objects compose it in virtue of their activity's constituting a life. Let us call such a composite object an *organism.*

What is an organism like? I think we know enough "principles of composition" (in the sense of Section 4) to have a fairly clear picture of organisms. A clear enough picture to maintain plausibly that organisms in the present sense have just the properties that we associate with the things we normally call "organisms." And this is not surprising, since we normally suppose that the things we call "organisms" have parts and that the properties of organisms are at least to some extent determined by the properties of their parts. The thesis that the properties of organisms are not wholly determined by, do not wholly supervene upon, the properties of their parts, is sometimes called holism. According to holism, even a complete and correct list of principles of composition would not enable a perfect reckoner—the Laplacian Intelligence, say—to reckon the properties of wholes from the complete truth about the intrinsic properties of and the relations that hold among the parts that compose the wholes. Whether holism is correct, I do not know. Like most of my contemporaries, I am strongly inclined to think it is not correct, though I can't put my finger on what my reasons for thinking so are. Fortunately, none of the questions I attempt to settle in this book will require a decision about the correctness of holism.

What about the thesis that was called *Uniqueness* in Section 4? Could it be that, for some xs, those xs simultaneously compose two organisms? I do not see how this could be. Since lives are jealous, those two organisms would have to share the same life. But if at a given moment the same particles compose them, and if the activity of those particles constitutes just one life, then what could individuate the two organisms? (Suppose that somone believed that in addition to waves, there were "swells": substances or continuants that stood to waves as organisms stand to lives. Since waves can serenely pass through one another, this person ought to believe that at a certain moment the xs might compose two swells—at the same moment as that at which their activity constituted two waves. No such possibility seems to exist in respect of lives and organisms.) There are philosophers who will say this: My body and I are both organisms and, at any given time, have all the same proper parts (this case is logically similar to the case of the lump of gold and the gold statue). But, as I have said, I do not understand this sort of use of 'body'.

If, therefore, the particles of matter whose activities constitute lives thereby compose objects, it seems reasonable to identify the objects they compose with the objects ordinarily called organisms and to suppose that, for any xs, if the activity of those xs constitutes a life, then those xs compose exactly one organism. (This is a fortunate result, for, as an examination of the formal truths about composition laid down in Section 5 will show, the logic of parthood and composition is much simpler and more intuitive if *Uniqueness* is true.) We may note that if our answer to the Special Composition Question is correct, and if a thing is an organism just in the case that it is composed of objects whose activity constitutes a life, then the following biconditional (which is of the right logical form to be an answer to the General Composition Question) is true:

The xs compose y if and only if

y is an organism and the activity of the xs constitutes the life of y.

But this biconditional cannot in fact serve as an answer to the General Composition Question.

Consider the harmless-looking little word 'of'. It is this word and not the showier 'organism' that does the work that is required to turn our answer to the Special Composition Question into something formally suitable to be an answer to the General Composition Question. That 'organism' does no work toward that end can be seen from the fact that we could just as well have written the right-hand constituent of the biconditional like this: 'the activity of the xs constitutes the life of y'. But we cannot eliminate 'of' from this sentence—or only in favor of an essentially equivalent device, like the possessive case or some phrase containing 'have'. Now, what does 'of' mean here? Just this, I think: 'x is the life of y' means 'there are zs such that the activity of those zs constitutes x and x is a life and the zs compose y'. Therefore, although I am willing to grant that the biconditional displayed above is true, I am unwilling to describe it as a satisfactory answer to the General Composition Question, for it contains, in disguised form, a mereological term.

We shall in the next five sections take up the question of the correctness of our proposed answer to the Special Composition Question. We shall ask why one should suppose that the "if" part of the answer is right: Why should one suppose that in addition to the (presumably fairly minute) objects whose activities constitute lives, there are also the organisms that have or live them? And, of course, we shall ask why one should suppose that the "only if" part of the answer is right: Why should one suppose that the only composite objects are living organisms? It is, of course, the "only if" part of our answer that is likely to prove really controversial. Only a Nihilist is likely to be unhappy with the assertion that there are organisms. Let us for the moment assume the truth of the less controversial half of our answer: Let us assume that there are living organisms. In explaining what a life is, and having done so, in saying that the things called 'organisms' or 'living things' in everyday life are things that are composed of objects whose activities constitute lives in the sense explained, I have presented a certain picture, rather an abstract one, of the nature of a living organism. This picture is a philosophical picture (stripped of its atomism, it would be Aristotle's picture), but it is not a philosopher's picture. That is, it is not a picture that could only come to be as a product of the attempts of philosophers to deal with their peculiar preoccupations. Let me present two fine expressions of this picture, one by a biologist and one by a neurophysiologist. The first passage I shall quote (it is by J. Z. Young) has been quoted by David Wiggins, but it deserves to be quoted frequently.

> The essence of a living thing is that it consists of atoms of the ordinary chemical elements we have listed, caught up into the living system and made part of it for a while. The living activity takes them up and organizes them in its characteristic way. The life of a man consists essentially in the activity he imposes upon that stuff.[32]

The second passage is by Jonathan Miller:

> The nature of the physical universe is such that the mere existence of a living organism, the mere fact that it is distinguishable from its environment, means that it is in a state of jeopardy. By the middle of the nineteenth century physicists were forced to acknowledge that the physical universe tends towards a state of uniform disorder, a leveling down of all observable differences, and that left to themselves things will cool, fall, slow down, crumble and disperse.
>   In such a world the survival of form depends on one of two principles: the intrinsic stability of the materials from which the

object is made, or the energetic replenishment and reorganisation of the material which is constantly flowing through it. The substances from which a marble statue is made are stably bonded together, so that the object retains not only its shape but its original material. The configuration of a fountain, on the other hand, is intrinsically unstable, and it can retain its shape only by endlessly renewing the material which constitutes it; that is, by organising and imposing structure on the unremitting flow of its own substance. Statues preserve their shapes; fountains perform and reperform theirs.

The persistence of a living organism is an achievement of the same order as that of a fountain. The material from which such an object is made is constitutionally unstable; it can maintain its configuration only by flowing through a system which is capable of reorganising and renewing the configuration from one moment to the next. But the engine which keeps a fountain aloft exists independently of the watery form for which it is responsible, whereas the engine which supports and maintains the form of a living organism is an inherent part of its characteristic structure.

The fact that the mechanisms responsible for maintaining life are virtually indistinguishable from the structures they support is one of the reasons why it took so long to identify their existence. Even primitive biologists knew that the maintenance of life was a strenuous labour, but in the ancient world work was invariably performed by laborious devices, so that when human beings first began to speculate about their own characteristic 'go', they understandably sought the explanation in the most unremittingly strenuous parts of the living body: those organs that seemed to go on their own, those physiological actions whose very spontaneity suggested that they were the prime movers of the living process. For more than 2,000 years, the heart, blood and lungs were regarded as the principal agents of life. Modern biology came into existence only with the recognition that the vital impetus was distributed throughout the living tissues of the body, and that the heart, lungs and blood, far from being responsible for life, were kept alive by biochemical processes which they shared with all other structures of the living body.[33]

In connection with Miller's comparison of a living organism to a fountain, it is interesting to remark that the fountains that are ourselves flow a good deal faster than one might suppose. The "rate of flow" is different for different types of tissue; to take one example, only about half the atoms that made up your liver five days ago are within your liver today. (We should remember that if our proposed answer to the Special Composition Question is correct, there are no such things as marble statues or fountains. I merely note this fact; a defense of this position is not a part of the project of the present section.) Professor Young says that an atom can become a momentary part of a living thing by being caught up into the life of that thing. I shall adopt this figure and I shall frequently talk of one object's being caught up in the life of another. (I say 'in' rather than 'into' because I shall have more occasion to talk about the ongoing state of a thing's being "caught up" than I shall have occasion to talk about the transition that resulted in that state.) We may spell out this way of talking in terms of the vocabulary we have already introduced: to say that x is caught up in a life is to say that there are ys whose activity constitutes a life and x is one of the ys. Given our answer to the Special Composition Question, it follows that x is a (proper) part of something if and only if x is caught up in a life.[34] (This is a stronger thesis than Young's, which at most commits him to the "if" half of this biconditional.) It follows, moreover, from our answer to the Special Composition Question and our identification of the things that have, or live, lives with "organisms," that the following biconditional holds:

x is a proper part of y if and only if

y is an organism and x is caught up in the life of y.[35]

(We could drop the word 'proper' from the left-hand side if we added the words 'x is y or' to the right-hand side.)

I will close this section with a description of several episodes in which an object comes to be caught up in the life of an organism. It is my hope that this will give the reader an intuitive feel for the biological, or quasi-biological, concepts that I have introduced in this section.

Alice drinks a cup of tea in which a lump of sugar has been dissolved. A certain carbon atom that is part of that lump of sugar is carried along with the rest of the sugar by Alice's digestive system to the intestine. It passes through the intestinal wall and into the bloodstream, whence it is carried to the biceps muscle of Alice's left arm. There it is oxidized in several indirect stages (yielding in the process energy, which goes into the production of adenosine triphosphate, a substance that, when it breaks down, provides energy for muscular contraction) and is finally carried by Alice's circulatory system to her lungs and there breathed out as a part of a carbon dioxide molecule. The entire process—Alice began to do push-ups immediately after she had drunk her tea—occupied the span of only a few minutes.

Here we have a case in which a thing, the carbon atom, was (very briefly) caught up in the life of an organism, Alice. It is, if the position I have put forward in this section is correct, a case in which a thing became however briefly, a *part* of a larger thing when it was a part of nothing before or after. ("But didn't you say that the carbon atom had been part of a lump of sugar and became part of a carbon dioxide molecule?" I confess I did. I was speaking of parthood loosely, as I speak of motion loosely when I talk of the sun's "rising" or "moving behind the elms." In Section 11, I shall attempt to show how such loose talk can in principle be eliminated.) Moreover, I regard this case as a typical or central case of an object's becoming and then ceasing to be a part of an enduring thing. I would contrast it with the following case. Suppose the lump of sugar also contained a certain strontium atom ("contained" in the sense that the strontium atom was spatially inside the lump of sugar). This atom was also carried to Alice's intestine and, quite by chance, somehow passed into her bloodstream. It circulated within her many times and, owing to various chance encounters, participated in various chemical reactions. Several hours later, it was eliminated by Alice's excretory system. Despite the superficial similarity of the two cases, the strontium atom was never caught up into Alice's life and thus never became a part of her. A sufficient, but not a necessary, condition for this is the fact that strontium is not one of the sixteen or so chemical elements that are the only elements involved in those chemical reactions that collectively constitute the life of a human being. We must, as this example shows, distinguish between a thing's being caught up in the life of an organism and a thing's merely undergoing some complex series of motions or changes of state that are due to the effects upon it of the processes that constitute that life. (Consider once more our "club" of automata. A component that is first a part of a wild automaton, and then of a captured automaton, and then of a detached subassembly that had once been part of that automaton, and then a part of a newly constructed club member, and finally lies in the club's scrap heap, is a component that is analogous to an atom that is for a time caught up in the life of a living thing. A component that becomes accidentally wedged into a crevice in one of the club members and is carried about for a long while, undergoing a complex series of motions as a result, is analogous to our strontium atom.)

The story of our carbon atom is a close paraphrase of a story told by J. Z. Young. After telling this story, he says, "Can we say that [the carbon atom] has ever formed part of the living tissue of the body? Many people when asked this question quickly answer 'No'. . . ." In my view, this quick answer derives from the fact that many people take human artifacts and their parts to be the typical or central cases of the part-whole relation. A central goal of this book is to try to persuade people to adopt another "paradigm" of the part-whole relation.

Let us assume for the moment that our carbon atom did become a part of Alice. ("Well, just *when* and *where* did it become a part of her?" This is an important question to which we shall return in Section 17. It is not less important for being misconceived.) We have, then, a case in which an object becomes part of an already existing object. We may call such cases cases of *assimilation*. Formally, we may say that x *assimilates the ys at t* just in the case that the ys become parts of x at t and x exists throughout some interval that includes t but of which t is not the earliest member. (Not all cases of assimilation in the present sense involve digestion or respiration. Suppose, for example, that I am given an eye transplant. Then I assimilate the atoms and the cells that made up the transplanted eye.)

There is another way than by assimilation in which an object may become a part of a thing. We may call this second way *generation*. Formally, we may say that x *is generated out of the ys at t* just in the case that the ys come to compose x at t and x does not exist before t (or, if a thing can go out of existence and then once more come into existence: 'x does not exist at any moment in some interval ending in t') and the ys do exist before t. (I am not going to bother about distinguishing between cases in which there is a last moment of a thing's nonexistence and cases in which there is a first moment of a thing's existence. Such distinctions are pretty, but they have nothing to do with physical reality.) At the moment at which Alice assimilated the carbon atom, the atoms that composed her at that moment came to compose her at that moment, since one of them at least had not composed her earlier. But she was not generated out of them at that moment, since she existed before that moment. If, however, God were to take certain atoms and, all in an instant, make a living cat out of them, then He would cause it to be the case that that cat was generated out of those atoms, and each of them would become a part of the cat—would be caught up in its life *ab initio*—without being assimilated by it. Or, to take a more common case, a sperm and an egg unite to form a zygote. Then the zygote is generated out of the atoms that had composed the sperm and the atoms that had composed the egg. (But the zygote is not generated out of the sperm and the egg, since the sperm and the egg do not come to compose the zygote.)

The opposite of generation is *corruption*. Formally: x is corrupted at t just in the case that, for some ys, the ys are two or more and the ys cease to compose x at t and x does not exist after t (or: x does not exist at any moment in some interval beginning with t) and the ys do exist after t. To be corrupted, in other words, is to go out of existence by coming apart. If a thing ceases to exist but is not corrupted, then we shall say that it has been *annihilated*. Formally: x is annihilated at t just in the case that x exists at t and x does not exist after t (or: x does not exist at any moment in some interval beginning with t) and nothing that is a part of x at t exists after t (or: exists at any moment in some interval beginning with t).

10. Why the Proposed Answer to the Special Composition Question, Radical Though It Is, Does Not Contradict Our Ordinary Beliefs

The thesis about composition and parthood that I am advocating has far-reaching ontological consequences: that every physical thing is either a living organism or a simple. (For suppose there is something that is neither a simple nor an organism. Since it is not a simple, it has proper parts. Since it is not an organism, then, if the thesis I am advocating is correct, it has no proper parts.) We might, in fact, think of simples as degenerate organisms, in the sense of 'degenerate' in which, for instance, a line segment is sometimes called a degenerate ellipse. An organism may be thought of as a thing whose intrinsic nature determines how it is to change its parts with the passage of time. Thus, a table could not be an organism since, if there were tables, they could change their parts purely as the result of the application of external forces. (An organ transplant is *not* a case of organism's changing its parts purely as the result of the application of external forces. See Section 15.) A simple fits this abstract characterization of what it is to be an organism: its intrinsic nature determines that it is always to be composed of the *same* parts. If we adopt this way of talking, we can say that all physical objects are organisms, either degenerate or living.[36]

The Proposed Answer, therefore, is consistent with the existence of simples. Does it *require* the existence of simples? That is, does it entail that organisms are composed of simples? There would seem to be two ways to avoid this conclusion. First, one might suppose—it can be argued that this is Aristotle's view of the matter—that organisms have no proper parts, that they are entirely composed of absolutely continuous stuffs. (Strictly speaking, this does not entail that there are no simples, but rather that living organisms are simples, albeit they are continuously assimilating and eliminating matter.) I take it, however, that we now know empirically that living organisms are not composed of absolutely continuous stuffs. Secondly, one might suppose that organisms have proper parts and that every proper part of an organism has proper parts. It is easy enough to propose models on which this thesis is true. Suppose, for example, that space is continuous and that every region of space that lies within the boundaries of an organism (or every such region topologically suitable for occupation by an object) is occupied by a part of that organism. I have argued elsewhere[37] that this supposition is false, but, true or false, it is not consistent with the proposed answer to the Special Composition Question. It is obvious that, while some regions of space inside an organism may be occupied by organisms, some of them are not. A second model, one that does not face that difficulty, is this: An organism like a man or a cat is composed of smaller organisms, cells; and cells in their turn are composed of "subcells" (whose activity constitutes the life of the cell); "and so ad infinitum." Again, however, I take it that we know empirically that this is false. I know of no model for the mereological structure of organisms that is consistent both with the thesis that there are no simples and with the empirical facts. (And, anyway, current physics strongly suggests that quarks and leptons and gluons and photons have no proper parts and that all organisms are composed of quarks and leptons and gluons and photons.)[38] I shall, accordingly, assume that if the proposed answer to the Special Composition Question is correct, then all organisms are composed of simples. That is, I shall suppose that, for every organism, there are xs such that the xs are simples and the xs compose that organism. Note that this does not entail that, for every organism, and for any xs, if those xs compose that organism, then those xs are simples.

Most philosophers I have talked about these matters with think that my ontology contains too few objects. One philosopher (Peter Unger) thinks it contains too many. In the present section, I shall attempt to take some of the sting out of the charge that I believe in too few objects. (I shall put off till Section 17 the less pressing problem of answering the charge that it contains too many.) I shall show that my view, though radical, is not so far from being rational that it does not deserve a hearing.

Before I do this, however, I want to do what I can to disown a certain apparently almost irresistible characterization of my view, or of that part of my view that pertains to inanimate objects. Many philosophers, in conversation and correspondence, have insisted, despite repeated protests on my part, on describing my position in words like these: "Van Inwagen says that tables are not real"; ". . . not true objects"; ". . . not actually *things*"; ". . . not substances"; ". . . not unified wholes"; ". . . nothing more than collections of particles." These are words that darken counsel. They are, in fact, perfectly meaningless. My position vis-à-vis tables and other inanimate objects is simply that there *are* none. Tables are not defective objects or second-class citizens of the world; they are just not there at all. But perhaps this wretched material mode is a part of the difficulty. Let us abandon it. There are certain properties that a thing would have to have to be properly called a 'table' on anyone's understanding of the word, and nothing has all of these properties. If anything did have them, it would be real, a true object, actually a *thing*, a substance, a unified whole, and something more than a collection of particles. But nothing does. If there were tables, they would be composite material objects, and every composite material object is real, a true object, actually a *thing*, a substance, a unified whole, and something more than a collection of particles. But there are no tables. I hope I have made myself clear.

Is my thesis absurd? Why? The argument, I think would be something like this:

> According to your proposal, there are no such things as tables or chairs or rocks or mountains or continents or stars. But there just obviously are such things as these. Therefore, your theory is wrong. In fact it's *so* obvious that there are such things as these that your theory is absurd.

Now these words can be interpreted in various ways. I believe that the strongest argument that can be found in them is the following, an argument that was invented, or at least made famous, by Moore:

> Your position, if it rests on anything at all, rests on certain arguments. But the premises of these arguments, whatever they may be, could not possibly be so worthy of belief as what you are denying, *viz.* that there are such things as tables and stars.

Is this really true? What it *would* be true to say is this:

> . . . the premises of these arguments, whatever they may be, could not possibly be so worthy of belief as the thesis that when English-speakers, immersed in the ordinary business of life, utter sentences like, 'There are two very valuable chairs in the next room' or 'There are stars larger than the sun', they very often say true things.

But I do not deny this. In fact, I affirm it. "Now, *look.* 'There are two very valuable chairs in the next room' entails 'There are chairs', which is what you deny." The objection is misconceived. 'There are two very valuable chairs in the next room' and 'There are chairs' are sentences, not propositions. Therefore, they neither entail nor are entailed and they are not the objects of affirmation and denial. Moreover, any of the propositions that an English speaker might express by uttering 'There are two very valuable chairs in the next room' on a particular occasion—there are, of course, many such propositions, owing to the indexical elements in the sentence—is, I would argue, consistent with the propositions that I, as metaphysician, express by writing the words 'There are no chairs'.

This reply may strike some philosophers as a desperate, ad hoc evasion of a very cogent point. But, really, whatever the merits of the present case may be, this sort of maneuver is common enough. Here are three examples of similar cases. (1) I am a vociferous defender of the Principle of Noncontradiction. You ask me whether it's raining. I answer, "Well, it is and it isn't." You remind me of my allegiance to the Principle of Noncontradiction. I reply that the proposition I expressed by saying "It is and it isn't" is consistent with the Principle of Noncontradiction. (2) I deny that there are sense data, after-images, pains, or other objects of immediate sensory awareness. One day you hear me complain of a nagging pain in my left shoulder. You say, "There—you admit that there are pains!" I reply that the proposition I express when I say "There's a nagging pain in my left shoulder" is consistent with my denial that there are objects of immediate sensory awareness. (3) I accept the Copernican Hypothesis. One day you hear me say, "It was cooler in the garden after the sun had moved behind the elms." You say, "You see, you can't consistently maintain your Copernicanism outside the astronomer's study. You say that the sun moved behind the elms; yet, according to your official theory, the sun does not move." I reply that the proposition I expressed by saying "It was cooler in the garden after the sun had moved behind the elms" is consistent with the Copernican Hypothesis. This last example is particularly instructive. When I speak the words 'the sun moved behind the elms', I am reporting a fact. I am reporting a real alteration in the relations of external objects. Perhaps the words I use constitute what is in some sense a misleading description of this fact, but they do at least get one thing literally right: Taken literally, they report an alteration in the spatial disposition of external objects and an alteration in the spatial disposition of external objects really does occur and is the basis for the report. Thus, 'The sun moved behind the elms' is not, even from the point of view of the most fanatical astronomical literalist, a report of a nonexistent, fabricated, or imaginary event; it is not like, say, 'The sun moved rapidly back and forth across the sky'. It may describe an actual event in a misleading or loose or even a wrong way, but the event it describes or misdescribes is there to be described or misdescribed. Something similar may be said about 'There are two very valuable chairs in the next room'. This sentence, when it is successfully used to report a fact, does report a fact about the existence of *something*. This much is shown by the fact that if the next room were wholly empty of matter, then what was expressed by this sentence would be false by anyone's standard. We may say that this sentence is "essentially existential," meaning that it can be used to report a fact, and that a correct paraphrase—correct by the most pedantic and literalistic standards—of this sentence into the language of formal logic must start with an existential quantifier. (In a similar spirit, we could say that 'The sun moved behind the elms' was "essentially alterational.") In Section 11 we shall take up the question of what literally correct paraphrases of sentences like 'There are two chairs in the next room' should look like. I believe that the fact that such sentences can be used to say what is true and the fact that they are essentially existential together account for the *feeling* we have of making an assertion of existence, one that is objectively correct, when we utter them in appropriate circumstances. But from the three premises, (1) a certain man has said (using the words in their standard English senses) "There are two chairs in the next room," (2) what he said was true, and (3) what he said must be represented formally as an existential quantification, we cannot infer that there are chairs.

My position, therefore, is that when people say things in the ordinary business of life by uttering sentences that start 'There are chairs . . .' or 'There are stars . . .', they very often say things that are literally true. (" 'Literally'? What does that mean?" Well, they can be *right*, in whatever sense someone can be right if he says that the sun traversed 59 minutes of arc during our conversation.) I can say this because I accept certain theses in the philosophy of language. Some people, I suppose, would reject these theses. These people would say that when I said "It is and it isn't" and "The sun moved behind the elms," I said something false. If I agreed with them, I could not reply to the Moore-style objection to my ontology in the way that I have. Since I do not propose to defend my philosophy of language in the present work, I think it is worth pointing out that even if I did accept the austere philosophy of language that ascribes falsity to typical utterances of 'The sun moved behind the elms', I could nevertheless respond to "Moore's gambit" in a way that is very much like the way I have responded to it. If someone maintains that 'The sun moved behind the elms' expresses a falsehood, he must still have some way to distinguish between this sentence and those sentences (like 'The sun exploded' and 'The sun turned green') that the vulgar would regard as the sentences that expressed falsehoods about the sun. He will require what we may call a "term of alethic commendation" which he can correctly apply to 'The sun moved behind the elms' and withhold from 'The sun exploded'. Let us suppose that his term of alethic commendation is 'expresses a falsehood that for most practical purposes may be treated as a truth'. (It will make no real difference what term of alethic commendation we consider.) If, I say, I accepted this austere philosophy of language, then I should be more cautious about what I granted to a philosopher who attempted to refute my position by an argument in the style of Moore. I should not be willing to say that people who uttered things like 'There are two very valuable chairs in the next room' very often said what was true. I should be willing to say only that they very often said what might be treated as a truth for all practical purposes.

Mention of Moore brings to mind "common sense." Does my position not fly in the face of common sense? I do not think so. This is not because I think that my position is in accord with "common sense," but rather because I do not think that there is any such thing as the body of doctrine that philosophers call common sense. There is common sense: Common sense tells us to taste our food before we salt it and to cut the cards. It does not tell us that there are chairs. Now, in addition to common sense there is what we might call Universal Belief: that body of propositions that has been accepted by every human being who has ever lived, bar a few imbeciles and madmen; which is accepted even by Spinoza and Bradley when the madness of philosophy is not upon them. Is the existence of chairs—or, at any rate, of things suitable for sitting on, like stones and stumps—a matter of Universal Belief? If it were, this would count strongly against my position, for any philosopher who denies what practically *everyone* believes is, so far as I can see, adopting a position according to which the human capacity for knowing the truth about things is radically defective. And why should he think that his own capacities are the exception to the rule? It is far from obvious, however, that it is a matter of Universal Belief that there are chairs. In fact, to say that any particular proposition that would be of interest to philosophers belongs to the body of Universal Belief is to put forward a philosophical thesis and no trivial one. It is difficult to settle such questions, in part because there are a lot of things that one might express by uttering "philosophical" sentences like 'There are chairs', and some of them might be things that are irrelevant to the concerns of ordinary life. Moreover, the distinctions among various of these things may be subtle: It may be that the intellectual training provided by dealing with ordinary matters ill equips one to appreciate them.

In my view, my general thesis about what there is—that the only physical things are simples and living organisms—is not inconsistent with anything believed *ubique et ab omnibus*. In my view, my metaphysic does not shut me off from Universal Belief. I shall try to show why I think this is so by telling a fable, the story of the bligers.

When the first settlers arrived in the hitherto unpeopled land of Pluralia, they observed (always from a fair distance) what appeared to be black tigers, and they coined the name 'bliger' for them. "Bligers" were even more shy of human beings than ordinary tigers, and they were never suspected of harming human beings or even of carrying off a chicken. The Pluralians were an intensely practical race of farmers who never hunted for sport, and, since nothing needed to be *done* about bligers, bligers were seldom in their thoughts. Occasionally, Pluralians would make idle remarks along the lines of 'There's a bliger crossing that field', and that was about the extent of their interaction with bligers. A few centuries after the settlement of Pluralia, however, a foreign zoological expedition discovered that, in a way, there were no bligers. "A bliger (*Quasi-Tigris Multiplex Pluralianus*)," their report read, "is really six animals. Its 'legs' are four monkey-like creatures, its 'trunk' a sort of sloth, and its 'head' a species of owl. Any six animals of the proper species can combine temporarily to form a bliger. (Combinations lasting for several hours have been observed telescopically.) The illusion is amazing. Even a trained zoologist observing a bliger from a distance of ten meters would swear that he was seeing a single, unified animal. While the purpose of the combination is doubtless to protect its members from predators by producing the illusion of the presence of a large, dangerous carnivore, we can only guess at the evolutionary history of this marvelous symbiosis."

Are there any bligers (in the story)? I think not. But I do not suppose that a Pluralian says anything false if he says "There is a bliger crossing that field," any more than I would suppose that he says something false when he says "The sun is rising" or "That cat is sharpening its claws." But what do I mean when I say that there are no bligers? I am obviously not denying that there are occasions on which six animals arrange themselves in bliger fashion (as we might say). But it does not follow from this fact that there are bligers. That is, it does not follow that six animals arranged in bliger fashion compose anything, and that is what I mean to deny when I say that there are no bligers. Or put my thesis this way. Consider six animals arranged in bliger fashion; consider the region of space that they collectively occupy; there is no one thing that just exactly fills this region of space.

What I mean by saying that there are no chairs is precisely analogous to what I mean by saying that there are no bligers. To make things as simple as possible, let us suppose that chairs—if there are any— are made entirely of wood and let us suppose (though nothing remotely like this is true) that any object that is "made entirely of wood" is composed of simples called 'wood-particles'. Now consider those regions of space that, according to those who believe in the existence of chairs, are occupied by chairs. Call them chair-receptacles. One of these chair-receptacles is beneath me as I write. Call it R. I concede the truth of this proposition:

(A)   The chair-receptacle R is filled with rigidly interlocking wood-particles; the regions immediately contiguous with R contain no wood-particles; the wood-particles at the boundary of R (that is, the wood-particles within R that are not entirely surrounded by wood-particles) are bonded to nearby wood-particles much more strongly than they are bonded to the non-wood-particles immediately outside R; the strength of the mutual bondings of wood-particles within R is large in comparison with the forces produced by casual human muscular exertions.

What my answer to the Special Composition Question entails the denial of is not (A), but rather the two following theses (and, therefore, the proposition that either of them is entailed by (A)):

(B)   There is something that fits exactly into R.

(C)   There is something that the wood-particles within R compose.

Now if either (B) or (C) were true, there would be a chair. If either of them is false, then there are no chairs. (Or, at least, there is no chair in R.) Because it is (B) and (C) that I deny, and not (A), I am a metaphysician and not a madman. (I once actually met a madman who denied the existence of the moon. But *I* deny the existence of the moon, since it is neither an organism nor a simple. I deny that anything is a sphere of rock two thousand miles in diameter. What makes the man I met a madman and me a mere metaphysician? Part of the answer, no doubt, is that my denials are more systematic and coherent than his: he thinks that there's a *special* reason for denying the existence of the moon. But even in the particular case there are differences. He thinks that there is nothing in the "lunar receptacle." I say that the lunar receptacle contains untold myriads of things; I simply deny that these myriads compose a single thing. Moreover, I think that when people say "Men have walked on the moon," they say something true. He thinks they say something false; in fact, he will not even grant that what they say expresses a falsehood "that for most practical purposes may be treated as a truth.")

What I differ from most philosophers about (though perhaps most philosophers have not thought about material objects in just these terms) is this: They believe that (A) entails (B) and (C) and I do not. But whether this entailment holds is a very subtle metaphysical question. I do not think it is absurd to suppose that (A) might be true and (B) and (C) false. The possibility is at least worth examining.

I have been arguing that my position is not absurd and is not at variance with Universal Belief. A good many philosophers may feel that it is absurd for all that, and at variance with Universal Belief as well. They may want to accuse me of a philosophical ploy that Saul Kripke has described in these words:

> The philosopher advocates a view apparently in patent contradiction to common sense. Rather than repudiating common sense, he asserts that the conflict comes from a philosophical misinterpretation of common language—sometimes he adds that the misinterpretation is encouraged by the 'superficial form' of ordinary speech. He offers his own analysis of the relevant common assertions, one that shows that they do not really say what they seem to say. . . .
>
> Personally, I think such philosophical claims are almost invariably suspect. What the claimant calls a 'misleading philosophical misconstrual' of the ordinary statement is probably the natural and correct understanding. The real misconstrual comes when the claimant continues, "All the ordinary man really means is . . ." and gives a sophisticated analysis compatible with his own philosophy.[39]

I would make two points.

First, my view is not in patent contradiction with common sense, because, as I have said, there is no such body of extra-philosophical belief as "common sense." There are, of course, various philosophies like "the Scottish philosophy of common sense" or "Moore's philosophy of common sense" that my view contradicts, but then they contradict one another. (There may be some sort of problem of self-reference here. I can imagine a philosopher telling me that my assertion that there is no such thing as what philosophers call common sense is in patent contradiction with common sense.)

Secondly, I am not proposing an analysis of common language. I am offering a metaphysical theory. The only thing I have to say about what the ordinary man really means by 'There are two valuable chairs in the next room' is that he really means that there are two valuable chairs in the next room. And we all understand him perfectly, since we are native speakers of our common language. In my view, this sentence is sufficiently empty of metaphysical commitment that the proposition it typically expresses is consistent both with the thesis that (A) entails (B) and (C) and with the thesis that (A) does not entail (B) or (C), and that is all I have to say about the meaning of sentences of ordinary language. In a similar vein, I would say that what is ordinarily expressed by 'It was cooler in the garden when the sun had moved behind the elms' is consistent with both Ptolemaic and Copernican astronomy. (It may be that the word 'moved' occurs in the idiom this sentence exemplifies because the first people to use this idiom accepted some geocentric account of the apparent motion of the sun. But that would not entail that an astronomical theory was built into the *meaning* of this idiom.)

I will close this section with a remark about the ordinary man. If you were to tell the ordinary man that I thought that there were no chairs, he would probably think I was mad. But you would have misled him about my thesis. He would understand you to be saying—given his education and interests, what else could he understand you to be saying?—something that implied that whenever anyone uttered a sentence like 'There are two valuable chairs in the next room', that person was under an illusion of some sort. He would think that I regarded utterers of this sentence as he (perhaps) regards utterers of the sentence 'There are two horrible ghosts in the next house'. But my assertion (and yours and his) that there are no ghosts is not like my assertion that in Pluralia there are no bligers. My assertion that in Pluralia there are no bligers is not meant to deny that reports of bligers are reports of a real and unified set of phenomena. My assertion that there are no ghosts is meant to deny that reports of ghosts are reports of a real and unified set of phenomena. When people say they see ghosts, I believe (and I presume you do, too) that either there is nothing there, or, if there is something there, it's not the same sort of thing on each occasion. When Pluralians say they have seen a bliger, there generally is something there, and it's generally the same sort of thing. My assertion that there are no chairs is like my assertion that there are no bligers. But that is something that you will not convey to the ordinary man when you tell him that I think that there are no chairs, just as you would not have conveyed to the sixteenth-century ordinary man what Copernicus believed about the motion of the sun if you told him that, according to Copernicus, the sun does not move.

11. The Topic of the Previous Section Continued: Paraphrase

If I am right, then all facts of the sort that most philosophers would say were facts about artifacts, and about nonliving "natural" objects like stones, are facts about the arrangement of simples. If this position is, as I have been arguing, not absurd, then it should be possible to paraphrase the sentences of ordinary language that most philosophers would say expressed facts about things like chairs in language that refers to no material things but simples.

I shall try to make it seem plausible that such paraphrasis is always possible by showing how to accomplish one reasonably difficult case of it. I should, of course, like to be able to show that such paraphrasis is always possible. But to do that, I think, it would be necessary to discover a general, universally applicable way of paraphrasing ordinary sentences of the kind we are interested in. And to do that, I should require a much more systematic understanding of these ordinary sentences than I (at any rate) possess. I am not even sure how to characterize with any precision the class of sentences I wish to be able to paraphrase.

The really difficult problems of paraphrasis will be the ones that involve either multiple quantification, identity through mereological change ('This is the house that Jack built'), or accident and essence ('This table might have been longer than it is'). I shall leave the problem of paraphrasis of sentences apparently implying the identity of an artifact through a change of parts or accidents till we look systematically at the topic of artifacts in Section 13. The problem of paraphrasing multiply quantified sentences will be sufficiently taxing for the moment.

We owe to Quine the general methodological insight that a philosopher who denies the existence of objects of a certain sort had better be prepared to give an account of multiply quantified sentences, some of whose existential quantifiers bind variables that apparently range over objects of that sort. Before Quine's studies in the methods of ontology enjoyed their present salutary influence, a philosopher who denied the existence of, say, properties, would tell us what to do about sentences like 'This is a square, red block'; nowadays, if he knows his trade, he will tell us what to do about sentences like 'There is a color and there is a shape such that no block of that color is of that shape.' Let us consider the problem of how to paraphrase the sentence 'Some chairs are heavier than some tables' in language that does not appear to make reference to, and does not appear to presuppose the existence of, anything material besides simples. I shall help myself to three variably polyadic predicates: 'are arranged chairwise', 'are arranged tablewise', and 'are heavier than'. The xs are arranged chair- (table-) wise if they fill a chair- (table-) receptacle and satisfy certain other conditions that can be gleaned from an inspection of proposition (A) of the preceding section.[40] For the xs to be arranged chairwise is as much a matter of their contrast with their surroundings as it is of their distribution in space. Thus, the simples occupying a chair-shaped and chair-sized region of space that falls entirely within a certain tree are not arranged chairwise, though they would be if the rest of the tree were stripped away. Simples arranged chairwise do not, of course, compose a chair or anything else (unless there should be chair-shaped living things). The third predicate, which could also be written 'are collectively heavier than', seems to me to be unproblematical. There is nothing unclear about such sentences as 'The weights on the left-hand balance are (collectively) heavier than the weights on the right' and 'The pebbles in the jar are heavier than the jar and the lid'.

We are now ready to consider a paraphrase of 'Some chairs are heavier than some tables':

There are xs that are arranged chairwise and there are ys that are arranged tablewise and the xs are heavier than the ys.

(We may note that this paraphrase does not presuppose the existence of material objects of any particular kind. Therefore, it satisfies the requirement that it presuppose the existence of no material objects other than simples. Of course, if our proposed answer to the Special Composition Question is right, then it is doubtless true that, for any xs, if those xs are arranged tablewise or chairwise, then those xs are all simples.) This paraphrase involves plural quantification. But anyone who feels more at home with sets and ordinary quantifiers than with plural quantifiers could write instead:

> There is an x such that x is a set and the members of x are arranged chairwise and there is a y such that y is a set and the members of y are arranged tablewise and the members of x are heavier than the members of y.

In general, if we employ a method of paraphrasis that does not involve plural quantifiers, then we shall have to press some sort of object into service to enable us to keep track of the items in our domain of quantification. There are, we suppose, no tables; we philosophers who supposed that things sometimes added up to tables were mistaken. There is, we maintain, no table over there, but only certain things arranged tablewise. But if we are going to refer to those things in lieu of referring to a table, we shall need to call them something—say, 'those things over there that are arranged tablewise'. And if we are going to translate multiply quantified sentences involving physical-object common nouns like 'table' into sentences involving no physical-object common nouns, or none but 'simple', then we shall have to employ some device that allows us to "mimic" the quantificational structure of the original sentences—for it is almost certain that a successful paraphrase (whatever our standards of success may be) of a multiply quantified sentence will have a quantificational structure that in some way corresponds to the quantificational structure of the original. There would seem to be two ways to accomplish the sort of paraphrasis that is our current interest. We can either employ plural quantifiers, or else we can introduce some sort of nonphysical object that automatically, by its nature, sorts physical objects and thus allows us to keep track of them. Sets are obviously qualified for this work, since a set automatically sorts things into those things that belong to it and those that don't. But we could use other kinds of nonphysical object—such as regions of space, each of which automatically sorts things into those that fall within it and those that don't. If, for example, one wanted to paraphrase sentences apparently about artifacts into sentences that did not appear to be about artifacts and did not wish either to employ the apparatus of plural quantification or to assert the existence of sets, one might render 'Some chairs are heavier than some tables' in this way:

> There is an x such that x is a region of space and the things that fall within x are arranged chairwise and there is a y such that y is a region of space and the things that fall within y are arranged tablewise and the things that fall within x are heavier than the things that fall within y.

Which of these paraphrases is "best" is a question which does not much interest me and which I shall not pursue. I prefer the first, but only because the use of plural quantification enables the paraphraser to avoid having to make a seemingly arbitrary choice between objects of singular quantification—between sets and regions—to perform a function that is essentially one of bookkeeping. (And there are doubtless other objects than sets and regions that might perform this function.) But this is not a strong or fundamental reason for preferring the first paraphrase. One might point out, in defense of the second, for example, that ordinary quantification and set theory are much more studied and much better understood than plural quantification.

The main logical feature that unites our three paraphrases and separates them from the original is that, where the original, at least when it is translated into the quantifier-variable idiom in the obvious way, contains ordinary predicates like 'x is a table', the paraphrases contain variably polyadic predicates like 'the xs are arranged tablewise'. (In the first paraphrase a plural quantifier binds the free plural variable in these predicates. In the other two paraphrases the free plural variable is eliminated in favor of an open plural referring expression—for example, 'the members of x'—containing a singular variable bound by an ordinary quantifier.) What does this feature do for us? Why is it a good thing? In short, why bother to construct paraphrases that have it? Well, our present purpose is only to argue (by example) that such paraphrase is possible. Our answer to the Special Composition Question entails that there are no material objects but organisms and simples, and our suggested technique of paraphrasis enables us to escape some of the more embarrassing consequences of this position. When someone says "Some tables are heavier than some chairs," there is obviously something right about what he says. Our technique of paraphrasis enables us to capture what it is that is right about what he says—or such is my hope. To say this much, of course, is not to point out an advantage of our paraphrases over the originals, but only to point out why someone who accepts my answer to the Special Composition Question finds it expedient to have such a technique at hand. An appreciation of the *advantages* of the paraphrases over the originals must wait on an examination of the application of this technique to such problems as the Ship of Theseus. We shall devote Sections 13, 14, and 15 to this examination. I anticipate what will be said there by saying this much: If there are no artifacts, then there are no philosophical problems about artifacts: If situations that, according to the common philosophical view, involve the persistence of artifacts through a change of parts in fact involve no artifacts at all but only rearrangements of simples, then there are no problems about the persistence of artifacts.

Having, I hope, made it seem plausible that in a large class of cases it is possible to paraphrase sentences that contain artifactual common nouns into sentences that contain no physical-object common nouns (and, a fortiori, no physical-object common noun but 'simple'), I shall sometimes make assertions by writing sentences that contain terms like 'table' and 'chair'. Whenever I do this, I am to be taken as claiming to be able to produce a paraphrase of the sentence I have written that, but for considerations of space and English prose style, I should be willing to put in its place. I shall sometimes apologize for my apparent reference to and quantification over things I deny the existence of by describing these things as "virtual objects."[41] And I shall talk of the "virtual parts" and "virtual properties" of virtual objects. I am not to be taken as thinking that virtual objects are a type of object, any more than the nominalist who allows himself apparent reference to "virtual classes" is to be taken as thinking that virtual classes are a type of class. (My position and that of the nominalist of the preceding sentence are not strictly parallel, by the way. He can allow himself apparent reference to virtual classes but not even apparent quantification over them; I can allow myself apparent quantification over virtual objects.)

Before leaving the topic of paraphrase, I will revert briefly to a topic touched on in the preceding section and emphasize that paraphrases are not supposed to capture the meanings of their originals. (My use of the word 'paraphrase' is therefore somewhat loose, but I do not know of a word that would be better.) When the ordinary man utters the sentence 'Some chairs are heavier than some tables' (in an appropriate context, and so on and so on), he expresses a certain proposition, and one that is almost certainly true. But I do not claim that this proposition *is* the proposition that, for some xs, those xs are arranged chairwise and for some ys, those ys are arranged tablewise, and the xs are heavier than the ys. If these are two distinct propositions, what is the relation between them in virtue of which the latter is a "paraphrase" of the former (or the sentence expressing the latter is a paraphrase of the sentence expressing the former)? An analogy will show how I conceive this relationship. Consider the two sentences

The sun moved behind the elms.

Owing to a change in the relative positions and orientations of the earth and the sun, it came to pass that a straight line drawn between the sun and this point (which is on the surface of the earth) would have passed through the elms.

The first of the two sentences is a sentence of ordinary language. And there is certainly some sense in saying that this sentence appears to imply that the sun moves. And it does not appear to me to be wholly unintelligible to say that the second sentence "describes the same fact" as the first. But the second sentence does not even appear to imply that the sun moves. For that matter, it does not even appear to imply that the earth rotates. It is consistent with both Ptolemaic and Copernican astronomy. (Unlike 'Owing to the diurnal rotation of the solar sphere, it came to pass that a straight line . . .' or 'Owing to the diurnal rotation of the earth, it came to pass that a straight line . . .'.) It therefore not only "describes the same fact" as 'The sun moved behind the elms', but, like that ordinary sentence (*I* contend that the ordinary sentence has this feature), is neutral with respect to competing astronomical explanations of the apparent motion of the sun. For all that, it does not seem right to say that the two sentences are identical in meaning or express the same proposition.

My position is that the relation of the paraphrase of 'Some chairs are heavier than some tables' to that sentence is precisely analogous:

(A)   The paraphrase describes the same fact as the original.

(B)   The paraphrase, unlike the original, does not even appear to imply that there are any objects that occupy chair-receptacles.

(C)   The paraphrase is neutral with respect to competing metaphysical theories, *viz.* the "received" theory, that there are objects that occupy chair-receptacles, and the theory I have proposed, according to which there are no such objects.

(D)   The original, though it doubtless does not express the same proposition as the paraphrase, has the feature ascribed to the paraphrase in (C): It is neutral with respect to the question whether there are objects that fit exactly into chair-receptacles.

It is in virtue of these properties of the relation between the paraphrase and the original that I call the paraphrase a "paraphrase" of the original.

No doubt many philosophers will dispute (D). They will want to say that 'Some chairs are heavier than some tables' (or the proposition expressed by typical utterances of this sentence) *does* entail that there are objects that fit exactly into chair-receptacles. And some philosophers may want to say that 'The sun moved behind the elms' (or the proposition expressed by typical utterances of this sentence) *does* entail that the sun moves. (That is, does entail the thesis asserted by a Ptolemaic astronomer when he utters the sentence 'The sun moves' in the course of an astronomical debate with a Copernican.) Philosophers of these two persuasions and I disagree on a point of the philosophy of language. Whichever side in this disagreement may be right, it should now be clear what I am claiming for the sentences I call paraphrases.

12. Unity and Thinking

We have proposed the following "Moderate" answer to the Special Composition Question:

($\exists y$ the xs compose y) if and only if
the activity of the xs constitutes a life.

I have done my best to explain the content of this answer, and I have argued that this answer is not absurd. But to argue that an answer to a certain question is not absurd is not to argue that it is correct. Why should anyone suppose that this answer is correct?

I do not suppose that it is possible to prove a philosophical thesis, particularly a far-reaching and radical one. Moreover, the best reasons for accepting a philosophical thesis are generally of a sort that it is hard to capture in consecutive prose. The best reasons for accepting a philosophical thesis generally involve the ways in which a host of more or less unrelated problems, convictions, observations, and arguments interact with that thesis. I think that the best reasons for accepting my proposed answer to the Special Composition Question are available only to the philosopher who has examined the great philosophical puzzle cases about endurance in the light provided by this answer. We shall presently conduct an examination of some of these cases in that light. Nevertheless, it is possible to produce some arguments in the narrow sense—arguments having identifiable premises and a discernible logical structure—that support our answer. These arguments are perhaps rather weak, but I do not think they are entirely worthless and I shall devote the present section to them.

I begin with a point made in Section 8: Nihilism is false because (1) I exist, and (2) if I exist, I have parts. But what about (1)? Why should I suppose that I exist?

There are various arguments that, if I accepted them, would force me to concede that I did not exist. The only arguments that support this unattractive thesis that seem to me to be worth taking seriously (and I think they are worth taking more seriously than many philosophers do) are various arguments having to do with vagueness. We shall consider one of these arguments in Section 17.

The main arguments for the thesis that one exists are, of course, due to Descartes.

Why should I think that I exist? Why should *who* think that *who* exists? To raise the question whether one exists is to presuppose that one exists; even an omnipotent deceiver could not deceive one about one's own existence, owing to the fact that one would have to be *there* in order to be deceived. (Imagine an omnipotent deceiver who boasted, "This morning I deceived Zeus. Although he doesn't exist, I made him think that he did.") In addition to the argument from the incoherency of denying one's own existence, Descartes employs a second argument: *Cogito, ergo sum.* Presumably this argument is not really (as Hobbes thought it was) of the same logical form as *ambulo, ergo sum.* Presumably Descartes meant by saying '*Cogito, ergo sum*' that he was in some sense directly aware of a thinking being, a being about whose existence he could not be mistaken, and that this being would have to be himself, since, for any being distinct from himself, he *could* be mistaken about that distinct being's existence.

These arguments have been challenged by various empiricists, such as Hume and Russell. A "composite photograph" of the various empiricist counterarguments would look something like this. An occurrence of the question 'Do I indeed exist?' is a certain succession of ideas; suppose there are three of them, and call them *a, b,* and *c.* For this question to have an asker, however, is for the members of a certain very large set of ideas that contains *a, b,* and *c* to compose something. And the question whose occurrence is the succession *abc* can be correctly answered yes only if it has an asker: only if the members of that very large set of ideas compose something. But from the fact that *a, b,* and *c* occur in succession, it does not follow that there are χs such that *a, b, c,* and the χs compose something. An omnipotent deceiver could not, it is true, deceive any thinking being (any being composed of ideas in the right way) into thinking falsely that it existed. But it could cause an occurrence of the question 'Do I exist?' on an occasion when the answer to that question was no. And even if one does exist when one asks oneself whether one indeed exists, one has no right to be sure, without further argument, that this is not one of those occasions. A similar point applies to the second argument. Even if one does exist, the most one is aware of at any given moment is a succession of ideas; one is not aware of a thinking being, of a being composed of the members of some large collection of ideas of which the ideas one currently perceives are but a few.

Now, I find this all perfectly unintelligible. To mention just one difficulty among many, I do not understand what it means to say that I am composed of ideas. Whatever things compose me, they are all of them material—or, at any rate, are no further from being material than quarks and electrons are. But perhaps a materialist who doubts that I exist, or who rejects the Cartesian arguments for this conclusion, might offer an argument that is in some ways analogous to the argument of the empiricists.

He might say this: "Consider those simples that we should normally say composed you. Suppose we're wrong about them. Suppose they don't compose you. Suppose they don't compose anything. Suppose, if you like, that Nihilism is true and that two or more simples never compose anything. Nevertheless, the simples that would compose you if there were such a thing as you—if there were any composite objects—stand to each other in just the causal relations they would stand in if they composed you: The same electrical currents flow, the same chemical reactions take place, and so on. Now, as a good token-token materialist, you believe that each of your particular, occurrent thoughts is identical with some particular physical process in your head. But even if these particles we're talking about compose nothing, that doesn't stop all these processes from going on, and thus it doesn't prevent the occurrence of thoughts. Perhaps, then, the thought that, according to vulgar opinion, is your wondering whether you exist can't be so described; perhaps it's no one's thought. Still, it occurs. Therefore, perhaps, there are occurrences of the question 'Do I exist?' on occasions on which the answer to that question is no."

A less dramatic way to put this point would be the following. "You have offered paraphrases of sentences about artifacts into sentences that refer only to simples. Why do you suppose that the same thing can't be done in respect of sentences about you and other thinkers? Why couldn't we introduce a variable polyadic predicate—say, 'the xs are arranged intellectually'—and paraphrase talk apparently about thinkers into talk that refers only to simples?"

I have no knock-down response to this challenge. What I am going to say will perhaps be thought to beg the question, but it is the best I can do.

Consider the sentences 'The sun shines' and 'The shelf supports the books'. According to the view I am advocating, there are no stars to do any shining and no shelves to do any supporting. Still, as one might put it, the shining and the supporting somehow get done. How, in my view, do they get done? Well, they get done in virtue of the cooperation of simples. The simples that are arranged shelfwise cooperate to support weight; the simples that are arranged siderially cooperate to produce light. Our initial impression is that there is a certain huge object, the sun, that does a thing called shining. Later, under the influence of our theory, we decide that what we took to be the product of the activity of a single object was the product of the joint activity of many. Our initial impression is that there is a certain middle-sized object, the shelf, that does a thing called supporting weight. Later, under the influence of our theory, we decide that what we took to be an accomplishment of a single object was an accomplishment of many.

Could *this* be true: Our initial impression is that there is a certain object, I, that does a thing called thinking; later, under the influence of our theory, we decide that what we took to be the activity of a single object was the activity of many? Peirce says somewhere that one's thinking is really no more than a persistent habit of cooperation among one's brain cells. Couldn't he be right? In fact, couldn't we go him one better and say that one's thinking is really no more than a persistent habit of cooperation among certain simples? And if we have the cooperating simples, what need have we for *one*?

In my view, we do have a need for "one," that is, for the individual thing that thinks. I do not see how we can regard thinking as a mere cooperative activity. Things can work together to produce light. They may do this by composing a single object—a firefly, say—that emits light. But things that work together to produce light are not forced, by the very nature of the task set them, to produce light *by* composing a single object that emits light. And things that work together to support weight are not forced, by the very nature of the task set them, to support weight *by* composing a single object that holds things aloft. (As regards the second case, it seems obvious enough that it is no argument for the thesis that Tom and Tim have a mereological sum to point out that they are carrying a beam: Tom's activity and Tim's activity are jointly sufficient to account for the fact that the beam remains aloft and moves along.) But things cannot work together to think—or, at least, things can work together to think only in the sense that they can compose, in the strict and mereological understanding of the word, an object that thinks. (I am, incidentally, using 'think' in a very liberal sense, sufficiently liberal that I will count such items as *feeling pain* as instances of thinking.) Now, surely, planning for tomorrow or feeling pain cannot be activities that a lot of simples can perform collectively, as simples can collectively shine or collectively support a weight? One is reminded, when one considers this question, of the so-called Chinese Room examples that figure in debates about artificial intelligence.[42] One popular reply to the arguments in which these examples figure is that it is the *system* (the system consisting of the man, the rule books, and the scraps of paper) that does the thinking. This may or may not be a good reply, but it does seem to presuppose the following thesis: There is a certain object, a real and not a virtual object, a "system," which is such that the man and the books and the scraps of paper compose it. Thus the proponents of the "systems" reply do not suppose that thinking can be a cooperative activity: They suppose that there is one object that does the thinking and differ from their opponents in believing that such an object, a system consisting of a man, some books, and some paper, is the sort of thing that *can* think. It is, of course, a consequence of our answer to the Special Composition Question that there are no systems (except, possibly, individual living organisms), although there are no doubt objects that cooperate systematically. I believe that those philosophers who deny that the Chinese Room can think are actually motivated by an inarticulate realization that the "system" supposedly composed of the human rule-follower, the rule books, and the scraps of paper does not exist; an inarticulate realization that these individual objects (supposing *them* to exist) are the only things *there*; a realization that they do not add up to anything. But, I would judge, these philosophers, having failed to raise the Special Composition Question, misdescribe the source of their intuitions by conceding (not explicitly; they concede by failing to dispute) that there is such a thing as the man-book-paper system and proceeding to argue that it is not the sort of thing that thinks. But once the existence of the "system" is conceded, the battle is lost; worse, the whole dispute degenerates into cloudy exchanges about whether a "system" can have the same causal powers as a human brain. (It should be evident from the preceding, by the way, that if my answer to the Special Composition Question is correct, computers—computers of the sort IBM sells—cannot think. They cannot think because they do not exist.)

I therefore exist. And yet I have parts. (Someone might argue that the Cartesian arguments we have employed are valid only on the assumption that the subject is an immaterial being, and hence a being without proper parts. I don't see this. It seems to me that Descartes's arguments for his own existence can be evaluated independently of what the evaluator knows or believes about his own nature; they are simply neutral in relation to questions about the metaphysics of thinkers. I concede that Descartes believed that he could deduce his immateriality from the fact that he was the sort of being whose existence could be proved by "Cartesian" methods. But you, I hope, will concede that his attempted deduction of this conclusion was irremediably invalid.) Therefore, there is at least one case in which a material being has parts. When, in general, does this happen? What allows a material being to have parts? What makes this possible?

We have argued that this state of affairs is possible because it is actual. And our argument for the conclusion that it was actual depended on the notion of thinking: We argued that a thinking being existed and was composite. But we did *not* argue that the fact that this being was a thinking being in any way explained or accounted for the fact that it was a composite being. A proof of actuality is a proof of possibility, but such a proof does not invariably explain the possibility whose existence it demonstrates, for we may very well know that a certain thing is actual (and hence possible) and nevertheless have no explanation of how such a thing could be possible. For example, the absence of money from a bank vault may prove that someone entered the vault during the night, and, if it does prove this, will a fortiori prove that it was *possible* for someone to enter the vault during the night. But the absence of money will in no way explain how it was possible for someone to enter the vault. We can easily imagine officials of the bank and the police saying both that it is undeniable that someone was in the vault and that they have no idea how anyone could possibly have got into the vault. We may also note that, in a case like this, no one will suppose that the absence of money from the vault is even a part of the explanation of how someone could enter the vault: Everyone will suppose that if someone could get into the vault and take money from it, a person could also get into the vault by the same method, whatever it may be, and, if he chose, take no money.

In my view, the fact that I am a thinking being shows that there is at least one composite material object. But it does not explain how it is possible for there to be a composite material object. The fact that I think presupposes but does not explain the fact that certain simples compose something. And I do not suppose that the fact that I think is even a part of the explanation of the fact that certain simples are capable of composing me. I see no initial reason to deny that the factor that accounts for the unity of those simples might exist in the absence of thinking. It is possible (for all I know) that I might cease to think—that I might lose the very capacity for thought—and continue to exist. It is possible (for all I know) that there are composite objects that are essentially incapable of thought. And if there are such objects, the mereological unity of the simples that compose them may be due to precisely the same factor to which the mereological unity of the simples that compose me is due.

When I reflect on the matter, it does not seem to me that thinking has anything to do with my existence. The capacity for thought (even the capacity for sensation) seems to be, metaphysically speaking, a rather superficial property of myself. It may be the most valuable or important of my possessions, the sine qua non of an existence that is of any value whatever to me. There is no reason to suppose—whatever Saint Anselm and Descartes may have thought—that mere existence is a valuable thing. But the fact that a certain feature of a being is of preeminent, even transcendent, value to that being does not even seem to show that that feature is metaphysically essential to it. Descartes, of course, believed that his essence not only contained but *was* thinking. His arguments for this conclusion, however, are fallacious. His real reason for thinking this, whatever arguments he may have devised, seems to me to have been this: If one arranged in thought the objects of one's awareness according to their perceived distance from oneself (compare Moore: "I am closer to my hands than I am to my feet"),[43] one would place one's thoughts at the very center. One's thoughts seem to be as close to one as anything could be. The other things—the hands and feet and eyes—are "out there" and hence not a part of one. The thoughts are "right here" and hence a part of one. I do not say that these words, or anything like them, have been offered as an *argument* by Descartes or by anyone else. I do say that their content is responsible for the plausibility of Descartes's conclusions and (since the more plausible the conclusion of an argument, the less critical the audience to whom the argument is addressed) explain the perennial popularity of Descartes's arguments.

If thinking is not my essence, what is? What is the ground of my unity? That is, what binds the simples that compose me into a single being? It seems to me to be plausible to say that what binds them together is that their activities constitute a life, a homeodynamic storm of simples, a self-maintaining, well-individuated, jealous event. But if I exist because the activity of certain simples constitutes a life, then it would be wholly implausible to suppose that I exist and that no other organisms do. If I exist, then you do too, and so all other human beings. That is to say, if in one case in which simples are arranged "anthroponomically" they compose an object, then in all cases in which simples are arranged anthroponomically they compose an object.

Might it not be that simples (or any other objects) compose an object just in the case that their activity constitutes a *human* life? Might it not be that the xs compose something if and only if the xs are arranged anthroponomically? This would be an arbitrary position indeed. If objects whose activity constitutes a human life compose something, then so do objects whose activities constitute a feline or a murine life. ("But the notion of life is a vague notion. Not all lives are like the lives of human beings and cats and mice. What about bacterial and viral lives? Don't the lives of the lower links of the Great Chain of Being trail off into vague, temporary episodes of molecular interaction? Where will you draw the line?" I shall discuss these questions in connection with the general topic of vagueness in Sections 17, 18, and 19.[44])

It would, I have suggested, be arbitrary to say of any simples whose activity constitutes a life that they fail to compose an object. If this suggestion is correct, then the 'if' half of our answer to the Special Composition Question is correct. But what about the 'only if' half of the answer? That, after all, is the really radical part of the answer. Why should one suppose that there are no artifacts and stones and heavenly bodies? If it is arbitrary to suppose (given that simples arranged anthroponomically compose a human being) that simples arranged pigwise do not compose pigs, then, surely, it is arbitrary to suppose that simples arranged penwise do not compose pens? Surely a pen (or a stone or a star) would normally be taken to be as much a central or perfectly clear or paradigmatic case of an existent object as people and pigs are? Why stop with organisms?

The answer (insofar as I have an answer) is threefold. (1) Cartesian arguments show that we are forced to grant existence to *some* organisms (to the ones that think, at least), owing to the fact that thinking cannot be understood as a disguised cooperative activity. But *all* the activities apparently carried out by shelves and stars and other artifacts and natural bodies can be understood as disguised cooperative activities. And, therefore, we are not forced to grant existence to *any* artifacts or natural bodies. (I have not, of course, proved this general statement. I have done no more than give examples. Perhaps the example of paraphrase given in the preceding section and the discussion of cooperative activity in the present section have gone some way toward making this general statement plausible.) (2) What answer to the Special Composition Question would generate artifacts and natural bodies? *Contact, Fastening, Cohesion, Fusion,* and Universalism would generate various of these things, though they might generate more or fewer of them than the friends of artifacts would be comfortable with. *Contact,* for example, does not obviously provide us with cups, since it is not obvious that one should say that the simples within a certain cup-receptacle are in contact. And if *Contact* does provide us with cups, then it also provides us with an object that is the sum of the dinner table and the complete service for eight that is laid out on it. (As a further bonus, it generously provides us with a host of metaphysical problems about this complicated domestic object; does it, for example, cease to exist when the saltcellar falls to the floor, or does it simply cease to have the saltcellar as a part?) In any case, all these answers are demonstrably wrong. Perhaps some answer of the *Series* type will generate all the comfortable furniture of earth (and will generate no discomfiting spare furniture, like tables-cum-services-for-eight). But we in fact know of no plausible answer of the *Series* type. If we supposed that there were no material objects but organisms and simples, we should be relieved of the task of trying to devise an answer to the Special Composition Question that would accommodate them. (3) It is not only discomfiting spare furniture that generates embarrassing metaphysical problems. The comfortable furniture of earth can be very embarrassing indeed. If we supposed that there were no material objects but organisms and simples, we should be spared these embarrassments.

Let us now turn to the metaphysics of artifacts.

13. Artifacts

Imagine a desert, a true desert wherein nothing grows and there is nothing but sand. Imagine that a regiment of the Foreign Legion arrives at a certain location in this desert with orders to secure the local caravan routes against banditry. The first thing the legionnaires do is to build a fort. They have brought bulldozers, and they push the sands of the desert about with these machines till the formerly level desert looks like this:

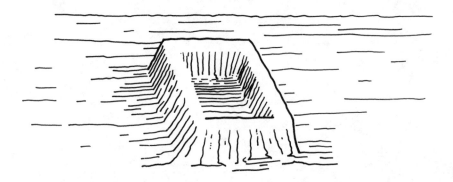

Have they brought anything (a fort, say?) into existence? I should say that they have not. They have, to use a phrase I used earlier, rearranged the furniture of earth without adding to it. The blades of their bulldozers have pushed grains of sand—or simples arranged grainwise—about and piled them in a militarily useful way, but they have not brought even one object into existence. (But if one of the legionnaires said, "We have built a fort," he would thereby assert a true proposition.) The fort, there-fore, is a virtual object. It may serve as a model in our thinking about artifacts. Other artifacts differ from it only in that the virtual objects that are their "parts"—the virtual objects that get cobbled together in the course of their construction—differ from one another in size, shape, and other properties more than grains of sand differ from one another, and in that these "virtual parts" are typically bonded together by a more diverse set of physical forces (the fort is held together, above the granular level, entirely by gravitation and friction). But these differences are of no ontological consequence.

I do not know what most philosophers would say about our fort. But some philosophers, at least, have described a similar case in a way that is radically incompatible with the picture I have tried to paint in the preceding paragraph. The case I have in mind is the case of the lump of gold and the (at least momentarily) conterminous golden statue. This case was introduced in Section 2 when we were discussing the thesis that any objects have at most one sum. I briefly mentioned there that some philosophers contend that the lump and the statue are numerically distinct. I wish now to discuss this contention more carefully. Since it will be convenient for my purposes to imagine a statue made of a stuff that can be easily worked with the fingers, I shall, like a singularly incompetent alchemist, change gold to clay.

Suppose that a sculptor comes upon a nondescript lump of clay and kneads it into the shape of a man. According to the philosophers I am thinking of, the sculptor thereby brings an object—a statue—into existence. But (these philosophers say) the lump of clay continues in existence. It occupies the same space as the statue and has the same shape and weight and color and texture, but it retains its separate identity. We must suppose this (these philosophers tell us) because there is something *there* that has properties that the statue does not have. These are, roughly, the properties that Descartes ascribed to his famous piece of wax. There is, for example, something there that can be kneaded into any of an infinite number of forms, most of them radically different from its present form. But the statue does not have this property. It cannot be radically deformed. Even a modest deformation would destroy it. This object which is not the statue and which can persist through radical deformation is, of course, the lump of clay. (Some philosophers would say that, in addition to the statue and the lump, there is a third thing, the clay, which, unlike the lump, can survive being scattered to the four corners of the earth. I shall not discuss "the clay," for it seems to me to raise no problems of principle beyond those raised by the lump.) And it is not only this dispositional or modal property that the lump of clay does not share with the statue. The historical properties of the lump are also different from those of the statue, since the lump has been in existence longer than the statue.

Any philosopher who takes this position on the statue and the lump will presumably reject our assertion that the legionnaires have brought nothing into existence with their bulldozers. He will say (presumably) something like this: Lying in the desert floor when the Legion arrived, mixed with many others of its kind, was a certain *mass of sand*; the bulldozers prodded this mass of sand till it was fort-shaped (separating it from the others of its kind in the process), thereby producing a new object, a fort, an object that differed from the now fort-shaped mass of sand in its modal and historical properties—but only in those.

This seems to me to be an incredible view. Let us consider the case of the statue and the lump. Suppose the statue and the lump both exist (though I in fact deny that either of them exists). Then, surely, the words 'the statue' are simply a name that applies to the lump at various points in its career; the property *being a statue* is possessed by the lump wherever the lump is of the right shape. (Note that this is just what the proponent of the numerical distinctness of the lump and the statue says vis-à-vis the property *being spatially coincident with a statue*: This property is possessed by the lump whenever the lump is of the right shape.) If you take this incredible view, then, I think, you should also take the view that whatever *outré* shape a lump of clay might have, that lump is spatially coincident with an object with which, though the two are distinct, it shares all its momentary properties. Pick up a lump of clay and knead it into some complicated and arbitrary shape. Call anything essentially of that shape a gollyswoggle. Did you bring a gollyswoggle into existence? I should think that if our sculptor brought a statue into existence, then you brought a gollyswoggle into existence. 'Statue-shaped' is a less definite shape predicate than 'gollyswoggle-shaped', and one we have a use for, and our sculptor intended to produce something statue-shaped while you, presumably, did not intend to produce anything gollyswoggle-shaped. But these facts would seem to be irrelevant to any questions about the existence of the thing produced; if you can make a statue on purpose by kneading clay, then you can make a gollyswoggle by accident by kneading clay. But if you can make a gollyswoggle by accident by kneading clay, then you must, as you idly work the clay in your fingers, be causing the generation and corruption of the members of a compact series of objects of infinitesimal duration. That is what seems to me to be incredible.

If, despite these considerations, you are still inclined to believe in the statue that is distinct from the lump of clay, consider this. We have a snake, a very long, thin, tough snake. Without cutting or otherwise injuring the snake, we weave it cleverly into a hammock (using an art that we have) and suspend the hammock between two trees. We are therefore artisans. We have caused there to be a hammock where there was no hammock before. Nonetheless, we have not augmented the furniture of the world but only rearranged it. If we imagine our snake to be an intelligent being and imagine him to reflect on the question 'Is there an object—a hammock—that is numerically distinct from me but currently spatially coincident with me?' then we do a grave disservice to the intellectual reputation of our helpless creature of fiction if we make him answer this question in the affirmative. A really *intelligent* intelligent snake in the curious circumstances we have imagined will conclude, after only a very brief moment of reflection, "No, no . . . there's nothing here but me." If we, too, are intelligent, we shall agree with him.[45] But if we do agree that the snake momentarily becomes a hammock, then, surely, we should also agree (if we believe in any of these things at all) that the lump of clay momentarily becomes a statue and the mass of sand momentarily becomes a fort. But why believe in any of them? Why (just to focus our intuitions) believe in the mass of sand? Assuming the grains of sand to exist—and of course, I don't believe in *them*, either— what reason could there be to believe in the mass? I can think of no reason but an adherence to Universalism, and Universalism, as we have seen, is false.

There are, therefore, no tables and chairs, and there are no other artifacts—with the unlikely exception of a few things like our living hammock. Artisans do not create; not, at least, in the sense of causing things to exist. They rearrange objects in space and cause bonding relations to begin to hold or to cease to hold (as in the case of the sculptor who chips away at a block of marble) between objects. But, in the last analysis, the labors of Michelangelo and the most skilled watch- maker are as devoid of true metaphysical issue as the labors of our legionnaires. All these people are simply shoving the stuff of the world about. (I hope it is not necessary to say that this description of the labors of artisans, important as it is for metaphysics, has no consequences whatever for aesthetics in particular or the theory of value in general. Consider economic value. Suppose it is necessary for a certain scientific purpose to position two pieces of equipment that are about one hun- dred miles apart in such a way that the distance between them is known to within one one-hundred-thousandth of a centimeter. Scientists might spend three weeks and ten thousand dollars in doing this and consider the time and money well spent. The precise relative placement of the two devices, then, is a "thing" of considerable economic value, and probably a very fragile and carefully protected one. But no one would suppose that in so placing the two pieces of equipment the scientists have brought something into existence. They have arranged preexistent things to their liking and thereby created economic value. Vermeer arranged preexistent things to his liking and thereby created aesthetic value. Value can reside in the arrangement of a plurality of things; it need not have a single object as its vehicle.)

Now, if there are no artifacts, then there are no philosophical problems about artifacts. Or, at least, those philosophical problems that we should have said were "about artifacts" are real problems only to the extent that the sentences that are used to state them can be translated into sentences that can be clearly seen to imply the existence of no physical objects but simples and organisms. And I know of no traditional problem about artifacts that can survive that sort of translation. This is particularly true of problems of identity and persistence through mereological change. The greatest and most profound of the classical problems about the identity of artifacts is the puzzle of the Ship of Theseus. (I trust that anyone who has been willing to read this far knows the story.) The answer to the Special Composition Question I have proposed has, of course, a short way with this puzzle: There are no ships, and hence there are no puzzles about the identities of ships. But, although this much is quite true, it can be elaborated. Let us tell the story of the Ship of Theseus in language that does not make even apparent reference to ships. (To simplify this project, let us suppose that those virtual objects called 'ships' are composed entirely of simples called 'planks'. Or, if you like, we could say that in telling our story, we are treating the planks as "honorary simples," since their individual identities are not in question and since their virtual parts and relevant virtual causal properties are invariant throughout the story. This is a useful device that allows us to use homely words like 'plank' and therefore allows us to tell our story with a minimum of stage-setting. But if anyone insists on it, we can replace our talk of planks with talk of simples arranged plankwise.)

Once upon a time, there were certain planks that were arranged shipwise. Call them the First Planks. ('The First Planks' is a rigid plural designator, like 'the British Empiricists'.) One of the First Planks was removed from the others and placed in a field. Then it was replaced by a new plank; that is, a carpenter caused the new plank and the remaining First Planks to be arranged shipwise, and in just such a way that the new plank was in contact with the same planks that the removed plank had been in contact with, and at exactly the same points. Call the planks that were then arranged shipwise the Second Planks. A plank that was both one of the First Planks and one of the Second Planks was removed from the others and placed in the field and replaced (according to the procedure laid down above), with the consequence that certain planks, the

Third Planks, were arranged shipwise. Then a plank that was one of the First Planks and one of the Second Planks and one of the Third Planks. . . . This process was repeated till all the First Planks were in the field. Then the First Planks were caused to be arranged shipwise, and in just such a way that each of them was in contact with the same planks it had been in contact with when the First Planks had last been arranged shipwise, and was in contact with them at just the same points.

It is not a part of this story that any ships begin to be or cease to be or ever are. All that happens in the story is that planks are rearranged, shuffled, brought into contact, separated, and stacked. But at no time do two or more of these planks compose anything, and no plank is ever a proper part of anything. And this is not a defect in the story or in my way of telling the story. Nothing of philosophical interest has been excluded from the story. *Everything* that went on is represented (somewhat abstractly, I admit) in my description of the way in which planks were shuffled during a certain interval. There are, therefore, no philosophical questions to be asked about the events I have described. In particular, there is no such question as 'Which of the two ships existing at the end of the story is the ship with which the story began?' for the story ended as it began: with no ships at all.

"But we *do*, in the ordinary business of life, utter identity sentences that refer to artifacts. And, in uttering these sentences, we sometimes say things that are true and sometimes say things that are false. If we say, 'This is the house that Jack built' and it is the house that Jack built, then we're right, and if it's the house that Jill built, then we're wrong. How would you account for this difference?"

How seriously should we take the singular terms in these identity sentences? Suppose that it turns out that the Martians don't say "This is the house that Jack built"; suppose they say something that translates literally as "These were arranged housewise by Jack." ("These whats?" Well, *this* what? "This house." These things arranged housewise.) I can see no reason to think that the Martians couldn't "get along in the world" as well as we do. But is our sentence superior metaphysically to the Martians', in that it contains the singular demonstrative 'this' and the count-noun 'house' and a verb of agency, 'built', that, unlike the Martians' 'arranged', takes a singular object? Does our sentence more adequately reveal the structure of the world than the Martians'? I do not think so. I would add that I don't think that the Martians' language is superior to ours. It may be that theirs "more adequately reveals the structure of the world," in the sense that it lacks certain features that are likely to mislead philosophers who are attempting to describe the structure of the world and who are, consciously or unconsciously, guided in these attempts by the structure of the language they use to talk about the world. But language did not evolve for the purpose of guiding philosophical speculation. That's not what it's *for*. (This is a point about the biological history of language. But almost the same point can be made about the histories of particular languages. Languages do not evolve for the purpose of guiding philosophical speculation. That's not what they're *for*.) It may be, therefore, that a language in which one must say 'it is raining', or in which one may use 'exists' as a predicate, is ontologically treacherous in ways that other imaginable languages are not. But this no more reflects adversely on such languages than the fact that some wine bottles make bad rolling pins reflects adversely on those wine bottles.

Paraphrasis like our retelling of the story of the Ship of Theseus or our earlier reparsing of 'Some chairs are heavier than some tables' is of philosophical interest mainly because it provides us with alternatives to our ordinary idioms, alternatives that may be pressed into service when philosophers subject those idioms to dialectical pressures they were not designed to withstand. Consider a simple identity problem about houses. The Wise Pig built a house entirely of bricks (honorary simples), ten thousand of them. That was three generations ago. Over the years his industrious descendants have replaced two thousand of these bricks. Assuming that there is such a thing as the house the Wise Pig built and that there is a house here now, then either the house here now is the house the Wise Pig built or it isn't or the Law of the Excluded Middle requires some sort of amendment.[46] If you think that there are, in the strict, philosophical sense, houses—if you think that when bricks are arranged housewise, they compose something—then you are faced with the problem of choosing one of these alternatives. But suppose that we insist that when questions about the identity of artifacts are being strictly debated, we conduct the debate in a language that refers to nothing besides simples and living organisms and abstract objects. If we follow this rule, we shall be able to formulate no *philosophical* questions about the identities of artifacts at all. The only questions we shall encounter are ones like these: 'Were there bricks arranged housewise then?'; 'How many of the bricks that were among those that were arranged housewise then are among those that are arranged housewise now?'; 'What has been done with the bricks that have been replaced?'

My position, therefore, is this: I am just as willing as you are to use sentences containing 'house' or 'ship' in the ordinary business of life. But if you begin to insist that the things we are talking about strictly and in every respect conform to such general logical principles as the Law of the Excluded Middle, then I shall insist that we have departed from the ordinary business of life and I shall consequently insist that we adopt a language capable of bearing the weight of a full and comprehensive adherence to the Law of the Excluded Middle: a language that refers to nothing besides simples and living organisms and abstract objects. After all, this is essentially what I should do, and what you would do, in many other circumstances. If you get sticky about strict adherence to the Principle of Noncontradiction—if, that is, you insist that even the surface structure of my sentences never be of the form 'p and not p'—then I shall stop saying "It is and it isn't" in response to "Is it raining?" and instead talk of mists. If you insist that every piece of language that has the syntactical form of a singular referring expression denote an object and that every predicate expression concatenated with such a referring expression express a possible property, I shall stop saying "The average father has 1.3 children" and say that the number of children divided by the number of fathers is 1.3. If you insist on raising the question whether the bliger we see before us is the bliger we saw last week, then I shall refuse to use the count-noun 'bliger' at all and talk of animals arranged in bliger fashion. In so retreating to other sorts of language, I, of course, implicitly claim that the language to which I have retreated is such that anything *true* that can be said in the original language can be said in the "language of refuge."

Does our language of refuge (the language employed in the paraphrases of multiply quantified sentences in Section 11) actually provide us with a satisfactory refuge? That is hard to say. Certainly there are some things that can be said, or can apparently be said, in ordinary language that do not seem to be sayable in the language of refuge. Here is a salient example: 'The very same house that stands here now has stood here continuously for three hundred years'. Anything we can say in the language of refuge seems at once too vague and too informative to be a correct paraphrase of this sentence. Suppose we were to try this: 'There are bricks arranged housewise here now and there have been bricks arranged housewise on this spot at every moment during the past three hundred years, and at any two moments during those years that were separated by only a short interval, the bricks arranged housewise at those two moments were pretty much the same bricks, and the bricks on this spot have always been arranged in pretty much the same way'. This statement seems too vague because it contains explicitly vague phrases like 'short' and 'pretty much the same' that do not correspond to any explicitly vague elements in the original. This statement seems too informative because the story it tells is overly specific; surely there are other histories than this of the bricks that (as we would ordinarily suppose) make up a house that would lead us to say that the same house had stood here for three hundred years? (Couldn't a whole wing have been added to the house in a feverish burst of labor? Couldn't a wing have been torn down even faster? Couldn't a house retain its identity through such catastrophic modifications?)

One might attempt to elaborate our paraphrase to take account of these difficulties. But although I have no argument for this, I believe that no paraphrase of 'The very same house that stands here now has stood here for three hundred years' into the language of the rearrangement of bricks is possible. Or, at least, I think that this is true if the paraphrase must refer only to bricks and their mutual relations, because I think that the original sentence makes covert reference to the activities and intentions of intelligent beings with respect to the rearrangement of bricks.

Let us imagine a situation in which certain persons—"we"—have very definite intentions with respect to the arrangement of a few objects—say, three. Suppose that we arrange three pencils on a table to form a triangle. Suppose we take a solemn oath to maintain this arrangement in as nearly its original form as is possible. (Perhaps we believe that this arrangement wards off malignant forces.) Suppose that the content of what we promise to do looks, in detail, something like this:

If the pencils should become disarranged, whoever notices this will immediately rearrange them as they were before.

If any of the pencils should disappear, a search for it will be made; if it can't be found or is damaged, a pencil as nearly like it as possible will be provided to take its place.

The arrangement will be checked at least once an hour to see whether either of the above matters needs to be attended to; a schedule of those responsible for doing this is posted on the bulletin board.

We may imagine that we form a society and induct new members to carry out these duties when old members die or apostasize. Suppose it is now three hundred years since the foundation of the society and that in that period seven pencils (including all the original ones) have disappeared and have been replaced. The content of a diary or log of the society's activities over the years, or the protracted and complex event the course of which is recorded in such a diary, will be what I shall call a "history of maintenance." A history of maintenance begins with an arrangement of objects (typically, virtual objects) and is constituted by the activities of a group of intelligent beings acting in accordance with the prescriptions of a "constitution" (such as the one consisting of the above three rules and some rules about the replacement of society members) to maintain that arrangement. At any given point in a history of maintenance, we may say that that history has certain "current objects": the objects that are then arranged in the pattern that that constitution was instituted to maintain. In our example, at any given time three pencils are at that time the current objects of the history of maintenance.

A more realistic example of a history of maintenance might be provided by the history of a woodpile. Logs are initially piled in a certain way, and these logs are replaced according to an informal constitution in effect among the people who use the pile. Or, again, our legionnaires presumably act according to the prescriptions of a certain constitution in maintaining the arrangement of grains of sand pictured above; if they did not, the desert would soon be level once more. The piled logs, then, are the current objects of a history of maintenance, as are the piled grains of sand. And, as I have argued, a house differs from a sand fort or a woodpile only in that the virtual objects that compose it and the physical forces that ensure the stability of their arrangement are more various. And a house, of course, normally has a history of maintenance. (Even if a house has never received any repairs, there are normally people whose responsibilities and dispositions to carry them out would lead them to repair it under certain circumstances—as we might say, there are no entries in the log, but the rules for making them have been established. And this much is sufficient for the house's having a history of maintenance.)

We may paraphrase 'The very same house that stands here now has stood here for three hundred years' as follows:

There are bricks (or, more generally, objects) arranged housewise here now, and these bricks are the current objects of a history of maintenance that began three hundred years ago; and at no time in that period were the then-current objects of that history arranged housewise anywhere but here.

(If we removed the last clause, we should have a paraphrase of 'The house that stands here now has existed for three hundred years'.) No doubt this paraphrase could be improved. Consider, for example, this difficulty. Suppose that the bricks virtually composing a house stood on this spot until a short while ago, when they were taken apart by a capricious demon and immediately once more arranged housewise, but according to a wholly different design. Then the original sentence would express a falsehood even when it was understood in the loose and popular sense. But the paraphrase might very well be true, for it might be that the blocks continue to be the objects of a three-hundred year old history of maintenance; if those responsible for maintaining the house immediately begin to pull apart the demon's handiwork and to put the bricks back the way they were before, then we should know that this was so. A second difficulty: suppose everyone in the world dies suddenly from a cause that leaves the bricks undisturbed. Then there is no longer a history of maintenance of which the bricks are the current objects, but 'The house exists' continues to express whatever sort of truth it expressed before all constitutions become void.

I think that these examples can be met. For example, we might say that certain bricks are "properly current" objects of the history of maintenance that figures in our story if they are current objects of that history and, if they are now arranged housewise, are not arranged housewise owing to the application of forces that operate independently of the constitution that belongs to that history. (In our first example, the bricks that are here and now arranged housewise are not properly current objects of the history of which they are current objects, since their present housewise arrangement is due to a demon whose activities are not a part of that history.) Having introduced this concept, we might modify our paraphrase to read '. . . are the properly current objects . . .'. As to the second example, perhaps it would suffice to add a clause along the lines of '. . . or if they are not the current objects of any history of maintenance, they are arranged pretty much as the last history of maintenance of which they were the objects left them'.

Doubtless other cases could be devised that would necessitate further elaboration of the technique of paraphrase that I have introduced by example. (For example, what about things like wineglasses that are never repaired if they are damaged? What about things like cigars that are, in a sense, made to be destroyed?) I will not go further into the matter, for I am convinced that the proposal I have made is on the right track: Statements that are apparently about the persistence of artifacts make covert reference to the dispositions of intelligent beings to maintain certain arrangements of matter. We might compare statements of this sort with statements apparently about the persistence of constellations ('The heavens change slowly; the constellations of today are the constellations the Greeks named'), which make covert reference to the perspectives of actual or possible observers of the heavens.

This proposal has the virtue of explaining certain puzzling tendencies we have in our talk about the persistence of virtual objects. Why do we want to say that Uncle Henry's old Ingersol is now in pieces on the jeweler's worktable, and that there are no watches in the jeweler's scrap bin, even though fifty watches could be constructed (in a hundred thousand possible ways) from the gears and springs therein? Answer: Because the gears and springs spread out on the jeweler's table are the current objects of a history of maintenance and none of the gears and springs in the scrap bin is (that is, there are no xs such that the xs are in the scrap bin and the xs are the current objects of a history of maintenance).[47] Why is it at least a joke to say that this is my great-grandfather's axe, though it has had two new heads and five new handles since his day? Why have we at least a tendency to say that this ship is the original ship of Theseus, even though the planks that Theseus originally trod are elsewhere and are arranged in relation to one another just as they were when he trod them? The answer in each case lies in the fact that certain (virtual) objects now before us are the current objects of a history of maintenance.[48]

The theory of artifacts that I have proposed in this section does not answer every philosophical question about artifacts. In the remainder of this section I shall address five questions about artifacts it leaves unanswered. My treatment of these questions is intended to provide examples of ways in which the theory might be extended and applied. But it is conceivable that a philosopher who accepted the theory might prefer other treatments of some or all of the questions.

The first question: What about additions to, or extensive structural modifications of, an artifact? Can't a new wing be added to a house? When the old north wing burns down, can't the owners decide not to have it rebuilt? Can't a house be extensively rebuilt in ways that cannot be described in terms of the addition or subtraction of rooms or wings? Can't a house retain its identity though such episodes, in whatever sense it is it can retain its identity through the gradual replacement of its component bricks? Aren't there analogous questions about ships and bridges—and even about watches and shoes? I would suggest that plausible answers to these questions can be given within the framework of the theory I have proposed if we assume that the "constitutions" that underlie at least some sorts of history of maintenance permit significant increases or decreases in the number of the current objects of those histories or permit significant changes in the way the objects are arranged, much as the constitution of a state might permit a significant increase or decrease in the number of cabinet ministers, or significant structural changes in ministerial organization. (In that case, it might be more appropriate to speak of a history of maintenance and modification than simply of a history of maintenance, but I shall keep the original phrase.) If, as seems reasonable, a history of maintenance may be governed by a constitution having this feature, then there is an obvious way of writing paraphrases of sentences apparently about the persistence of artifacts through reconstruction. Here is a model paraphrase: 'When it was built, that house over there was smaller, since it wasn't until 1952 that the garage was added' is paraphrased as 'The initial objects of the history of maintenance of those things arranged housewise over there collectively occupied less space than those things over there do, since it wasn't until 1952 that the then-current objects of that history included things arranged garage-wise'. If anyone is made uneasy by the contrast between the simple and idiomatic original sentence and its strained and involuted paraphrase, let him reflect on the contrast between the simple and idiomatic sentence 'The sun moved behind the elms' and its strained and involuted paraphrase (p. 112).

The second question: What about modal or counterfactual sentences apparently about artifacts? That is, sentences such as 'This house could have been larger' or 'If this house were larger, it would be easier to see from across the river'? A paraphrase of the former can serve as a model: 'These things arranged housewise are the objects of a history of maintenance which is such that it could have had objects that collectively occupied more space than these things in fact do'. It will be noted that this suggestion implies that our ability to assign truth or falsity to the propositions expressed by sentences like 'This house could have been larger' depends on our ability to identify events in counterfactual situations. We can assign truth-values to such sentences only insofar as we are able to say of an actual history of maintenance that *it*, that very event, would have been going on under certain counterfactual circumstances.[49]

The third question: What about sentences in which there occur words or phrases that are apparently proper names of artifacts—sentences like 'Buckingham Palace is commodious'?[50] We may note that events, like continuants, can have proper names: 'World War II', 'the French Revolution', and so on. But then there is no reason why a history of maintenance couldn't have a proper name—a name like, say, 'the Buckingham Palace History'. (Proper names of histories of maintenance need not contain proper names—or apparent proper names—of artifacts. One could introduce a proper name for a history of maintenance simply by pointing and saying something along the lines of "See those things arranged palatially? Call the history of maintenance of which they are the current objects 'Winifred'.") If so, then 'the current objects of the Buckingham Palace History are arranged commodiously' would seem to be an acceptable paraphrase of 'Buckingham Palace is commodious'.

This suggestion can, of course, be combined with the previous suggestion to provide a way of paraphrasing sentences like 'Buckingham Palace could have been even more commodious'.

The fourth question: What about self-maintaining artifacts? We could imagine a machine that repaired and otherwise maintained itself. Or, if you like, we could imagine a lot of machine parts so arranged as to preserve certain features of their mutual arrangement against entropic dissolution, by exploiting in a flexible way the opportunities presented to them by their environment. Such parts would never be the objects of a history of maintenance in the sense of a history of operations performed on them by external, purposive agents. In another, more liberal sense of 'history of maintenance', of course, they would be the objects of a history of maintenance that was identical with their own mutual operations. Wouldn't there be at least as much reason to say that such machine parts would compose a real, persisting object as there is to say the same thing of the atoms or simples whose activity constitutes the life of an organism?

Well, perhaps. I have not, strictly speaking, said that there are no artifacts, but only that (besides simples) there are only living organisms. Remember our intelligent snake, which was momentarily an artifact. If a super-biologist of the future were to make an amoeba "directly" out of atoms, perhaps that amoeba would be both an artifact and an organism. Perhaps Dr. Frankenstein's creature was both an artifact and an organism. And perhaps a machine that could maintain itself would be an organism. (Perhaps our club of automata is an example of such a machine: I see no reason to think that an organism, as a matter of conceptual necessity, must be a spatially connected object.) When people talk about the possibility of scientists' "creating life," they are normally thinking of the possibility of creating living things whose largest nonliving virtual parts are large organic molecules: things that have the kind of life we and dogs and amoebas have. But perhaps there can be living things that have springs and diodes or assemblies of these as their largest nonliving virtual parts. It is hard to say. Whether it is hard to say because the possibility of such "living machines" is remote from our experience and we have only the vaguest shadow of an idea of what they are supposed to be like, or whether it is hard to imagine simply because the concept of life is vague, is itself hard to say.

Someone generally sympathetic with my position might think it needs to be made more flexible. Such a person might suggest that the kind of event that should figure in a correct answer to the Special Composition Question is a kind of which "soft" or "organic" or "biological" lives are a special case, a kind that might have as members not only soft lives but "hard lives": events constituted by the mutual operations of nonliving virtual objects that are large enough to be visible. I am not irremediably hostile to this suggestion. Neither am I prepared to endorse it.

The fifth question: "Histories of maintenance are in some respects like what you have called lives. They are certainly homeodynamic events. Why not exploit this similarity and 'get' artifacts in your ontology? More formally, why not give the following answer to the Special Composition Question?

($\exists y$ the xs compose y) if and only if

the activity of the xs constitutes a life or the xs are the current objects of a history of maintenance.

This answer goes against all my deepest instincts. The question whether certain things constitute a life is a question about the relations they bear to one another and about nothing else. The question whether certain things are the current objects of a history of maintenance, however, is a question about those things and other things as well. We might say that acting so as to constitute a life is an "internal" multigrade relation and that being the current objects of a history of maintenance is an "external" multigrade relation. My deepest instincts tell me that composition is an internal relation and that, therefore, a proper answer to the Special Composition Question must take the form of a statement that asserts a necessary extensional equivalence between the relation expressed by 'the xs compose something' and some internal multigrade relation. Or we might avoid speaking of external and internal relations and say simply that a proper answer to the Special Composition Question must conform to the following principle:

If the xs compose something, and if the ys perfectly duplicate the xs (both in their intrinsic properties and in the spatiotemporal and causal relations they bear to one another), then the ys compose something.

Consider, for example, some blocks that are piled towerwise. Suppose God were to create a perfect atom-for-atom (or simple-for-simple) duplicate of each block and that someone were to pile the duplicates into a tower in exactly the way the originals are piled. (That is, suppose someone were to cause the following to be the case: For each x, y, and R, if x and y are two of the original blocks and R is a causal or spatiotemporal relation, the duplicate of x bears R to the duplicate of y if and only if x bears R to y.) Then the duplicates compose something (a tower of blocks, presumably), if and only if the originals compose something.

The "liberal" answer to the Special Composition Question that we are considering does not conform to the Duplication Principle (so to call it). Suppose that a child emptied a bag of blocks on to the floor, and that some of these blocks by chance fell in such a way that they were piled towerwise; suppose that no one noticed this. Suppose that the child piled some other blocks in exactly the same way when she was visiting a doting and sentimental aunt, who resolved to maintain these blocks just as she had left them as a memorial of her visit. If the "liberal" answer is correct, then the blocks of the latter case compose something and the blocks of the former case do not, which violates the Duplication Principle. (We may note that the Duplication Principle rules out any metaphysic according to which the existence of physical things depends on the attitudes or mental activity of human beings or other observers of the world. If there were no human beings—or Martians or whatever—then there would be stars and electrons and mountains if and only if there are stars and electrons and mountains in actuality. Our conceptual activity may involve a lot of boundary drawing, but drawing a boundary around a filled region of space does not make it the case that there is some one thing that exactly fills that region. If the mutual causal operations of the things in that region can do that, they need no help from the mental activities of external observers, and if they can't do that, no external activities can help them to do it.)

Now, it might be argued that the central thesis of this book, the Proposed Answer, does not conform to the Duplication Principle. Suppose (the argument might proceed) that there is someone exactly like me—right down to the subatomic level—except that he has lost his right ear. Let the xs be the atoms that compose him, and let the ys be the atoms that compose me, exclusive of the ones making up my right ear. Then, according to the Proposed Answer, the xs compose something, but the ys, which perfectly duplicate the xs in their intrinsic properties and in their relations to one another, do not compose anything. And this consequence of our supposition violates the Duplication Principle. I reply that the supposition is impossible, owing to the fact that the activities of the atoms adjacent to my right ear are affected by the presence of the atoms that (virtually) compose that ear, and thus they do not reproduce the activities of the atoms in the corresponding position in my mutilated counterpart, which compose scar tissue and are adjacent to nothing but air. More generally, if the xs compose a mutilated organism, then there could not be *y*s such that the *y*s perfectly duplicate the *x*s and the *y*s are properly among some objects that compose an unmutilated organism. (A Universalist could put the point this way: no proper part of an unmutilated organism could be a perfect duplicate of a mutilated organism.) "But suppose that at the very instant your counterpart's ear was cut off, it was replaced with some inorganic appendage that perfectly duplicated the causal powers of the severed ear. Then the atoms adjacent to the 'interface' would behave exactly as they would have behaved if the ear had not been cut off." If the "appendage" *perfectly* duplicated the causal powers of the severed ear, right down to the atomic level, it would have to be an atom-for-atom duplicate of the ear and would thus not be "inorganic." The atoms that virtually composed it would immediately be assimilated by my counterpart, who would thereby become a perfect duplicate of me.[51] And that outcome would not contradict the Duplication Principle.

I do not know how to defend my instinctive allegiance to this principle except by trying, as I have tried, to present the principle in as attractive a light as possible. At any rate, it is easy to see why someone with my instincts would reject an answer to the Special Composition Question that essentially involved the concept of a history of maintenance.

There is a second reason for rejecting any such answer. Consider once more the Ship of Theseus. We have said that an appeal to the notion of a history of maintenance explains why we have a strong tendency to say that the "maintained" ship is the ship whose boards Theseus originally trod. But let us not forget that we also have a strong—perhaps a stronger—tendency to say that the "reassembled" ship is that ship. If we accept an answer to the Special Composition Question that entails that planks arranged shipwise can compose an object, then we shall be faced with the task of reconciling these opposing tendencies, and that is a task it would be pleasant to avoid. (Note that there is no tendency to identify a "reassembled" *organism* with the "original." If God were to "reassemble" the atoms that composed me ten years ago, the resulting organism would certainly not be *me*.)

In this section, we have discussed certain sentences of English, sentences like 'This house has stood here for three hundred years', that are usually discussed in connection with "the problem of identity across time." But if our answer to the Special Composition Question is correct, these sentences cannot have any very intimate connection with that problem (whatever, exactly, that problem may be), for in that case there are no houses or other artifacts, and thus there is no problem about their persistence through time.

In the next section, Section 14, we shall examine the persistence through time of the only objects there are, organisms and simples. (We shall also examine the problem of counterfactual identity or "identity across worlds" for organisms and simples.) In Section 15 we shall discuss a special but important problem of identity across time for organisms, the problem of the "brain-transplant."

14. The Identities of Material Objects

When, in general, do organisms persist through change? Can we discover a general statement of the rules that differentiate cases of alteration from cases of substantial change among organisms? If we can do this, then we shall have a large part of the solution to "the problem of identity through time" in one sense of those words. I say 'in one sense' because, unless I have them wrong, some philosophers think there are deeper problems about "identity through time" than the problem of saying under what circumstances it occurs. I say 'a large part' because, if our answer to the Special Composition Question is correct, then every concrete object—I assume that there is no problem of identity through time for abstract objects like numbers or propositions—is either an organism or a simple or is not material at all. Immaterial concrete objects, if such there be, fall outside the scope of this book. We shall raise the question of the persistence of simples later in the present section.

In discussing the possibility of *Series*-style answers to the Special Composition Question in Section 7, I remarked that it would be nice to have an answer to the Special Composition Question that (unlike *Series*-style answers and unlike Simple Bonding answers) at least suggested an approach to the great puzzle-cases about the identity across time of material objects. And I promised that the answer I should eventually provide would suggest an approach to these cases. We have already seen how the Proposed Answer deals with the case of the Ship of Theseus and other puzzles involving artifacts—it deals with them as atheism deals with the problem of evil and nominalism with Russell's Paradox. But what about puzzles like those posed by the notorious case of the "brain-transplant," puzzles about organisms? We shall see that our answer to the Special Composition Question indeed suggests an approach to these puzzles. In order to appreciate this approach, however, we must first see what if anything our answer has to tell us about the persistence of an organism through time in ordinary cases—in cases in which the organism is not undergoing radical surgery or any other out-of-the-way adventure. Does our answer to the Special Composition Question (unlike *Series*-style and Simple Bonding answers) suggest an answer to the question 'When, or under what conditions, does one and the same organism continue to exist'? (I say 'suggest' rather than 'entail' because I doubt whether any answer to the Special Composition Question can logically commit its adherents to any thesis about the persistence of objects through time.) I believe that there is one answer to the question about the persistence of organisms that will seem much more natural or congruous than any other answer to one who accepts our Proposed Answer to the Special Composition Question. I believe that Locke has already hit upon something very like this answer. Speaking of an oak, he says:

> We must therefore consider wherein an oak differs from a mass of matter; and that seems to me to be in this, that the one is only the cohesion of particles of matter anyhow united, the other such a disposition of them as constitutes the parts of an oak, and such an organization of those parts as is fit to receive and distribute nourishment, so as to continue and frame the wood, bark, and leaves, &c., of an oak, in which consists the vegetable life. That being then one plant which has such an organization of parts in one coherent body, partaking of one common life, it continues to be the same plant as long as it partakes of the same life, though that life be communicated to new particles of matter vitally united to the living plant in a like continued organization, conformable to that sort of plants. For this organization being at any one instant in any one collection of matter, is in that particular concrete distinguished from all other, and is that individual life which existing constantly from that moment both forwards and backwards, in the same continuity of insensibly succeeding parts united to the living body of the plant, it has that identity which makes the same plant, and all the parts of it parts of the same plant, during all the time that they existed united in that continued organization, which is fit to convey that common life to all the parts so united.[52]

And speaking of animals:

> An animal is a living organized body; and consequently the same animal, as we have observed, is the same continued life communicated to different particles of matter, as they happen successively to be united to that organized living body.[53]

I do not, of course, agree with everything Locke says in his chapter "Of Identity and Diversity." I do not agree, for example, with his contention that *he*, a certain person or thinking substance, is not a living animal and is not, therefore, a man. More to the present point—since we are talking about the persistence of organisms and not about the question whether persons are identical with organisms—I do not accept the existence of "masses of matter" or "cohesions of particles of matter anyhow united." In Locke's view, an organism, such as an oak or a man, is at any given moment spatially conterminous with an object that is numerically distinct from it: a certain mass of matter; and, typically, the oak or the man will be conterminous with different masses of matter at different times. Each of the successive masses of matter associated with (say) me is a sort of momentary recipient of my life, which, its brief hour of cohesion done, it transmits to its successor. (Locke does not clearly say this, but I believe that there is only one way to develop his position with complete logical rigor: There are—in the strict and philosophical sense—no oaks or men; there are only "masses of matter"; talk of perduring oaks or men is a loose, conventional way of expressing certain facts about how masses of matter succeed one another in time.) In my view, however, there is nothing *there* but the oak or the man; if you want to call the oak or the man a mass of matter, that's all right with me, but I do not countenance any mass of matter numerically distinct from the living, persisting thing. (Compare what was said in Section 13 about the statue and the lump of clay.) In my view nothing ephemeral was ever conterminous with the aged oak, for nothing but the oak itself has ever been conterminous with the oak.

There would seem to be two unstated premises on which Locke's allegiance to "masses of matter" rests. First, some primitive answer to the Special Composition Question, *Contact*, perhaps, or, more likely, since he uses the word, *Cohesion*. Secondly, the thesis that the objects generated by this answer obey what one might call the Principle of Strengthened Mereological Essentialism: If the xs compose y, then y is essentially such that the xs compose it, and the xs are essentially such that if they compose z at t, then they compose z whenever they are arranged as they are at t. But since I reject *Contact* and *Cohesion* (and all other Simple Bonding and *Series*-style answers to the Special Composition Question) and reject any form of mereological essentialism, I reject the thesis that there are Lockean "masses of matter."[54] It is because I reject this thesis that I say that Locke's thesis about the persistence of living things is "very like" the right thesis about the persistence of living things.

The correct part of Locke's thesis about organisms may be stated in our terminology like this:

If an organism exists at a certain moment, then it exists whenever and wherever—and only when and only where—the event that is its life at that moment is occurring; more exactly, if the activity of the xs at t_1 constitutes a life, and the activity of the ys at t_2 constitutes a life, then the organism that the xs compose at t_1 is the organism that the ys compose at t_2 if and only if the life constituted by the activity of the xs at t_1 is the life constituted by the activity of the ys at t_2.

Let us call this principle '$Life$'. $Life$ tells us when organisms persist; but in order to apply it, we should have to know when lives persist. Now, I do not think that $Life$ would be useless or uninteresting to someone who was unable to provide an explicit criterion for the persistence of lives. In my view, one can lay down the conditions governing the persistence of the objects in a certain category only if one is allowed to presuppose the persistence of the objects in some other category. One may, of course, go on to lay down the conditions governing the persistence of the objects in this second category, but, obviously, one cannot take more than a finite number of such additional steps. Eventually one must be content with describing the persistence of some sort of object by reference to the persistence of some other sort of object in the absence of any general and explicit statement of the conditions of persistence for objects of that other sort. (Even such a simple criterion as 'An object that exists at t_1 still exists at t_2 if and only if there is a continuous, matter-filled path in space-time leading to t_2 from the position occupied by that object at t_1'—a criterion that, as we shall see, is doubtful even for Democritean atoms—presupposes the persistence of regions of space.) But these reflections, true though they are, do not absolve us of our obligation to say as much as we can about the persistence of lives. If nothing else, careful investigation might turn up facts, or plausible conjectures, about the persistence of lives that, in conjunction with $Life$, entailed false or implausible theses about the persistence of organisms.

Let us first examine the question of the temporal continuity of lives. If a life is going on at t_1 and is not going on at the later time t_2, is it possible for it once more to be going on at the still later time t_3? Can a life stop and then start again? Can a life fall into two parts separated by an inter-regnum or "intervitam" during which nothing is caught up in it? Let us examine some cases of lives that one might be inclined to regard as "gappy." Suppose that a man's heart stops beating and then he stops breathing; suppose that a doctor is able to start his heart beating again and that he recovers. We feel no doubt that the man who recovers is the man who was stricken. I shall assume that we are right. It follows that if the life of the man who recovers is *not* the life of the man who was stricken, then *Life* is false. But this case does not force the friends of *Life* to defend the thesis that a life can stop and then start again, since it is not clear that a man's life is not going on when his heart is not beating—or even when blood is not circulating in his veins and arteries (a circumstance that is not an invariable consequence of one's heart's not beating, owing to the availability of mechanical hearts and other such devices). I seem to remember that when the heart stops beating, the human organism will sometimes cause its arterial walls to contract, in a valiant and pathetic attempt to cause the blood to circulate; this indicates that the cells that compose the stricken man are still caught up in a continuing homeodynamic event. But we can imagine a more difficult case. Suppose we take a healthy cat and freeze it; suppose we reduce its body temperature to very nearly absolute zero by some technique (not currently available, by the way) that does it no irreversible organic damage. Suppose we then revive the cat. It seems clear that the revived cat is the cat we started with. (The phrase "the revived cat" strongly suggests, if it does not entail, that there is only one cat in our story. It would obviously be possible to tell the story in a way that did not entail, or even suggest, this. Consider it done.) But it also seems clear that the cat's life ceased when it was frozen. Life is the sum of a great many chemical processes, and no chemical processes at all are going on inside the frozen cat. And therefore, one might argue, the friends of *Life* must accept the possibility of discontinuous lives.

It is not altogether clear, however, that the life of the cat ceases when it is frozen. It may be true, or at least a good approximation to the truth, to say that all chemical processes within the frozen cat cease. (In order to avoid begging questions, we must regard the frozen cat as being, for all we know, only a virtual object). But it is not true that there cease to be any chemical *facts* about the cat. The atoms of which the feline corpse is composed continue to be bonded to one another by the complicated dance of electrons and photons that makes for solid matter. If they were not so bonded, the frozen cat would dissolve into atomic nuclei and free electrons; and it is a quantum-mechanical impossibility for electronic and photonic activity to cease. All the fragile molecules of life persist, properly arranged and bonded, inside the cat, maintained in their arrangement and (virtual) existence not by any homeodynamic process but by the mere absence of those random, disruptive surges of thermal energy whose effects it is the normal business of life to undo. Because all these chemical bonds persist unchanged in the frozen cat, and because these bonds were established by the operations of the cat's life, I find it attractive to suppose that the cat's life persists even when the cat is frozen. I would describe the frozen cat's life this way: Before the cat was frozen, its life consisted mostly of chemical reactions and various relatively large-scale physical processes (the breaking and establishing of chemical bonds, the movement of fluids under hydraulic pressure, the transport of ions); when the cat was frozen, its life was "squeezed into" various small-scale physical processes (the orbiting of electrons and the exchange of photons by charged particles). Its life became the sum of those subchemical changes that underlie and constitute chemical and large-scale physical unchange. But the life was *there*, disposed to expand into its normal state at the moment sufficient energy should become available to it. I, who am fond of oxymorons, would describe the frozen cat as a living corpse.

Perhaps this description will strike some readers as contrived and tendentious. It is not really essential to my position to suppose that our frozen cat is alive. If someone insists that the frozen cat is not alive, I do not think that he is misusing the word 'alive'. I would say that he was proposing a stipulative sharpening of the meaning of 'alive'; and that, I think, is just what I was doing in the preceding paragraph. If we use the word 'alive' in such a way that a frozen but undamaged (and revivable) organism is not alive, then I will distinguish two sorts of ways in which a life may cease: a life may be *disrupted* and a life may be *suspended.* The frozen cat is an organism whose life has been suspended. In general, a life has been suspended if it has ceased and the simples that were caught up in it at the moment it ceased retain—owing to the mere absence of disruptive forces—their individual properties and their relations to one another. (Actually, this is not quite right. The simples of which a cat is composed are, in my view, up-quarks, down-quarks, and electrons—and, perhaps, photons and gluons. And these never cease their activity, not even when they are parts of an object that is immersed in liquid hydrogen. It is the activities of relatively large virtual objects—molecules—that essentially cease at very low temperatures. I hope that my having noted the necessity for a revision to take account of this fact will absolve me of the responsibility for actually carrying it out.) A life that has ceased but was not suspended has been disrupted. We may be confident that the life of an organism which has been blown to bits by a bomb or which has died naturally and has been subject to the normal, "room-temperature" processes of biological decay for, say, fifteen minutes has been disrupted. Having made this distinction, I lay down the following two principles about the continuity of lives. If a life has been disrupted, it can never begin again; any life that is going on after its disruption is not *that* life. If a life has been suspended, it can begin again; if the requisite energy is supplied to the simples whose activity has been suspended, in a uniform, nondisruptive way, it *will* begin again. (Perhaps a gentle prod will be required; an electrical stim-ulus to the heart muscle of the just-thawed cat, or something of that sort.)

What about the organism whose life is suspended? Does it exist during the suspension of its life, or does it go out of existence when its life stops and come back into existence when its life starts again? (According to *Life*, remember, if a life is suspended and then begins again, the revived organism is the organism whose life was suspended.) It is not absolutely essential to my position to say that the organism exists when its life is suspended, but I feel inclined to say that it does. That it does is a consequence of *Life* and my earlier contention that the life of a frozen, undamaged organism—in the actual world, I think, suspending the life of an organism as complicated as a cat must come down to freezing the organism; other laws of nature might allow other types of suspension—continues at the subchemical level. But if we suppose that a frozen organism is not "alive," then we must fiddle with our principles govern-ing composition and persistence if we want the result that the frozen organism is a real (as opposed to a virtual) object and that it is the same real object that exists before and after the freezing. We must first modify our answer to the Special Composition Question if the frozen organism is to be a real object at all:

($\exists y$ the xs compose y) if and only if

the activity of the xs constitutes a life or the individual properties of the xs and their relations to one another are unchanging (at the level of activity at which the processes of life take place) and when the xs were last changing, their activity constituted a life.

And if we wish the frozen object to be the same object that the simples composing it composed when their activity last constituted a life, we must amend *Life*. Let us count stasis as a special case of "activity." Let us say that if the individual properties of the xs and their relations to one another are unchanging at t, and if, when the xs were last changing, their activity constituted a life, the activity of the xs at t "results from" the life that their activity lately *constituted*. (We could now express our revised answer to the Special Composition Question like this: The xs compose something if and only if the activity of the xs constitutes or results from a life.) Then let us rewrite *Life* in this way:

If the activity of the xs at t_1 constitutes or results from a life, and the activity of the ys at t_2 constitutes or results from a life, then the organism the xs compose at t_1 is the organism the ys compose at t_2 if and only if the life that the activity of the xs at t_1 constitutes or results from is the life that the activity of the ys at t_2 constitutes or results from.

We may say, therefore, that if *Life* is not to have implausible consequences for the persistence of organisms, then temporal continuity in at least the following weak sense is necessary for the persistence of lives: if a life is going on at t_1 and t_3, then for any time t_2 between t_1 and t_3 there must be objects whose activity at t_2 constitutes or results from that life.

If temporal continuity is necessary for the persistence of a life, might spatiotemporal and "material" continuity be jointly *sufficient* for the persistence of a life? That is: Suppose that the activity of the xs constitutes a life at t; suppose that a few of the xs cease to be caught up in that life and that the remnant continue to be caught up in a life; suppose that those of the xs that have ceased to be caught up in that life are "replaced"—that certain objects, the ys, come to be caught up in the life the remnant of the xs are caught up in, in such a way that the ys and the remnant of the xs constitute that life. Suppose that this sort of replacement happens a sufficient number of times that eventually none of the xs is caught up in the life that has evolved, by a continuous (and "insensible," as Locke calls it) replacement of the xs, from the life that was once constituted by the activity of the xs. Is this life the life that was constituted by the xs?

In many cases, cases of the more usual sort, the answer is undoubtedly yes. In these cases an ongoing life exhibits this sort of spatiotemporal and causal continuity, continuity of the sort that is illustrated by the example of the "club" of automata in Section 9. We may call this "Lockean" continuity. There are, nevertheless, episodes of biological change that raise the question whether life B, which is spatiotemporally continuous with life A, and which is connected with life A by that continuity of replacement that is the hallmark of Lockean continuity, may not be the life of a different organism from the organism having life A. And if it were a different organism, then the advocates of *Life* would have to deny that Lockean continuity was sufficient for the persistence of lives. Two of the "episodes of biological change" I have in mind are cell division and the early stages of embryonic growth. Cell division and embryonic growth raise questions about the application of the concept of Lockean continuity, which is admittedly a concept of which I have been able to give only an impressionistic and analogical characterization. That is, cell division and embryonic growth raise questions about when it is that we actually *have* a case of Lockean continuity. Another sort of episode, metamorphosis (particularly in invertebrates), suggests that two numerically distinct lives may be continuous with each other in just the Lockean sense. Let us first examine cell division.

An amoeba undergoes fission. What happens to the life of the amoeba? There would seem to be three possible answers. (1) The life divides. An instant before it began to divide, the activity of the xs constituted the life of the amoeba. An instant after the division is complete, the activity of the xs still constitutes a life, but there are ys and zs such that the ys and zs are the xs, and the ys are causally isolated (or very nearly so) from the zs, though all the ys interact with one another and all the zs interact with one another. This answer, in conjunction with *Life*, if pushed to its logical conclusion, would yield the result that (assuming that any two amoebas have a common "ancestor") all amoebas are virtual parts of a vast scattered object. Fortunately, answer (1) is ruled out by an intuitively appealing principle: If the activity of the xs constitutes a life, then none of the xs is causally isolated from the others. (I have said that I do not regard it as a necessary truth that an organism is a topologically connected object; but if some organism is composed of, say, two maximally connected parts— real or virtual parts—it is, in my view, a necessary truth that there must be some sort of interaction between the two "separated" parts of the organism. This interaction might involve radio waves or some other causal medium that did not need to propagate along a pathway made of living tissue. But I should think that the interaction would have to be continuous in time and space. The haphazard and intermittently operative web of causation that binds together a hive of bees is not tight enough to make an organism of the hive.) (2) The old life is transferred to *one* of the daughter cells; the other is somehow provided with a new life. This is arbitrary and absurd. (3) The old life ends; the life of each of the daughter cells is a new life. The xs cease to compose anything and their activity no longer constitutes a life; the activity of the ys begins to constitute a life and the ys begin to compose something—and so with the zs. (I am tempted to try to give a more fine-grained statement of the metaphysics of eucaryotic cellular fission, despite the fact that my knowledge of cytology is inadequate to the task. What follows is sheer speculation. [i] The cell dissolves, perhaps in late interphase just before chromosome doubling occurs. I mean the word 'dissolves' in an ontological rather than a physical sense: the life of the cell ends, and, though the simples that had composed the cell continue to cohere, they no longer compose an organism. The cell dissolves, in this sense, into a cohesive mass of cytoplasm in which there "swim" various small organisms. [ii] These organisms are mostly former virtual parts of the parent cell—chromosomes and various organelles such as the centrioles. [iii] Each chromosome splits lengthwise, the products being two copies of itself, and these

"new" chromosomes—chromatids—cooperate with the other temporary subcellular organisms to rearrange the matter of the former cell and
the chromatids themselves into two "arenas," each of which, like a pile of
logs that has been laid and is ready to become the site of a campfire, is
ready to become the site of a life. [iv] The arenas are walled off and
physically separated and in each a new life begins. The independent
organisms that had been the agents of the division of the matter that
would compose the daughter cells are absorbed into the daughter cells,
that is to say, they cease to exist and, loosely speaking, become virtual
parts of the daughter cells.) If this is right, then it follows that not all lives
that end, end in decay and physiological dissolution. If these speculations are correct, the question whether "Lockean" continuity is sufficient
for the persistence of a life is a rather tricky question, since it is a rather
tricky question when we have and when we don't have a case of Lockean
continuity. I should like to say, for theoretical reasons, that the life of
the cell has ceased when its chromosomes begin to split. But, at least as
far as I know, there is nothing in the observable facts of cell division to
prevent one from saying that the cell's life ends much later in the mitotic
process—at any time up to the actual physical separation of the daughter cells. But if the life of the amoeba ceases at *any* time before the physical
separation of the daughter cells, we have a case of a life ending without
any readily apparent break in the continuity of the processes of life.
Perhaps if I knew something about cellular metabolism during fission,
and, in particular, about the relation of the chromosomes to the metabolic processes taking place in the cytoplasm during mitosis, I should
revise my opinion about the point at which the life of a dividing cell
ceases and be willing to say that its life continues right up to the moment
of actual physical separation. But if I am right and the life of the cell ends
earlier than that, this would not necessarily violate the principle that
Lockean continuity is sufficient for the persistence of a life. We should
have Lockean continuity up to the point of physical separation only if, at
every moment prior to separation, the activity of the simples then caught
up in the process of cell division constituted some life or other. And the
fact that there is "no readily apparent break in the continuity of the
processes of life" does not guarantee this. My speculative description of
the metaphysics of mitosis in fact entails that throughout most of the
mitotic process there is no *one* life that is constituted by the activity of the
simples then caught up in that process (that is, the mitotic process is not
then a life); and this description—since it is true to the observable facts—
entails no break in the continuity of that process.

The questions about the continuity of life raised by sexual reproduc-
tion are even trickier than the questions raised by cellular fission.

A sperm unites with an egg. What happens, metaphysically speaking?

The following, I think. The sperm enters the egg and then each ceases to exist—the simples that compose the sperm cease to compose anything, and the simples that compose the egg cease to compose anything; then the simples that had composed the sperm and the simples that had composed the egg begin to compose something; what they begin to compose is a zygote. (Here, again, is an attempt at a more fine-grained description of this process, one based largely on ignorance. The entrance of the sperm causes the egg cell to undergo its second meiotic division, which constitutes the end of its life: the egg ceases to exist; it dissolves into a mass of cytoplasm in which there swim a sperm and various newly created subcellular organisms. The nucleus of the sperm approaches the haploid nucleus created by the second meiotic division of the egg, and they begin to interact. The sperm dissolves, not only ontologically but physiologically. The chromosomes of the sperm and the haploid egg nucleus and various subcellular organisms cooperate to arrange themselves and the available cytoplasm into an arena, the activity of the inhabitants of which will constitute the new life. The new life begins and the temporary organisms are absorbed by it. A new object, a zygote, now exists, generated out of the simples that had composed the sperm and the simples that had composed the egg.)

It is sometimes said that a zygote "develops into a new individual." There is certainly something in this statement, but it cannot be literally correct. To begin with, the zygote *is* a new individual, *ab initio*. In one sense, to say that it will develop into a new individual can no more be true than it can be true to say that an adult human being will develop into a new individual. Perhaps what is meant is this: The zygote will grow and change and one day become a mature canine or feline or human organism. If this is literally true, then—assuming that you and I are organisms—you and I were once zygotes.

I do not think that this can be right. The zygote is a single cell. About thirty hours (in the case of human beings) after fertilization, it will divide mitotically, and the immediate result will be two duplicates of it that adhere to one another. If what we have said about the metaphysics of cellular fission is correct, the zygote ceased to exist with this division. But in that case you and I have never been zygotes; whenever you and I came into existence, it was more than thirty hours after our conception. What alternative views of the metaphysics of early embryonic development are possible? A diagram may help us to focus our thoughts.

t_1 zygote

t_2 two-cell embryo, immediately after mitotic
                        division of zygote

What happens to the zygote (A) in this episode? There would seem to be three possibilities. (1) The zygote ceases to exist; at t_2, neither B nor C nor anything else is A. (2) The zygote replicates itself and continues to exist, adhering to its replica; at t_2, either B or C is A. (3) The zygote changes from a one-celled to a two-celled organism; at t_2, A is the mereological sum of B and C.

I favor possibility (1). Possibility (2) seems to me to be wholly arbitrary and implausible. In any case, possibility (2) is inconsistent with the thesis that you and I were once zygotes. Anyone who thinks that you and I were once zygotes must accept possibility (3).

Possibility (3) is, I think, no real possibility. I assume that the advocate of possibility (3) believes that after the division of A, there is no longer any such *cell* as A; if there were, it would be either B or C, and a thing would be a proper part of itself. No, the advocate of (3) must think that, at one point in its career, A had exactly one cell as a part—itself—and that later it had exactly two cells as parts. (Later still, he will say, A had millions of millions of cells as parts.) This way of thinking receives a certain amount of wholly illusory support from the phrase "one-celled organism." If there can be a one-celled organism, then, surely, there can be a two-celled organism? (If there can be a one-man band, then, surely, there can be a two-man band?) It's the small numbers that are the hard ones, one is inclined to think; once the possibility of an n-celled organism has been established, then there is no difficulty about the possibility of an $n+1$-celled organism.

But, really, a one-celled organism is just a cell. It has, it is true, exactly one cell as a part, but this is no fact about the world but merely the result of a linguistic stipulation, *viz.* that the word 'part' shall be so used that everything shall be called a part of itself. It does not follow, therefore, from the fact that the zygote is an organism, and hence a real object, that the two-cell embryo that replaces it is a real object. Why should we believe that there is something that B and C compose? They adhere to each other, but we have seen that that is no reason to suppose that two objects compose anything. The zygote was a single, unified organism, the vast assemblage of metabolic processes that were its life having been directed by the activity of nucleic acid in its nucleus. No such statement can be made about the two-cell embryo. No event, I should say, is its life. The space it occupies is merely an arena in which two lives, hardly interacting, take place. Therefore, given our answer to the Special Composition Question, it does not exist. Or, better, the simples that compose B and the simples that compose C do not jointly compose anything. Moreover, B and C do not compose anything.

But then when does a multicellular organism begin to exist? I do not know the answer to this question, and I am sure that it has no answer that can be discovered apart from a very detailed examination of the facts of embryonic development. It seems to me to be most implausible to suppose that the developing embryo is yet an organism if it is still at a stage at which monozygotic twinning can occur. Suppose I was once a mass of adhering cells that was still capable of splitting into two masses, each of which would have developed into an organism that was genetically exactly like me. Suppose, then, that this had happened. What would have become of me? Only one answer is even superficially coherent: I should have ceased to exist, and two new organisms would have been generated out of the cells that had composed me. I should prefer to think that if an embryo is still capable of twinning, then it is a mere virtual object. (Peter Geach has argued that an embryo that is still capable of twinning is a "mere blob of slime."[55] I take this to be a way of saying that it is a virtual object; strictly speaking, there are no mere blobs of slime. Geach's argument for this conclusion, incidentally, overlooks the "superficially coherent" possibility I mentioned above.)

Cells that are arranged embryonically begin to compose something when their activity begins to constitute a life. When is this? I do not know. Certainly not earlier than the inception of cell differentiation. Certainly not later than the development of a functioning central nervous system, which, in the case of human beings, takes place about twelve days after conception. (I talk here, and I have talked earlier, as if the activity of certain cells could constitute a life and as if those cells, in consequence, could compose an organism. But I think that this rarely if ever happens. Many of the simples that are caught up in my life are not caught up in the lives of any of my cells—those making up my blood plasma, to take just one example.) It is certain that there is no perfectly sharp answer to this question. Life essentially involves certain chemical processes. Take some interval of time that is extremely small in comparison with the time scale on which chemical reactions typically occur— say, an interval of the sort involved in typical operations of the strong interaction among elementary particles. The time scale on which that interaction operates stands to the time scale of typical chemical interactions as the time scale employed by railways stands to the time scale on which continental drift occurs. No sense can be found in any attempt to locate the beginning of a life within such an interval. But if there is no perfectly sharp answer to the question when a life begins, is there a moderately sharp answer? One at least as sharp as the answer to 'When was his umbilical cord cut'? I should like to think so. But I know of no guarantee of this. We shall explore the logical and metaphysical ramifications of the vagueness of the temporal boundaries of life (and hence of existence) in Section 19.

Another sort of difficulty for the thesis that Lockean continuity is sufficient for the persistence of a life is raised by the phenomenon of metamorphosis. Is the life of a caterpillar continuous in the Lockean sense with the life of the butterfly that "succeeds" it. Are their lives the same life? It might seem that the life of the caterpillar and the life of the butterfly present a reasonably clear example of Lockean continuity, and that, nevertheless, a fairly strong case could be made for their being two lives and not one. But attention to the biological details of the transition from caterpillar to butterfly tends to undermine the impression that the transition is a case of Lockean continuity:

Butterflies . . . undergo what is termed complete metamorphosis during a quiescent pupation stage. . . .
[T]he transformation involves virtually the complete dissolution of all the organ systems of the larva, and their reconstitution *de novo* from small masses of undifferentiated cells called the imaginal discs. In other words, one type of fully functional organism is broken down into what amounts to a nutrient broth from which an utterly different type of organism emerges.[56]

It would seem from this description that the activity of the atoms making up the "nutrient broth" does not constitute a life, and that the caterpillar-butterfly transition is therefore not a genuine case of Lockean continuity. (Compare my earlier speculations about cell division and my denial of Lockean continuity in that case. If two small caterpillars, rather than one butterfly, emerged from the nutrient broth, this would be logically and metaphysically exactly analogous to the emergence of two daughter cells from a cohesive mass of cytoplasm. Compare also the role of my cooperating "temporary subcellular organisms" and the cooperating "imaginal discs.") It would seem, therefore, that invertebrate metamorphosis does not constitute a clear counterexample to the thesis that Lockean continuity is sufficient for the persistence of a life. Moreover, this thesis does not (in conjunction with *Life*) have any obviously false consequences for the persistence of organisms: the same factors that lead us to say that the life of the caterpillar is not continuous with the life of the butterfly should, I think, lead us to say that the caterpillar and the butterfly are distinct organisms. It therefore seems reasonable to say that this thesis is either correct, or, at the very least, is an excellent rule of thumb that is not going to lead us astray in very many cases.

In this respect, Lockean spatiotemporal continuity may be compared with spatial continuity. We almost always locate the boundaries of an organism by using some sort of continuity criterion. (It might be hard to state it.) Sometimes this criterion could lead us astray, as it would if we judged that two superficially joined Siamese twins composed a single organism. (Some philosophers I have talked to have not been willing to accept without argument the proposition that Siamese twins are two distinct but fused organisms. Well, consider that mass of tissue that is shaped like two fused human beings. There will be two brains—virtual objects, of course—within this mass of tissue. Destroy one of the brains. You will then *immediately* have a fresh corpse fused to a human being: The activity of about half the simples virtually composing the large mass of tissues will have *suddenly* ceased to constitute a life. Sooner or later, within a few days at most, the remaining simples will cease to constitute a life. Sooner if the newly dead flesh contains some organ vital to the living flesh, later if not: If not, then the living twin will die of the diffusion into his system of the poisons produced by the bacteria effecting the decomposition of his twin—of a massive case of gangrene.) But it will not lead us astray in very many cases. Whatever may be true in cases of insect metamorphosis or embryonic growth or cellular division, in most cases of the sorts that concern us in everyday life it is fairly easy to say whether a given time marks the beginning (or the end) of a given life. It is clear that my life did not begin last week; I was not generated last week out of the parts that had composed a human being who had looked just the way I do now and who was spatiotemporally continuous with me. It is clear that if the event that is now my life is spatiotemporally continuous with a life that will be going on next week, then it *is* that life that will be going on next week. It is clear that my life was once the life of a child, and, with any luck, will one day be the life of an old man. It is not clear whether my life was once the life of a gastrula, or, indeed, whether a gastrula has a life. But it is clear that if gastrulae have lives, then one of those lives was spatiotemporally continuous with my life; and it is clear that a gastrula, superficially considered, *appears* to have a life and that one of these apparent lives would have appeared to be continuous with mine. It is not clear whether my life could one day be the life of a "brain-dead" man—or man-shaped mass of living tissue—attached to a heart-lung machine, or, indeed, whether a brain-dead man *has* a life; and it is clear that such a man (or mass of tissue) would superficially *appear* to have a life and that its apparent life might appear to be continuous with mine.

What is there to be said about these cases in which one finds it difficult to decide whether a certain connected region of space is occupied by a single organism or merely by a lot of cohering cells?[57] I can do no more than suggest that one look carefully at what is going on in the region that one is interested in. The first step is to ask whether the activity of the simples (or cells or whatever) that are to be found within that space constitute a homeodynamic event. An affirmative answer to this question would not absolutely settle the question whether that space is occupied by an organism, since not every homeodynamic event is a life. But I think that in most of the cases in which we have any practical interest, we shall have no doubt that if any homeodynamic event has the filled-up space that is the focal point of our attention as its "field of operations," then that event is a life. If, for example, the activity of the cells that compose (perhaps only virtually) a gastrula constitutes a homeodynamic event at all, then that event is no doubt a life. Moreover, if there is no homeodynamic event to be found, then there is no organism to be found. When I consider a gastrula carefully, it seems to me to be clear that the cells that make it up are not caught up in a common life. Do it an "injury"—detach a few cells from it, say—and it will not "heal": there will be no mobilization of the collective resources of its component cells directed toward the restoration of its original structure. It no more has a metabolism than does a human pyramid at the circus: The individuals that virtually compose it metabolize individually, but it does not. Nothing directs its growth: Its growth is the sum of the uncoordinated growth and fission of its component cells. (Uncoordinated in the sense that none of the component cells adjusts the rate of its growth or the time of its fission in response to environmental conditions caused by the growth and fission of the other component cells—but no doubt the activities of the component cells are coordinated by a "pre-established harmony.") If all this is right, the gastrula is not an organism. Therefore, if the central metaphysical thesis of this book is correct, it is a virtual object, like a mass of swarming adders or a bliger or a chair; it is not really there; it does not exist; the cells arranged in gastrula fashion compose nothing. When I consider the gastrula carefully, all this seems to be true. But, of course, if embryologists knew more, or if I knew more about what embryologists do know, or if I reflected more carefully on the logical consequences of what I do know, things might seem otherwise to me. Similar remarks apply to the case of "brain-death." I am inclined to think that the cells that are being kept alive by the heart-lung machine virtually compose a mere man-shaped mass of tissue (a ventilated corpse, as someone has called it). But this is a very ill-considered and ignorant judgment. My purpose in the present section is not to settle hard questions about the beginnings and endings of organisms, but to say something about the structure of these questions and about what a considered answer to them would involve. Of course, if I knew the answer to these questions, I would tell them to you, but I have only opinions.

I confess, therefore, to an inability to supplement *Life* with a coherent, general statement of conditions that are individually necessary and jointly sufficient for the persistence of an individual life. But, as I have remarked, we should have had to come to this state sooner or later, for to state necessary and sufficient conditions for the persistence of an object of one sort, one must appeal to persisting objects of some other sort: "explanations must come to an end somewhere." And it is not as if we had been able to say nothing about the persistence of lives. The argument I have given for the conclusion that my life is not the life of the zygote from which I developed, for example, seems to me to be very persuasive indeed. And, I think, in many particular cases it is possible to provide plausible arguments in support of theses about the identity or nonidentity of lives. We shall see a particularly important illustration of this in Section 15, when we examine so-called brain-transplants. This is possible in enough cases that it is useful to recast questions about the persistence of organisms as questions about the persistence of lives.

We have been discussing the question of the persistence of organisms. But (or so we have been supposing) there is another type of material substance than organisms. There is another type of concrete material object that endures and, as they say, "receives contrary predicates." Under what conditions do simples persist? I do not have much to say in answer to this question. There are two reasons for this. First, I do not know much about simples. The notion of a simple is a functional, not a structural or ontological notion. The term 'simple' was introduced into our discourse as a name for objects that play a certain role in the economy of the physical universe. If there are things that play this role, it is by no means evident what their nature might be. If current physics is right, then it seems fairly clear that the category "simple" comprises quarks and leptons and gauge bosons. But perhaps current physics is wrong—or is at any rate radically incomplete. (There are many types of quarks and leptons and they fall into a remarkably neat array of patterns. This suggests very strongly that these particles are arrangements of certain simpler particles. But there are other possible explanations of this neatness—perhaps there is only one kind of particle, which at high temperatures can be in many different states; perhaps an up-quark is one of these particles "frozen" permanently into one of its possible states in the incredible cold of the present universe, and an electron is another of these particles frozen into another of its possible states—and there are energetic considerations that seem to render impossible the thesis that quarks are systems of smaller particles.[58] And if current physics is more or less right about what fundamental particles there are, it nevertheless leaves us with mysteries about their persistence. An electron disappears from a certain orbit and an electron appears in a lower orbit, the difference in energy being accounted for by the emission of a quantum of electromagnetic radiation. Is the "new" electron in the lower orbit the one that was in the higher orbit? Physics, as far as I can tell, has nothing to say about this.

Even if we leave the difficulties of present-day physics aside and proceed on the assumption that metaphysical simples are good, old-fashioned Democritean atoms, we find difficulties enough. One might think that it would be easy enough to provide a criterion of persistence for Democritean atoms: The atom that is at L_1 at t_1 survives till the later time t_3 if and only if there is some continuous path through space-time from L_1-at-t_1 to a point L_3-at-t_3, such that for every point L_2-at-t_2 on this path, an atom is at L_2-at-t_2. Both the 'if' and the 'only if' components of this proposed criterion might be questioned.

As to 'only if'. Some philosophers think that it is at least conceptually possible for an object to "jump" from one point in space to another without passing through any intervening points. I do not myself think that this is possible. (It might, of course, be possible for some object to jump from one point in a three-dimensional space to another point in that space by following a path through a four-dimensional space of which that three-dimensional space is a subspace. I don't mean to rule out cases of that sort. I mean that I don't think it is possible for an object to get from one point to another without following a continuous path through *some* space. Moreover, since it is always possible, as a matter of mathematics, to regard any space S_1 as embedded in a space S_2 of a greater number of dimensions and to describe an object's apparently discontinuous adventures in S_1 as a "slice" of its continuous adventures in S_2, I should put my position this way: It is not possible for an object to get from one point to another without following a continuous path through some physically real space—that is, through some space that has physical properties.) But I do not know how to argue for the thesis that a physical object must always follow a continuous path through (some physically real) space.

As to 'if'. A Democritean atom can, presumably, be annihilated or come into existence *ex nihilo*. If that is indeed possible, then it would seem to be possible for a (say) motionless atom to be annihilated and for a descriptively identical atom to appear one second later in the space it had vacated. And, of course, the same holds for any nonempty interval of time (except, perhaps, for the interval that consists of a single instant). What about the empty interval? Could an atom that has t as the last instant of its existence occupy a region R at every time up to and including t, and a numerically distinct but descriptively identical atom, one that has t as the last instant of its nonexistence, occupy R at every instant later than t? If so, then the 'if' component of our proposed criterion is wrong. And I see no reason to rule that this case is impossible. I am, therefore, unable to state any criterion for the persistence of simples. Though this is disappointing, it is not too terribly upsetting. The primary problems about persistence with which this book is concerned have to do with the persistence of composite, material objects. A primary problem about such objects is whether they can be composed of different matter at different times. If we cannot supplement our answer to the question with a criterion that tells us when we do and when we don't have "different matter," this inability does not, per se, vitiate our answer. Now, I have a great deal of difficulty with an ontology that includes "stuffs" in addition to things, and additional difficulties with the notion of a most general kind of stuff called "matter." I prefer to replace talk of sameness of matter—our discussion involves the notion of matter only to the extent that it involves the notion of "same matter"—with talk of sameness of particles; and I prefer to avoid problems about the sameness of composite particles by talking only of the sameness of noncomposite particles. Thus, I prefer to replace sentences like 'The cat was composed of different matter at t_1 and t_2' each with its corresponding sentence about sameness or difference of noncomposite particles; in this case, 'The cat was composed of different simples at t_1 and t_2'. I suppose I am strongly inclined to think that talk about sameness of matter makes sense only insofar as it can be spelled out in terms of sameness of particles. Since, therefore, I am using 'same simples' talk as a replacement for 'same matter' talk, what I have said about 'same matter' talk applies to the case of simples: If we cannot supplement our answer to the question whether the same object can be composed of different simples at different times with a criterion that tells us when we do and when we don't have different simples, this does not, per se, vitiate our answer.

Problems about the persistence of objects through time are often described as problems about "identity" through time. I am not terribly fond of this piece of terminology, which I regard as the source of much philosophical confusion. But there is no doubt that questions about persistence *can* be framed in terms of identity: To ask whether an object that exists at t_1 lasts till t_2 is to ask whether the object that exists at t_1 is identical with an object that exists at t_2. We have, therefore, been discussing a problem that may be described as a problem about identity. Let us now turn briefly to another problem that may be described as a problem about identity: to what is sometimes called the "problem of identity across worlds." By this phase I mean to denote the problem of specifying the class of counterfactual circumstances in which an object that in fact exists *would have* existed. (The phrase is sometimes used as a name for various other problems: How could the same object have existed in different circumstances? What does it mean to say of some object that it would have existed in other circumstances? Suppose we were thinking of some object as having existed in other circumstances; how could we know that it was really that object that we were thinking of as having existed in those other circumstances? None of these "problems," in my view, is a real problem.[59]

What are the circumstances in which a given organism—one that in fact exists; there are no others—would have existed? Anyone who accepts our answer to the Special Composition Question and who accepts *Life* will probably want to say the following: An organism would have existed in certain circumstances if and only if its life—the event that is actually its life—would have been going on in those circumstances. (That is to say, having the life I in fact have is my essence; conversely, being *my* life is my life's essence.) But what can we say about whether a given life would have gone on under other circumstances? In some cases it is fairly clear what we should say. Whenever my life began, it was already going on when I was born. At that moment, various possible futures faced my life. A nurse, let us suppose, gave me a certain bottle, which she had picked at random from a large rack of bottles. I assimilated the content of the bottle, and various simples were caught up into my life. But the nurse's hand might as easily have fallen on a different bottle, in which case I should have assimilated different simples. The result of a sufficiently long series of similar divergences from the feedings I actually received would have been my being composed of entirely different simples from those that actually compose me. (Suppose for the sake of the example that I in fact have a twin brother. Suppose that on our fourth birthday the xs composed me and the ys composed him. It would be easy to tell a coherent story in which on that date the xs composed him and the ys composed me.) Would the life that would have been mine if I had been composed of different simples have been the life that is actually mine? That it would have been follows from our assumption that I am an organism and our principle of persistence for organisms, *Life*. If *Life* is correct, then my life was once the life of a certain newborn baby—the one who was given a certain bottle by a nurse. In the possible world, or possible counterfactual history, we have imagined, that same baby—I—persisted through a period of growth and development during which he (I) assimilated different simples—came to be composed of different matter—from the simples that I had, in actuality, assimilated during that period. Since the organism that emerged from this period of growth and development was, by stipulation, the same organism that entered it, its life was, by *Life*, the life of the organism that entered it. And, therefore, by the Principle of the Transitivity of Identity, the life of the organism that emerged from that period of growth and development is my life, despite the fact that it is constituted by the activity of different simples. That is: My life is constituted by the activity of certain simples; if the nurse had put her hand on the other bottle, and if a sufficient number of similar differences in my history of assimilation had occurred, then my life, the very life I actually have, would have been constituted by the activity of a wholly different set of simples.

Someone might object that, though I may have shown that the event that is in fact my life would have occurred under different circumstances, I have done this only by first stipulating those circumstances as circumstances under which I should have existed, and going on to apply our principle *Life* to this stipulation. "Call your present life Lambda-now. Call the life you had as a baby Lambda-then. Your argument may be represented as follows. First you assume that you would still have existed if you had been given (numerically) different food to eat. Then you use *Life* to establish that the life you would have had under those different circumstances of diet is Lambda-then, the life you had before the counterfactual circumstances diverged from the real circumstances. And you use *Life* to establish that Lambda-now is Lambda-then. And you conclude, by the Principle of the Transitivity of Identity, that the life you would have had is Lambda-now. This may be a valid, even a sound, argument. But it's not of much use in the present context, is it? You're interested in identifying lives in counterfactual situations with actual lives *as a means to* identifying organisms in counterfactual situations with actual organisms. But you proceed by assuming that a counterfactual organism is identical with an actual organism and then using that assumed identity as a premise in an argument for the conclusion that a counterfactual life is an actual life."

Well, the point of my argument was only to show that it is *possible* for the same life to exist in other circumstances, and even possible for the same life to have been constituted, at a given time, by the activity of entirely different simples from those whose activity in fact constituted it at that time. If my argument for that conclusion rested upon the premise that I should still have existed if I had been given numerically different food, at least this premise is one that most of us would find plausible. But I think it is possible to argue that a life could exist in other circumstances without presupposing that the organism composed of the simples whose activity constitutes that life could have existed in those circumstances. Suppose that I must drive a cow into one of two pastures, in which pasture she will spend the rest of her life: Suppose it is a matter of indifference to me *which* of these pastures I drive her into. Now, forget about the cow. Think only of her life—call it Zoe—an enormously complex homeodynamic storm of simples. In one of the fields are certain simples, the xs, arranged grasswise; in the other field, other simples, the ys, are arranged grasswise. Two possible futures confront Zoe: In one of them it will eventually be constituted by the activities of some of the xs; in the other it will eventually be constituted by the activity of some of the ys. (To simplify the example we ignore the fact that a cow would assimilate matter by drinking and breathing as well as by eating.) If a life can go on, if it can persist through time, it will go on by drawing certain simples into itself and expelling others. But, obviously, its capacity to go on in no way depends upon the numerical identity of the simples that are available to it. No life is such that it must next draw the xs into itself and cannot draw in the (similarly arranged) ys. Therefore, after the organism whose life Zoe is has been driven into one of the pastures and Zoe is constituted by the activity of (say) some of the xs, it will be true that Zoe could *then* have been constituted by the activity of some of the ys.

We may therefore say of a certain life that it could have been going on in quite different circumstances. But our example depends essentially on this feature of our imagined counterfactual circumstances: We imagine them to diverge from the actual circumstances only *after* the life we are talking about has begun, only after that life is *there* to be talked about and has, as we might say, got its identity established. But does the following schema describe a possible case: A certain life, which began at *t*, *would* exist in circumstances included in a counterfactual course of events that diverged from the actual course of events *before t* ? It seems obvious enough that this could happen if the divergent circumstances were causally unrelated to the life. If someone in Australia had said the word 'yes' instead of merely nodding his head—his actual behavior—a second before the moment at which my life in fact began (in the northeastern United States), there is little doubt that my life would have begun despite this difference in the order of things. But could a life have begun if the circumstances leading up to (as opposed to merely preceding) its beginning were substantially different from what they were in actuality? It would certainly seem so. The sperm and egg whose union initiated a chain of events that brought about my life might have united twenty-four hours earlier. It is at least plausible to suppose that their union under those circumstances might have initiated the same human life their actual union initiated. (It is even more plausible to suppose that it might have initiated the same zygotic life. In fact, it seems plausible to suppose that it *would* have initiated the same zygotic life.) Or again: I believe my life to have begun when the cells virtually composing a certain embryo began to cooperate in such a way that their activity constituted the life of a multicellular organism. Suppose a chemical had been introduced into my mother's womb that slowed down (but did not disrupt) certain biological processes in such a way as to delay the onset of this cooperative activity by an hour. It seems plausible to say that the life that the activity of these cells would have begun to constitute at 1:00 P.M. in this counterfactual situation is the life their activity began to constitute at noon in actuality. At any rate, we should not adopt any general metaphysical principle that would rule out such identities a priori: We should not want to lay it down as a general rule that a life could have existed only if its antecedents were identical in every respect with its actual antecedents.

But if we do accept the possibility that an organism, or its life, might have existed even if its antecedents were in certain respects different, we open a modal Pandora's box. To take just one example, let us suppose that when my life began, at t, it was constituted by the activity of a million cells, the xs. Now consider this counterfactual situation: Some time before t one of the xs died; when my life began, more or less at t, it was constituted by the activity of about a million cells, of which about 99 percent were among the xs; but some of the xs (the descendants of the dead cell) never came to be. Would the life that began under those circumstances have been the life that actually began? Should I have come to be under those circumstances? One is strongly inclined to answer yes. On the other hand, one recognizes that this answer places its advocates on a slippery slope. Consider the two-cell embryo, virtually composed of the cells A and B, the formation of which lies near the beginning of the chain of embryonic events that eventually produced my life. Suppose that A and B had become separated and that B had died without issue. Should I have existed if A and its descendants had had a successful embryonic career? If we answer yes, then we should answer yes to the same question with the roles of A and B reversed. But suppose the two-cell embryo had divided and both A and B had survived, the result being a pair of identical—that is, monozygotic—twins. I obviously couldn't have been both of them. Yet if I could have "developed from" A, it would seem, I could have developed from A whether or not B had lived, and if I could have developed from B, I could have developed from B whether or not A had lived. Therefore, I could not have developed from A and I could not have developed from B. I could not, therefore, have developed from any one cell other than the one cell I actually developed from. But if the xs are sufficiently numerous (it would seem), I could have developed from the more or less equally numerous ys instead of from the χs. But how numerous is sufficiently numerous? There is, presumably, no definite answer to this question. The counterfactual identity of organisms would seem to be an inherently vague topic. In Section 18 we shall try to deal with some of the logical problems raised by "vague identity."

To ask whether a given organism would exist in a situation in which its causal antecedents were different is, therefore, to ask a vexed question. To ask the same question about simples is to ask an even more vexed question. For want of a better way to think of them, let us once more think of simples as Democritean atoms. (I am fairly sure that similar problems would arise under any conception of simples.) Let us suppose that a simple, so conceived, began to exist at a certain time and place. Could that very same simple have begun to exist at some other time or at some other place? A simple, having no parts, must, if it comes into existence, come into existence *ex nihilo*. Our conviction that a composite object can come into existence at a time or place other than the time or place of its actual origin seems to rest entirely (at least so far as I can judge from reflecting on my own thinking on this matter) on our awareness that the parts out of which it was composed at the moment of its origin could have been joined elsewhere and could have been joined earlier or later. This conviction, by the way, seems to be shared by all philosophers who think that generation is possible. But on what could a conviction that a simple could have come into existence—*ex nihilo*, of course—at another time and place rest? On nothing that I can see. When I try to picture a simple's beginning its career at some point in space-time other than its actual point of origin (I do my picture-thinking with Democritean atoms), I experience what I earlier called a kind of ontological vertigo. And yet it seems hard indeed to say that for each simple there is a point in space-time such that it must begin at that point if it begins at all. How could a material object—or whatever a simple is—be related essentially to a mere point in space? And if this relation does hold, should we also say that no *other* simple could have begun at that point? Is there a possible world in which a simple that is not identical (numerically) with any actual simple originates at the point in space-time that is the point of origin, in actuality, of some other simple?

Someone might respond to these questions with the observation that they arise only if we assume that simples have a beginning in time; perhaps we should not assume that. Now, it seems empirically unlikely that the physical world is made up of objects that have no beginning in time. But even if the world did have that unlikely feature, this would not solve the problem. Consider any two simples that are exactly alike in their intrinsic properties. (Consider any two Democritean atoms which are exactly alike in size and shape and density and which differ only in the paths they have followed through the void.) If simples have no beginning in time, then each of them has "already" passed along an infinite trajectory. Could they have exchanged trajectories? Is there a possible world in which each has traced out the path through the void that was, in actuality, traced out by the other? Contemplating this question, I again experience ontological vertigo. But, assuming that there are simples all of which have infinite histories, what is the alternative to supposing that two of them could have "exchanged trajectories"? The alternative would seem to be to suppose that each of them has an initial infinite segment of its trajectory essentially. (If any simple could have had a different trajectory "all the way back," all of them could have; if all of them could have, then, it would seem, any two simples identical in their intrinsic properties could have exchanged trajectories.) More precisely, the alternative would seem to be to suppose that each simple and its actual trajectory are related as follows: in every possible world in which the simple exists at all, its trajectory coincides exactly with its actual trajectory up to some point in time. (It may be noted that this statement of the essential relation a simple bears to its trajectory applies to the "finite" case—the case in which simples come into existence *ex nihilo*—as well as to the "infinite" case: whether or not simples must be infinitely old, either this statement holds true of them or else two simples could coherently be imagined to have exchanged roles.) But how could a material object be essentially related to a mere trajectory through space? (We may observe that the very feature of simples that makes them relatively unproblematic as regards "identity through time"—their having no parts—makes them highly problematic as regards "identity across worlds.")

Someone might respond to these questions with the observation that they arise only if we assume that simples could have existed under other circumstances; perhaps we need not assume that. Perhaps we could adopt a David Lewis–style Counterpart Theory and treat apparently indispensable statements that are apparently about what actual simples are, or would be, doing in nonactual circumstances, as being really about what their counterparts are, or would be, doing in those circumstances. (Presumably, both the intrinsic properties of simples and their trajectories count in making judgments about whether a given simple in world A is the counterpart of a given simple in world B. Presumably, people with different theoretical or practical interests might weigh these two factors differently.) I do not believe that Counterpart Theory gives a correct account of the relations between modality and identity. But I cannot discuss Counterpart Theory here. For the present, I will point out that the question whether Counterpart Theory is correct does not really mesh with the modal problems about simples and organisms that are our present concern. Counterpart Theory, essentially, reduces all problems about counterfactual identity to problems about choosing appropriate similarity relations. That is, Counterpart Theory essentially eliminates problems of counterfactual identity as such. If there were no problems of counterfactual identity in general, there would be no problems of counterfactual identity about simples and organisms. And that, from my point of view, would be splendid. (There is certainly no reason that someone who accepted both my answer to the Special Composition Question and *Life* should not be a counterpart theorist—or no reason that derives specifically from these theses. An adherent of Counterpart Theory who accepted them would, presumably, specify the counterpart relation on organisms by saying something of approximately the following form: 'An organism x in one world is a counterpart of an organism y in another if and only if the life of x is a counterpart of the life of y; lives in different worlds are counterparts if and only if they are sufficiently similar in the following respects . . .'. But I think that there are problems of counterfactual identity and that someone who accepts my ontology of material objects—someone who accepts my answer to the Special Composition Question—and who does *not* accept some general theory of modality that, like Counterpart Theory, eliminates all problems of counterfactual identity automatically (as it were) faces some grave problems of counterfactual identity.

My only consolation is that anyone who has any very well-worked-out view of material objects is going to face equally grave questions. The Nihilist, in denying the existence of composite objects, avoids all problems of unity (of what we might call 'identity across space') and persistence ("identity across time") through a change of parts. The Universalist, though his case is a more complicated one, is in a position from which he can argue plausibly that he avoids all problems and unity and persistence. But neither of these Extreme views provides a refuge from the problems of counterfactual identity or "identity across possible worlds." The Nihilist need not worry about the counterfactual identity of composite objects, and the Universalist can avoid worrying about the identity of composite objects if he adopts some form or other of mereological essentialism (a doctrine which is not logically entailed by Universalism but which is a natural adjunct to it). But the Nihilist presumably believes in simples, for if he denies that there are simples, he denies that there is anything physical. And anyone who believes in simples faces (as we have seen) grave problems about counterfactual identity that are quite independent of what his ontology "does" with the simples.

Now, a Universalist may believe in material objects and deny the existence of simples. Suppose, for example, that, like Parmenides, a

certain Universalist believes that the universe consists of a single homogeneous sphere; and suppose he believes that this sphere has an infinite
number of parts, the set of which, S, satisfies these two conditions:
(1) every member of S has some other member of S as a proper part;
(2) the mereological sum of any members of S is a member of S. (To get a
picture of what he believes, we may suppose that, roughly speaking, he
believes that any region of space within the sphere which has a nonzero
volume and which is topologically suited for occupation by a material
object—perhaps a scattered material object—*is* occupied by a material
object. This is the most obvious kind of model for a Universalism without
simples, though others are possible.) But I find objects that have parts
but no simple parts at least as puzzling as simples. To raise just one
problem among many, consider any two congruent parts of our Parmenidean sphere. Each will have a certain history, though I am not sure
what constraints a Parmenidean Universalist might want to impose on
such histories. But, presumably, the constraints would be the same for
any two parts of the sphere of the same topological order and would
certainly be the same for congruent parts. Could, then, these two parts
have exchanged histories? Is there a possible world in which their roles
as reversed? Why or why not?

   This is very close to the counterfactual-identity problem for simples.
And very much the same problem must arise for any ontology of the
material world. You believe in quantities of matter? Could the roles of
two quantities of the same kind of matter (if there is more than one kind)
of the same measure have been eternally exchanged? You believe in filled
regions of space? Could the roles of two filled regions of space have been
eternally exchanged?

   This sort of question shows, I think, that every ontology of the material
world will find some questions about counterfactual identity hard to
answer. (Of course, it is open to the proponents of any ontology of the
material world to adopt Counterpart Theory or some other "wholesale"
method of dealing with the problem. I mean that an ontology of the
material world will invariably face grave problems about counterfactual
identity if it incorporates the proposition that at least some material
objects are such that they, those very objects, would exist under other
circumstances.) This being the case, I cannot regard it as a decisive
objection to my theory that it cannot provide answers to various questions about "identity across worlds"; the failure of any theory to do so
shows that the questions are not well understood.

15. Brain Transplants

A brain is removed from the cranial cavity in my head and put in the cranial cavity in yours, and vice versa. Each is "hooked up to" the brainstem in its new home in the appropriate way. Who, then, is who, and who is where?

Most philosophers would say that, in Daniel Dennett's words, where my brain goes, go I. (These are Dennett's words but not his doctrine. He has written an amusing story that he says he intends to function as an "intuition pump": That is, we are supposed to think of our "intuitions"— what I would call our beliefs—about personal identity and the brain as forming a stagnant pool, the content of which Dennett's story puts into motion and perhaps even transfers elsewhere.[60] When we hear Dennett's story, we are supposed to become doubtful about the slogan 'Where my brain goes, go I'. My intuition remains unpumped and my consciousness unraised.) I share this tendency. In the present section I shall attempt to justify it. I shall attempt to show that it is a natural consequence of the principles governing the unity and persistence of organisms (that is, the Proposed Answer and *Life*) that I have presented and defended in Sections 9 through 14.

Suppose one of your fingers has been cut off. Then you have become smaller and lighter: Your weight has been reduced by perhaps an ounce and your volume by perhaps a cubic inch. And you have been maimed: Your anatomical structure is no longer that dictated by the blueprint embedded in your genes, and the mechanisms of homeostasis distributed throughout your tissues are incapable of restoring that dictated structure. (At least they are incapable of restoring it unless someone manipulates your environment in a very delicate way. If the severed finger were positioned accurately against the wound—the wound that is now a section of your boundary—and if various hydraulic problems were solved, the homeodynamic event that is your life might invade its former precincts and the particles composing the severed finger once more be caught up in that life. If the initial gains of this invasion could be consolidated, then the genetically dictated structure would be restored.) We might note that, if your finger were anaesthetized when it was cut off, you might not even notice at the time of its loss that you had been diminished. You might begin a certain complicated and continuous piece of close reasoning or literary composition before the loss of the finger and finish it afterward.

What about the severed finger? In the strict, philosophical sense, there is no severed finger, since the activity of the simples that would compose that finger if there were such an object do not constitute a life. Nor, for that matter, was there an unsevered finger. Before the finger was cut off, the simples that virtually composed it were all caught up in a life, but their activities did not constitute that life: They were only a few of the simples whose activity constituted that life. After the finger was cut off, however, they were not caught up in a life at all. (That is, no life was such that all of them were caught up in it. But perhaps each of them was still caught up in the flickering life of some dying cell.) A severed finger is a virtual object, the cells that virtually compose it being held together only by the mereologically impotent forces of physical cohesion. A helpful model for thinking of the severed finger is an empire, some part of which—a part that corresponds to no political subdivision of the empire—is suddenly isolated from the rest by an unforeseen natural disaster, and whose inhabitants immediately fall into anarchy. If we imagine the effects of the natural disaster removed and the anarchic section of the empire becoming suddenly once again subject to imperial rule, we find an instructive model for a surgically rejoined finger.

What I have said of fingers, I might have said of arms or legs. A person who suddenly loses his limbs dwindles and is maimed but continues to exist. And we might imagine—though the case would have to be rather contrived—that some complicated train of reasoning or episode of artistic creation that this person is engaged in proceeds uninterrupted through his radical alteration in size and shape and weight.

What about a still more radical alteration? Suppose we cut off your head. And suppose we arranged an elaborate mechanism to keep your head alive: a pump to pump blood at the proper pressure into and out of the severed head along the same route that your heart had pumped it, an artificial lung to oxygenate the blood, an artificial kidney to remove waste products from it, artificial glands, and so on. What shall we say of this case? The same, I think. You have dwindled and are maimed but you continue to exist. You now weigh about ten pounds and would fit in a hat box.

If this seems implausible, suppose we tell the story this way. Consider a man who, owing to irreversible damage to his sensory and voluntary nervous systems, is numb and paralyzed from the neck down. Imagine that you are visiting him and that, in response to one of your remarks he delivers some rather complex piece of connected discourse—say,

> The First Folio has 'and a table of green fields'. For a long time it was thought that it should be 'and 'a babbled of green fields'. But actually the correct reading is probably 'on a table of green frieze'; someone corrected a copy of the 1632 to read that way, and that doesn't seem to me to be a correction anyone would make as a guess. It's so uninspired and arbitrary that it's probably right. But most editions keep 'babbled' because it's a fine line.

It takes him about thirty seconds to say these words. Let us suppose that over the course of these thirty seconds a certain demon, as powerful as he is frivolous, steadily removes the paralyzed and numb limbs and trunk of the speaker, finishing his grisly task just at the words 'fine line'. (We, of course, suppose that the demon employs his extraordinary powers to pump oxygenated blood at the proper pressure and along the proper routes into and out of the man he is systematically pulling apart.) Imagine that you are watching a really good film—special effects by Industrial Light and Magic, Inc.—that follows this scenario. Imagine the alert, interested eyes of the speaker fixed on your own (or on the eyes of the character in the film whose viewpoint the audience shares); imagine the rise and fall of the voice—the demon supplies a resonant cavity to replace the vanished chest—and the developing, communicated meaning of the words the voice speaks as it unfolds and is grasped by you. Surely you are confronted with a single mind, one that holds together from the beginning to the end of this speech? And, surely, this mind is the mind of a certain thinking being, one who retains his identity throughout the speaking of these words? And what candidate is there for this thinking being but the living organism whose stuff is being pared away by the demon at a rate of five pounds per second?

Or put the argument this way. No one supposes that when a man becomes paralyzed from the neck down he ceases to exist—not if the newly paralyzed man can talk and think and feel in as normal a manner as is consistent with the fact of his paralysis. No one would doubt that, if a scholar who had recently become paralyzed delivered the above speech about the textual history of a line in *Henry V*, then the word 'me' that occurred in that speech would refer to a certain man, the speaker, or that the speaker had recently been unparalyzed. But if we concede that much, what importance shall we concede to the paralyzed trunk and limbs of the man? They are *causally* important, of course, since they contain organs causally necessary to the paralyzed man's continued life. But would replacing them with a machine that did the same work make a difference to the identity of the person associated with the unreplaced head, to the identity of the speaker of the words that issue from its mouth? If you were paralyzed from the neck down, would you refuse the gift of a "robotic" trunk and complement of limbs on the ground that the replacement of the paralyzed flesh with mechanical surrogates would cause you to cease to exist?

If a man may become a severed head, then he may become a naked brain—the famous brain in a vat. (In fact, I would suppose that a man could become a *part* of a brain, but I will not discuss the possibility of becoming maimed in a way that is even more radical than that involved in having all one's tissues but one's brain tissue cut away.) One might suspect that this would be impossible on logical grounds. One exists; one's brain exists; and two things cannot become one thing. (Two things can become one as a sperm and egg can: There can come to be an object such that some of the simples that compose it once composed one thing and the remainder of the simples that compose it once composed another. But there cannot be an object that used to be one thing and also used to be another.) The solution to this paradox is simply that one's brain does not exist. There is, of course, a lot of pinkish grey, spongy tissue in one's head, but this tissue does not (its constituent cells or simples do not) compose an object. One has no parts larger than a cell. This is shown by the very fact that we should be faced with a contradiction—displayed above—if there were an object that was one's brain. (And, of course, this fits nicely with our answer to the Special Composition Question, since the activity of the simples within one's cranial cavity does not constitute a life. One's brain is a virtual object. It follows that any answer to the Special Composition Question that "generates" proper parts of human beings larger than cells—larger than those proper parts of human beings that are themselves living organisms—is wrong.) The naked brain in the vat is three pounds of pinkish grey, spongy tissue; the cells that compose it were once entirely within someone's head. But it, the living object in the vat, was never a three-pound pinkish grey object in someone's head, for there was nothing in that person's head larger than an individual cell. It, the living object in the vat, was recently a 150-pound, four-limbed object. It has shrunk, or, rather, has been whittled down. It was once a normal man. It is now a radically maimed man, a man who is about as maimed as it is possible for a man to be. The case of the brain in the vat is logically not much different from the case of the man who has lost an arm: The latter was recently a 150-pound man and has lost about six pounds of bone and blood and tissue; the former was recently a 150-pound man and has lost about 147 pounds of bone and blood and tissue. (But this does not entail that the person who says in the ordinary business of life—say, in writing an anatomy text—"The brain is a three-pound mass of pinkish grey, spongy tissue in the cranial cavity" says something false, just as the Copernican Hypothesis does not entail that someone who says in the ordinary business of life—say, in setting the mechanism of an automatic tracking telescope—"The sun moves across the sky at a rate of one quarter of a degree per minute" says something false.)

Let us now look at a "brain transplant" from the perspective provided by these reflections. We must first note that these words are a misnomer. This is true for two reasons. First, there are no brains, and, therefore, they can't be transplanted. But this is the objection of the precisian, of someone who insists on calling Grand Central Station 'Grand Central Terminal'. The same sort of objection, if we took it seriously, would keep us from talking of eye transplants or heart transplants or the movement of the sun in the sky or of the shadow of a tree on the grass. A more serious objection is that, assuming that it is acceptable to talk of transplanting virtual objects, we are talking about transplanting the wrong virtual object.

Call the virtual part of a human being that is "the rest of him besides his brain"—the virtual object such that it and his brain virtually compose him—his brain-complement. A so-called "brain transplant" is really a brain-complement transplant. When the brain and the brain-complement of x are surgically separated from one another, the simples that had virtually composed the virtual object x's brain suddenly come actually to compose the actual object x; the simples that had virtually composed the virtual object x's brain-complement before the separation continue to compose a virtual object—that is, they continue to compose no object at all. (And, of course, the simples that had composed x before the separation now compose no object at all.) The same things are true, *mutatis mutandis*, of y's brain and y's brain-complement and the simples that had virtually composed these two virtual objects. When x in his new, diminished form is brought into contact (in just the right way, of course) with the mass of tissue that had been y's brain-complement, then the surgical lesions heal and the life of x spreads out almost instantaneously from the three pounds of pinkish grey, spongy tissue that had been its temporary, cramped abode to encompass and govern the tissue that had once been the stuff of y's brain-complement.

This story is logically similar to our earlier story of the severed and rejoined finger. But there is an important difference. The flow of a human life into a rejoined severed finger is, from a purely physical point of view, largely the flow of oxygen- and nutrient-bearing circulatory fluids. But it is not the job of the brain to provide the brain-complement with oxygen and nutrients; quite the other way round, in fact. The flow of a human life from a naked brain (a radically maimed human being) into a severed brain-complement is largely a flow of electrically and biochemically encoded information.

When we told the story of the severed finger, we employed a political analogy. It may be helpful to extend this analogy and to adapt it to our present purposes.

Imagine an empire. The empire is governed almost entirely from the Imperial Palace. Though there are "local specialists" within the palace, there are no governors or satraps who reside in the territory they administer. There is a constant flow of information out of (instructions) and into (intelligence) the palace. The flow of information directs the flow of hundreds of commodities around the empire (a tiny percentage of which is consumed by the palace) and the local administration of the courts and the police.

Now, imagine that some catastrophe isolates the palace: No instructions can leave it and no intelligence or materiel can enter it. The citizens of the empire are so unused to the exercise of individual initiative (we may imagine) that almost all organized activity ceases. Farmers continue to eat their own produce, but no one distributes the surplus and everyone who is not a farmer begins to starve. The irrigation workers wander away from their posts or starve and the flow of water to the farms ceases. Soon even the farmers are starving. But even before things had come to this pass, the empire had ceased to exist. The moment the flow of coordinating information from the palace had ceased, the former citizens of the empire had ceased to be bound together into a single political unit. Or, rather, the empire did not quite cease to exist; it shrank to comprise the isolated palace staff. Its political life continued but this life suddenly came to be constituted by the activity of a few hundred bureaucrats, where, a moment before, it had been constituted by the activity of millions of farmers and artisans. If the effects of the catastrophe that had isolated the palace are removed so that information can once more flow out of and into the palace, then a "wave-front" of information will move outward from the palace at the maximum speed at which the technology of the empire permits the transmission of information, and the outer limits of this wave-front will be at any moment identical with the de facto boundaries of the Empire. When this wave-front comes up against the former de jure boundaries of the empire, it will halt—things outside those boundaries having no disposition to respond to the information it carries—and the empire will be the size it was before the isolation of the palace. (Does this all seem too neat? Well, remember that our empire is an idealization. A real empire, composed of real human beings, would have local authorities capable of exercising individual initiative if isolated. And even if it didn't, it would contain people who would assume authority the moment they had the chance. To get the right picture, suppose that all the citizens of the empire but the palace staff are slaves as Aristotle imagined slaves to be, or suppose that they are the deltas and epsilons of *Brave New World.*)

One logical feature of this story deserves close attention. The empire, as I have said, shrinks suddenly to comprise only the members of the palace staff. But this does not mean that there was a preexistent political entity distinct from the empire that the empire "became," for, we may stipulate, the palace staff were not, before their isolation, the sole citizens of anything. (Something like this *could* happen, however. H. G. Wells's Martians might have caused the citizens of the Austro-Hungarian Empire to become, at a stroke, identical with the citizens of Austria, a preexistent political unit.) The fact that there was no preexistent political entity distinct from the empire that the empire became corresponds to the fact that, when one's brain and brain-complement are separated and one shrinks to a three-pound object, there is no preexistent material object, initially distinct from oneself, that one becomes. But *could* that happen? Could one become something preexistent, in a way analogous to the way in which the Austro-Hungarian Empire "becomes" Austria when the Martians obliterate Hungary? No. Nothing can become a preexistent object. For a thing to do so would be for it to violate the Principle of the Transitivity of Identity. And, indeed, Austria and the Austro-Hungarian Empire do not accomplish this impossible feat when Hungary ceases to exist: They merely come to have the same boundaries and the same citizens.[61] Could a human being do *that*? Could he come to be spatially coincident with a currently existing object (a real, not a virtual, object) that is at present a proper part of him? No. The largest proper parts of any human beings are individual cells. And no one could be pared away till he was the size of a cell. If, moreover, someone were, *per impossibile*, pared away till he was spatially coincident with a single cell, from which he was numerically distinct and which was a former proper part of himself, he and the cell would be composed of the same simples. But if the Proposed Answer is correct, the xs cannot simultaneously compose both y and the numerically distinct z, owing to the fact that a life is what we have called a "jealous" event.

We can now see why it is that "where my brain goes, go I." This is a trivial truth. It is like the proposition that where my finger-complement goes, go I. (Let us call the virtual object such that it and one's right index finger virtually compose one, one's "finger-complement.") At the present moment, neither my brain nor my finger-complement exists: Each is, like a table or a bliger or the shadow of a tree or a wrinkle in a carpet, a virtual object. If my right index finger or my brain-complement is cut off, then I become, as the case may be, my brain or my finger-complement (in the sense that the simples that had virtually composed my brain or my finger-complement come actually to compose me). If I am then brought up against an appropriate finger or brain-complement in the right way, my life will spread out to encompass the simples of which these virtual objects are composed and make them parts of me.

Looked at from the perspective I have tried to provide, the slogan 'Where my brain goes, go I' is indeed a trivial truth. But deep issues are nevertheless raised by our discussion of it. Richard Taylor has objected[62] to the above argument in a way I shall now paraphrase. Let us say that certain of the simples that compose me are "prepared to compose me" just in the case that they would compose me if they were suddenly to become causally isolated from the rest of the simples that compose me. (More formally: the xs are prepared to compose me if and only if there are ys such that the xs and the ys compose me and if the xs should suddenly become causally isolated from the ys, the xs would compose me.) It seems evident that the simples that currently virtually compose my finger-complement are (now) prepared to compose me and that the simples that currently virtually compose my finger are not prepared (and presumably could never be prepared, there being so few of them) to compose me. I have argued that the simples that now virtually compose my brain are prepared to compose me. I have argued for this conclusion by trying to make it seem plausible that the simples that currently virtually compose one's head are prepared to compose one, and by pointing out that brains would not seem to be much different from heads in this respect. Because I have argued in this way, I have been accused (by Taylor) of exhibiting a philosopher's prejudice in favor of the intellect. Consider those simples that currently virtually compose my brain-complement. If I am right, then these simples are not prepared to compose me. (Suppose they were; suppose my brain were separated from my brain-complement; then, if the simples that had virtually composed my brain before the separation had then been, as I have maintained, prepared to compose me, after the separation two distinct objects would be identical with me. In general, if the xs are prepared to compose me and the ys are prepared to compose me, then the xs and the ys must overlap; and they must overlap in a particular way: there must be zs such that the zs are among the xs and the zs are among the ys and the zs are prepared to compose me.) But why should I say that it is the simples that my brain comprises that are prepared to compose me; why is it not the far more numerous simples that my brain-complement comprises that are the simples are prepared to compose me? Is this conviction of mine anything more than a manifestation of the cerebro-centrism endemic among those who make their livings by sitting in chairs and thinking?

I have two replies.

Consider the object the vulgar call a freshly severed head. (I should prefer to call it a radically maimed human being, but this description is, I concede, tainted by my metaphysic.) Consider the object that the vulgar call a newly headless body. (I should prefer to call it a severed-head-complement and a mere virtual object, to boot. But this description is also tainted.) Let us suppose that an object of each of these types has been provided with an appropriate "life-support system." In my view the severed head is a genuine living organism and the headless body is not—though the latter, thanks to our ingenious if imaginary life-support system, may be composed entirely of living tissue. (A virtual object that is composed entirely of living tissue need not even seem to be an organism: witness a tangle of adders.) That is to say: The activity of the simples that compose a severed head constitutes a life; the activity of the simples that (virtually) compose a headless body does not constitute a life.

Is this not a wholly arbitrary position, a mere prejudice having the same roots as Moore's extraordinary conviction that he was closer to his hands than he was to his feet? After all, neither the head nor the headless body can survive (which means at least 'retain its shape and continue to be composed of living tissue') without its elaborate life-support system. An ordinary, unmutilated human being cannot, of course, survive without artificial aid in certain environments, like the deeps of the sea, but there are a few environments in which the normal human being needs no artificial contrivances for his life to continue. But both the head and the headless body require the resources of a technology more advanced than any actual technology if they are to retain their form and continue to be made of living stuff. Where is the difference between them to be found? In virtue of what does the activity of the simples composing the one constitute a life and the activity of the simples (virtually) composing the other fail to constitute a life?

I can answer these questions, in the sense that I can specify a difference between the head and the headless body. Whether this difference is a difference that makes a difference is the real question. Essentially, the difference is this: Give the severed head the proper environment and it will maintain itself, but the headless body will need a constant supply of "instructions" in the form of electrically transmitted information. Unlike the head, it will not be able to coordinate its activities. A life-support system for the head will be no more than an elaborate pump. A mechanical life-support system for the headless body must involve the functional equivalent of a computer. The contention that this difference does make a difference is a basic premise of my metaphysic. I can only try to paint a picture.

Again the picture is a political picture. Consider once more our idealized empire; consider it immediately after the isolation of the Imperial Palace. Suppose we wanted to keep each of the two groups of people— the farmers and artisans on the one hand, and the palace bureaucrats on the other—separately "alive." What should we have to do? To keep the palace "alive," we should only have to supply it with food and water and fuel and other such commodities. Suppose we set up an automated factory to do this. To keep the farmers and artisans "alive" as a group, however, we should have to provide them with a continuous flow of information—in the main, orders. Suppose we set up a computer whose programming enables it perfectly to duplicate the reception, processing, and transmission of information by the palace staff. (We may imagine, just to make things easier for the computer, that the palace transmits its instructions to the countryside by telegraph.)

I would describe the situation I have envisaged as follows. The empire—though perhaps it is no longer an "empire"—still exists and functions: It comprises the palace staff. (So much I have already maintained.) Whereas a moment before it was able, economically speaking, to make its own way in the world, it is now entirely dependent on an external "life-support system": the automated factory. The millions of farmers and artisans, however, are now the citizens of no state whatever, although they behave as if they were and perhaps think they are. A state essentially has a government, a seat of sovereign power—even if that government is a committee of the whole—and this "state" has none: what it has is a computer mock-up of the presence of a sovereign.

What I would say of the severed head and the headless body and their life-support systems is structurally analogous. The human being still exists and functions: He is the severed head. Whereas a moment before he was metabolically self-sufficient, he is now entirely dependent on an external life-support system. The millions of millions of nonbrain cells that are virtual parts of the severed brain-complement, on the other hand, are now proper parts of no object whatever, although they behave as if they were. This is because the flow of electrically and chemically coded information that directs their individual activities (and, as a consequence, directs their mutual activities) is not produced by the action of parts of an object they are also parts of, but by a machine, that is, by simples which are caught up in the life of no organism and which are arranged by human intelligence in such a way as to duplicate the flow of information originating in a brain. We should remember that the brain is not only the seat of our experience and our conscious thought; it is also the seat of our capacity to have lives; it is the seat not only of one's intellect but of one's entelechy.[63] A man may be in a coma from which he can never emerge, owing to irreversible brain damage, and yet continue to live. But cause the flow of electrical impulses from his brain into his spinal column to cease—by some as yet undiscovered technique of manipulating a flow of electrons that causes no organic damage—and he will die almost instantly. In short, a severed head-complement maintained by a life-support system is a virtual object the activities of the virtual parts of which must be coordinated by an external agency or *cybernetes.* The living severed head, however, is capable of holding *itself* together. It merely needs an unusual physiochemical environment, which its life-support system supplies.

Now, it might be objected that this answer presupposes too much of my theory and thus attempts to lift itself by its bootstraps. Someone might even object that my political examples, which are supposed to lend analogical support to my answer, have been misdescribed owing to a sort of feedback from my metaphysical convictions about organisms. What plausibility is there, really, in my assertion that the farmers and artisans "ruled" by a computer simulation of the Imperial Palace are citizens of no state? Isn't it much more plausible to suppose that they are citizens of a state whose sovereign is a computer? Well, that seems simply absurd to me. But suppose I'm wrong. Then the computer must be a part, if not a citizen, of the state it rules, since the ruler of a sovereign state cannot be an external entity. And, in that case, we should conclude by analogy that the severed brain-complement and its life-support system virtually compose a living organism—just as my brain and brain-complement virtually compose me. But in that case, the severed brain-complement is not itself an organism and, therefore, it is not an organism radically mutilated by surgery. The living severed head, the analogue of the isolated Imperial Palace, is the organism mutilated by surgery.

I said that I had two replies to the charge that my position was arbitrary in granting the status of an organism to a living severed head and in withholding that status from a living headless body. The above paragraphs constitute the first of these two replies.

The second reply turns on the kind of point that was the topic of Section 12. It consists simply in the observation that all the events and processes that take place within the living headless body may be regarded, without any particular intellectual difficulty, as involving only the cooperative activities of cells and simples: there is no need to suppose that there is anything larger than a cell or a simple *there*: Everything we observe when we look at the living headless body may be regarded as the sum of the effects of the individual activities of things that are too small to be observed individually. But this is not the case with the living severed head. Recall our example of the radically mutilated man who, in the course of his mutilation, and unaware that it is proceeding, discourses intently on the textual history of the depiction of Falstaff's death in *Henry V.* We might as easily have imagined that this man was radically mutilated from the beginning of his discourse. It is plain that in this case we should have a living, intelligent being who persists throughout the presentation of a connected series of utterances. If you think that this activity could be no more than the cooperative activity of numerous individually invisible things, then I have nothing more to say to you, for I have said what I have to say. But if you agree with me that, if the presentation of this connected discourse is not an illusion, then there must be one unified object that is its presenter, then you will see, I think, that we have a reason for believing that the severed head is an organism, a reason that is not a reason for thinking that the headless body is an organism. (I do not say that it is a decisive reason; only that it is a reason.) So, in the end, I do confer a kind of primacy on intellectual activity. But this is not because I think intellectual activity is so very fine, or because I make my living by this sort of activity—after all, the same point could be made about mere sensuous passivity—but for a very abstract sort of reason: I do not think that the apparent correctness of applying a predicate like 'is talking about the textual history of a line in *Henry V*' to a certain object can be explained in terms of the real correctness of applying some variably polyadic predicate to a vast number of cells or simples. (But remember that this argument does not involve any assertion that one's identity depends on one's mental activity. The continuity of one's mental life presupposes but does not explain one's identity through change. A man or woman no longer capable of any thought or experience might continue to exist and to be the same man or woman who had once been able to think and feel.)

I have been talking most recently about heads and head-complements. But don't the same points apply, with minor revisions, to brains and brain-complements? If they do, then the view of composition that I have been advocating would seem unequivocally to support the common conviction of philosophers that one follows one's brain. In a nutshell, the reason for this is that one's life—not simply one's mental life—is centered in the activity of the simples that virtually compose one's brain in a way in which it is not centered in the activity of any of the other simples that compose one.

16. Two Problems about Personal Identity: Memory and Commissurotomy

In the present section I will discuss some miscellaneous problems about the unity and persistence of thinking organisms. These problems are germane to the topic of this book but they do not fit neatly into its primary plan of organization. Readers who skip this section will miss nothing essential to the book as a whole, though they may be left with some unanswered questions.

I will first take up the question whether memory makes any contribution to the persistence through time of human beings. (It is, of course, obvious that there are connections between memory and persistence: If one remembers having recited *Daffodils* at school, then one did recite *Daffodils* at school, and if one remembers V-E Day, then one was alive on V-E Day. Memory, therefore, requires or involves or entails one's having persisted through a stretch of time. The question that concerns us is: Does one's having persisted through a stretch of time require or involve or entail memory?) It is important for us to consider this question because the popular thesis that memory is somehow intimately involved in the persistence of human beings is inconsistent with a premise of several arguments that I have given in earlier sections. I have supposed that human beings—you and I—are living organisms. And whatever the factors may be that constitute an organism's persistence though time— whether they be the factors enumerated in the principle I have called *Life* and in my discussion of this principle, or some other factors—these factors obviously do not include memory. An oyster is a perfectly good example of a living organism, but an oyster could hardly be said to have a memory; not, at any rate, in the sense in which a man, or even a mouse, has a memory. (And, surely, it would be entirely arbitrary to contend that if an organism is of the sort that *has* a memory, its persistence involves memory and otherwise does not involve memory.) It follows that if memory is an essential component in the persistence through time of human beings, then human beings are not organisms, and that many of the central arguments of this book (such as the argument in Section 8 against Universalism) rest on a false premise. (It might be possible for one to reconcile the thesis that memory is involved essentially in the persistence of human beings and the thesis that human beings are organisms if one were to view identity, and hence persistence, as not "absolute" but "relative." One might, on that view of identity, distinguish the persistence of human beings qua thinking beings or persons from the persistence of human beings qua living beings or organisms. One might, for example, maintain that, owing to some grave and pervasive failure of memory, the wizened human being who did so-and-so in 1890 was the same living organism as the fresh-faced human being who did such-and-such in 1830, but not the same person. Whether the idea of "relative identity" is coherent, however, is a question that lies outside the scope of this book, in which the classical or "absolute" conception of identity is presupposed.) Let us, therefore, examine the idea that memory makes an essential contribution to the persistence of human beings—to "personal identity," as they say.

Suppose I were to lose my memory, and not in the superficial way involved in all known cases of "amnesia" but in a much more fundamental way. The ordinary amnesiac is analogous to a library in which certain shelves have been locked and the keys that unlock them mislaid or scrambled or destroyed. I want a case analogous to a library in which every page of every book has been bleached white: a case of total oblivion. Suppose I drink of the springs of Lethe. The effect of a draft of Lethe, as is well known, is to obliterate the modifications that time has worked on certain molecules of ribonucleic acid in one's brain,[64] with the consequent obliteration of all the information that was encoded in those modifications. The effect is not the mere inaccessibility of that information; the information is *gone*. It is gone like a name writ in water and not like a name writ in lemon juice.

What is the effect of oblivion upon existence? Many philosophers think that when I drink of oblivion, I necessarily cease to exist. This proposition seems to me to be so obviously false that I do not know what to say about it. I have the feeling that I must be missing something. I can do no more than rehearse a very standard sort of argument, which, I am sure, is well known to everyone. This argument is, in my view, a good argument, in the sense that its premises seem to me to be obviously true, and that anyone who assents to them should assent to its conclusion. I suspect, however, that anyone who assents to its premises will already accept its conclusion.

Suppose that you have been informed that you must drink the waters of

Lethe one month from now and that you have no choice about this. Suppose you are also told that after you have drunk of Lethe, the organism which in my view is you, and which according to others is something called 'your body', will be subject to a week of ingenious torture—it will, of course, still have a functioning central nervous system—unless you agree to be tortured for one hour today. Suppose you are an ideally rational being who, all other things being equal, would agree without hesitation to be tortured for one hour today to avoid sixty-one minutes of torture in the remote future. Suppose you are an ideally selfish being who would not pay a penny to save anyone else from an eternity of torture. Which choice should you make? Well, I know which choice I should make: I should choose, without hesitation, to be tortured for an hour today. To have one's memory obliterated is a great misfortune (for most people; doubtless, some people would welcome it). But one can imagine greater misfortunes, even as misfortune is measured by ideally selfish beings. Death would be a greater misfortune, and so would the compounding of the misfortune of total oblivion by a week of subsequent torture. "But this just begs the question. You are assuming that you will survive the obliteration of your memory." Well, perhaps it does beg the question, whatever that is. But would you really choose not to be tortured today?

Peirce has a similar and in some ways more persuasive argument, which is built round the following case.[65] You must have an operation. You are given a choice between two kinds of anaesthetic. One is very expensive and is of the usual sort: It renders you unconscious. The other is free and is administered as follows. Just before the operation you are given a draft of Lethe. Just after the operation you are given a second draft of Lethe. Shortly after you have drunk the second draft, the memories that were obliterated by the first draft—and those alone—will be somehow restored to you. Which anaesthetic will you choose if you are ideally rational and ideally selfish? The trouble with this case is that it is not clear whether it makes sense to talk of the restoration of obliterated memories. Some will say that the "restored memories" would not be real memories of the events they seem to be about. And of those who say this, some might argue that to exchange one's memories for pseudo-memories would be to suffer a misfortune whose cost would have to be counted in making a rational decision about which anaesthetic to choose. And others might argue that pseudo-memories are an insufficient foundation for the persistence of a person through time.

In the 1950s there were philosophers who would argue the question whether "the criterion of personal identity" was a "bodily criterion" or a "memory criterion." It is not clear to me just what was going on or what was at stake in this dispute. In part, of course, it was a dispute about what evidence we typically use in deciding whether a person who has done some deed or has undergone some adventure is the same person as the one who has done some other deed or undergone some other adventure. And, in part, it was a dispute about which sort of evidence for a conclusion of this type is the strongest or most basic or most trustworthy. Suppose, for example, that someone could give a good description of a certain event, a description so detailed and exact and so very nearly correct that people would normally conclude that he had witnessed the event; but suppose he didn't match the description of any of the witnesses. Or suppose he perfectly matched the description of some witness to the event but was able to describe it in only the vaguest terms, and those inaccurate. In these cases, it was said, there was a conflict between the bodily criterion and the memory criterion of personal identity, and the question was raised, Which, if either, ought to prevail?

But, again, what is at stake in this dispute? One would like to say that these cases are simple cases of the conflict of two sorts of evidence. For one reason or another, human beings are good at telling one another apart by their appearances, though there are such things as doubles (not to mention identical twins), and a human being's appearance can alter, or be altered, drastically. And, normally, a person can describe an event as well as a witness to that event can only if he himself *was* a witness to that event; our memories would be of little use if this weren't so. Any two types of evidence that are not connected in some lawlike way (as someone's appearance and memories are not) can, at least in the imagination of philosophers, come into conflict. In a similar vein, we might imagine cases in which two kinds of evidence relevant to the authenticity of a diary (handwriting and accuracy of content, say) come into conflict. But this would not show that we had two "criteria" for the authenticity of diaries, and it would lend no sense to the question which of these two kinds of evidence was the more "basic." If a diary that has been represented as Hitler's is written in a hand that all the greatest experts swear is unmistakably Hitler's and yet recounts a visit to Potsdam (a dull and routine one) that it is absolutely certain, on independent historical grounds, that Hitler never made, then we who have an interest in the authenticity of the diary are faced with hard questions. Can a committee of the recognized experts on Hitler's handwriting render with great assurance a unanimous verdict that is just wrong? Could Hitler have been in the habit of inserting into his diary fictional accounts of events that, had they occurred, would have been perfectly routine? Is the accepted record of Hitler's movements mistaken after all? Hard questions indeed, and hard in large part *because* no particular sort of evidence is automatically more "basic" than other sorts. The same point applies to hard questions about identifying persons, such as the questions the friends, creditors, and heirs of Ambrose Bierce would have faced if, a year after Bierce's disappearance, someone had turned up claiming to be Bierce, looking exactly like Bierce, and having all his tricks of speech and behavior, but who made important misstatements about Bierce's past. The only thing one could do in such cases would be to try to construct various hypotheses that accounted for both the positive and negative evidence and to try to decide which hypothesis was the most reasonable.

So neither "bodily" evidence (appearance, scars, and so on) nor evidence based on the subject's memory (ability to tell reasonably correct stories about the past) is basic or "criterial" when it comes to deciding whether a human being who was present on one occasion was also present on some other occasion. Having settled this point, however, I have to confess that, in discussing it, I do not seem to be addressing the main point that is at issue in disputes over the "criteria of personal identity." Many of the disputants seem to have been taking it for granted that if one could show that "memory is the basic criterion of personal identity" (and it is not clear whether this is supposed to mean merely 'evidence based on the subject's memories is the decisive factor in disputes about personal identity' or is supposed to mean something more profound), then one would thereby show that a person's persistence through time was in some way a function of his memories. Thus, "the main point at issue" in disputes over criteria of identity is not really a point about what the evidence is that is relevant to deciding about the truth or falsity of certain propositions but is rather a point about the correct analysis (in some sense) of those propositions. It would seem that, in the minds of many of the philosophers who disputed about competing criteria of identity, the proposition 'Memory is the criterion of identity' did not mean 'Memory is the court of last resort in disputes about the identity of persons' but rather 'Facts about the identity of persons are just facts about the memories of persons'. But then how do questions about evidence fit into this dispute? The parties to the dispute seem to have regarded both of the following arguments as logically valid, or at least as cogent:

Evidence based on the subject's memories is the court of last resort in disputes about personal identity;

therefore, facts about personal identity are facts about memory.

Evidence consisting of observations of the subject's physical characteristics is the court of last resort in disputes about personal identity;

therefore, facts about personal identity are facts about physical characteristics.

Neither of these arguments is valid or, to my mind, even remotely plausible. Each represents a strong tendency in the philosophy of thirty years ago to see propositions of a given type as being, in the last analysis, propositions whose *subject matter* is just exactly facts of the sort that are commonly put forward as *evidence* for propositions of that type. (Thus, propositions about mental states were said to be, in the last analysis, propositions about behavior; laws of nature were said to be mere statements of exceptionless regularities.) Perhaps this tendency was a legacy of logical positivism, which had only recently been laid in its shallow and unquiet grave. Perhaps it stemmed from worries about the validity of induction. In any case, it was a mistake, though I do not propose to go into the question of why I believe it to have been a mistake. The two inferences I have written out are instances of this mistake, though this would be hard to show, since they are rather vaguely stated. Perhaps it does not make much difference for our present purposes whether the first of the two is valid, however, since, as I have argued, its premise and its conclusion are both false. (Its conclusion must be false if a person whose memory has been totally obliterated can continue to exist; *whatever* the thesis that facts about personal identity are facts about memory may have meant, it couldn't have been consistent with *that*.) And, although I think it is a mistake to suppose that "personal identity" has anything to do with the external marks that we typically use to reidentify people—one might as well say that the identity of pigeons had something to do with the leg-bands that are commonly used to reidentify them—I suppose I do think that facts about "personal identity" are in a sense facts about a person's physical characteristics, since being a living organism is (I suppose) a physical characteristic, though a very different sort of physical characteristic from those that the people who argued about criteria of personal identity were thinking of.

Proponents of the thesis that memory is the criterion of personal identity may protest that I have been attacking them on relatively peripheral issues and have ignored their strongest case. This case they have from the founder of their school, John Locke:

> For should the soul of a prince, carrying with it the consciousness of the prince's past life, enter and inform the body of a cobbler as soon as deserted by his own soul, everyone sees, he would be the same person with the prince, accountable only for the prince's actions.[66]

"If you were actually to witness an occurrence of the type Locke describes," I shall be told, "you would be converted to the view that facts about personal identity are facts about the persistence of memory and have nothing to do with the persistence of organisms. Organisms are not persons (you would be forced to concede), but merely the bodies of persons. You would see that the person goes where the memory goes."

But what, actually, am I being asked to imagine I have witnessed? A neutral account of it would go something like this.

I know a prince, Charlie, and a cobbler, Harry. One day the following seems to happen: Harry without warning begins to talk and act exactly as if he were Charlie. He exhibits both an unshakable conviction that he is Charlie and perfect knowledge of the most particular and intimate details of Charlie's life. Moreover, he acquires all Charlie's skills: a command of Greek, a mastery of horsemanship, and so on, skills which require a lifetime to acquire and which he had hardly known existed. But he can't mend shoes to save his life. (And, of course, all this happens, or seems to happen, to Charlie, but the other way round: He loses his horsemanship but becomes able to mend shoes.)

Should I be forced by this strange occurrence to concede that a person is not after all an organism and that the organism that had hitherto been "associated with" Charlie was now associated with Harry? Well, no, I certainly wouldn't say *that*. Better to say nothing than to talk nonsense. And, really, in such a case there would be a great deal to be said for saying nothing. The only thing that would be clearly true would be that something wholly mysterious had happened. What should one say if the Eiffel Tower suddenly sprouted wings and flew away? Probably there is nothing one should say, beyond admitting that one had no idea what the explanation of this phenomenon was. And the Harry-and-Charlie story is like that. If such a thing actually happened, none of us would understand it. Of course, it would not be hard to frame hypotheses that would save the appearances. For example, we might hypothesize that the Martians (who, as Norman Malcolm once observed, are wonderfully technologically advanced in the imaginations of philosophers) had performed something like plastic surgery—but much more complete and effective—on Harry, thereby causing him to look exactly like Charlie. But the framing of such hypotheses would be an idle exercise, for there would be no way to find out which of them was true. Many such appearance-saving hypotheses are possible. But the "hypothesis" that Harry and Charlie have "switched bodies" is not one of them, for there is no such hypothesis: these words make no sense at all.

Let us now turn to a problem that is about the unity (rather than the persistence through time) of thinking human beings. It was Thomas Nagel, I think, who first brought the puzzling facts about the results of "commissurotomy" to the attention of philosophers.[67] I propose to consider here only the implications that the data of commissurotomy studies have for the main theses of the present work. (Or, rather, I shall consider the implications of an imaginary "improvement" on these data.) Observations of patients who have undergone commissurotomy have suggested to some observers that present in each human brain there are two "consciousnesses" or "centers of mental life" or "psychic arenas" or "parallel streams of consciousness," one of them associated with one cerebral hemisphere and the other with the other hemisphere. And this, one might argue, could only mean that two thinkers or two subjects of experience are somehow present in the normal human brain. But if two thinkers are present in each brain, then two thinkers are present in each human being. Since each human being is a single multicellular organism (none of the interpreters of the data of commissurotomy has suggested, to my knowledge, that these data support the thesis that a normal human being is only apparently a single organism and in actuality is a fusion of two or more multicellular organisms, after the manner of a pair of Siamese twins), it would follow that thinkers or subjects of consciousness are not, as we have supposed, multicellular organisms. The alternatives to the thesis that thinkers are multicellular organisms would seem to be these:

—Thinkers are physical simples.

—Thinkers are single cells.

—Thinkers are immaterial.

—Thinkers are virtual objects.

—Thinkers are material but not simples or organisms; they are parts of organisms that are not themselves organisms (such as brains or cerebral hemispheres).

The first two of these theses would seem to be absurd on both empirical and conceptual grounds. The third thesis, that thinkers are immaterial, raises issues that lie outside the scope of this book. We shall simply assume that if there are really any thinkers, then at least some of them (you and I, say) are material. To suppose that thinkers are virtual objects is to suppose that, in the final analysis, there are no thinkers at all. (If we make use of the language of "virtual objects," we must be sure that we do not forget that *virtual object* is not a type of object. To say that shadows, as it may be, or wrinkles in carpets are virtual objects is to say that nothing among all the things there are is a shadow or a wrinkle, and that sentences that appear to be about shadows or wrinkles and appear also to express truths must be understood as shorthand expressions of sentences that do not even appear to be about shadows or wrinkles.) This is a perfectly absurd thesis, however. Of *course* there are thinkers. Of *course* there are subjects of consciousness. (But we have been over this ground before.) This sequence of eliminations leaves us with only one possibility: that thinkers are parts of organisms, parts that are not themselves organisms. But in that case there are material objects that are neither simples nor organisms, and the main thesis of this book (its answer to the Special Composition Question) is false.

The conclusions that some philosophers have reached on the basis of the data of commissurotomy, therefore, are ones that we must take seriously. But there is an annoying fact about these data that will complicate any attempt to do so. The data of commissurotomy are very complicated and raise many questions of interpretation. If certain of these questions were answered in certain ways, this would render the data harmless—harmless from our point of view, at least, although they might still raise difficulties for other philosophical positions. For example, it seems possible to interpret the data of commissurotomy this way: Only one cerebral hemisphere is a seat of consciousness; the structures present in the other hemisphere are a mere computational instrument that the thinking hemisphere, or the thinker whose thoughts are associated with that hemisphere, manipulates in thinking and perceiving; in the unusual situation produced by a commissurotomy, this computational instrument—and it is a very sophisticated and flexible instrument— occasionally exercises independent control of the organism's motor activities, producing the illusion that these activities are the manifestation of conscious thought. (If the main thesis of this book is correct, then a cerebral hemisphere is a virtual part of an organism, but there is no reason an organism cannot use one or more of its virtual parts as a computational instrument; consider someone's counting on his fingers.)

It might be thought that I should welcome the possibility of so interpreting the data of commissurotomy, since, if it is correct, it renders these data impotent to harm my thesis. This welcome interpretation of the data, however, rests on the fact that the cerebral hemispheres are rather unlike each other in the functions they perform and are sufficiently unlike each other that it is possible to insist that one of them is the locus of conscious thought and the other a mere computational device. (I say only that it is possible to insist this; I do not say this thesis is anything other than a desperate, ad hoc maneuver. I will not take sides in the debate about the *plausibility* of this thesis.) Now, it seems clear that we can easily imagine an organism that does not allow this escape hatch to the opponent of the "two streams of consciousness" school. We can imagine a single organism with two brains, each of which performs all the functions of the other, and in the same way. Since the theses of this book are supposed to be necessary truths, they are as vulnerable to refutation by imaginary physiology as by actual physiology, provided only that the imaginary physiology does not conceal some intrinsic impossibility. The advantage of actual cases in discussion of allegedly necessary truths is that what we know to be actual we know to be possible. But I can see no faintest hint of impossibility in the cases that I shall imagine, and, believe me, I have looked hard for it. I propose, therefore, to turn from the actual data of commissurotomy and confront some far more troublesome imaginary data.

Imagine an amoeba-like organism, the rough outline of whose structure is represented in the following diagram:

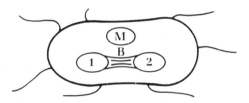

The creature—call it Cerberus—has two brains, which are labeled 1 and 2 in the diagram. (That is: there are xs and there are ys such that the xs are parts of Cerberus and are arranged cerebrally and the ys are parts of Cerberus and are arranged cerebrally and none of the xs overlaps any of the ys.) The two brains are connected by a sort of bridge or commissure (B) that allows information, in the form of electrical signals, to pass between 1 and 2. The two brains are for all practical purposes identical in physical structure (they are at least as similar as the brains of monozygotic human twins), and each is the seat of all those functions of which a human brain is the seat (including ratiocination and the processing of sensory information and the control of voluntary motion) except one: neither contributes any direction to the homeodynamic processes that hold the organism together: neither exercises any control over metabolism or the healing of traumatic lesions or antisepsis or respiration or pulse rate or anything of that sort. All such "maintenance"—insofar as it is localized—is under the control of a quite separate organ, M.

The two brains, 1 and 2, are so arranged and designed that each attempts to mirror the internal states of the other. (By way of analogy, imagine two men who are faced with the following "coordination problem": They must convince an observer that they are not two men but rather one man and his mirror image. And they must do this not simply by following a script they have been allowed to memorize before being subjected to the observer's scrutiny, but in a flexible and open-ended way in an unrehearsed situation that involves sudden adventures that are novel in their content and unpredictable in their timing. Each of the men will attempt to anticipate the other's movements and move at t in the way he expects the other to move at t. Each will try to make the movements that he believes it will be easiest for the other to anticipate. Each will "correct" his own movements if they are different from the other's and will do so in a way that is informed by his knowledge that the other will simultaneously be acting with the same intention.) This problem will be made easier for the two brains by the fact that each is receiving the same sensory "input" as the other (not counting the information that each is receiving *about* the other via B), by the fact that each is a structural duplicate of the other and thus shares its dispositions to respond to stimuli, and by the fact (we may imagine it to be a fact) that each of them is very "fast": We allow a certain margin for error in the synchronization of their states, and the speed with which they are capable of making satisfactory moves in the coordination game is sufficiently great that this margin is a comfortable one. Suppose, for example, that we count the brains as successful in their reciprocal state-matching game if their states are never out of synchronization for longer than one one-hundredth of a second; and suppose that each is able to decide what state to change to and to effect the required change in one one-thousandth of a second. (To return to our analogy, if our two men have nervous systems that are capable of responding to and processing an access of information in an interval that is an order of magnitude smaller than the interval that the nervous system of the observer would require to accomplish the same task, this will obviously greatly improve their chances of fooling him in the manner prescribed by the terms of their coordination problem.)

Neither of the two brains is any more intimately associated with any part of the periphery of Cerberus than the other. (This stipulation marks an important difference between our imaginary case and the actual connections of the human cerebral hemispheres with the periphery of the human organism.) We may imagine that each of the brains has exactly the same connections with all Cerberus' muscles, or with whatever effectors an amoeboid being like Cerberus may use in place of muscles. Since the states of Cerberus' two brains are synchronized to within a tolerance that is small in comparison with Cerberus' reaction time (we may imagine), the two brains send essentially the same signals to Cerberus' effectors—the information transmitted to Cerberus' periphery by either of his brains is entirely a function of the inner state of that brain—and thus no confusion results from the fact that each effector receives a duplicate set of signals. Each of Cerberus' voluntary movements is therefore an instance of "overcausation": when Cerberus moves pseudopod gamma, the motion of gamma is caused by a certain event in one of his brains and is also caused by a descriptively identical event in the other, and either alone would have sufficed for the occurrence of that motion. (We must also imagine that any signals sent from Cerberus' sense organs to his interior are "split" in such a way that an identical signal arrives simultaneously at each brain.)

One way to get an intuitive grip on Cerberus' inner dynamics would be to think of a guided missile that is being controlled, via radio, by two computers that are transmitting identical signals; in that case, the behavior of the missile would be the same whether or not both computers were running. (Even computers of the same make and model running identical programs would drift out of synchronization pretty quickly in such a situation. But we may imagine—and this strengthens the analogy—that the computers are able to exchange information by some means that is independent of their broadcasts to the missile, and that they are programmed to cooperate in the solution of a coordination problem like the one laid out above. We must also suppose that the intervals they require to resynchronize themselves are small in comparison with the intervals they are allowed for the solution of the navigation problems presented by the missile's changing situation.)

We might also attempt a political analogy, on the model of those we employed in Section 15. Conceive, if you can, a country that has two causally independent governments. One is responsible for internal affairs and the other for foreign policy. The former operates in much the same way as the Imperial Palace of our earlier examples: It has responsibility for the internal economy (in the broadest sense) of the country but has no power in matters of war, the balance of trade, diplomacy, or anything of that sort. Those matters are the business of the second government. Thus the two governments are related rather as Parliament and King in classical English politics, save that the "external" government has no power *whatever* in domestic matters, and, since the two governments are causally independent, the domestic government cannot attempt to control foreign policy by controlling the revenues of the external government, for it has no way to communicate threats or proposals to the external government. The external government may find that its supply of money has been cut off, of course, but it will have to guess why, even as you and I must guess the meaning of ominous internal symptoms.

If this is not sufficiently odd, we must go on to imagine that the external government is really two governments: two sovereigns who are set the coordination problem of mirroring perfectly each other's acts and decrees. They solve this problem (we suppose) and thus issue orders that are no more contradictory than those produced by conventional, unitary sovereigns. Various generals, merchants, and ambassadors are perhaps mildly puzzled by the fact that they always receive duplicate sets of instructions, but since the duplicates really are duplicates, this causes them no practical difficulty.

Perhaps the nature of Cerberus is now as clear as analogy can make it. (How could such a creature come to be? What explanation could there be, either in the Divine Mind or in natural selection, for the existence of Cerberus? Well, he seems clearly to be intrinsically possible. Perhaps we could imagine him to be the work of bored and frivolous genetic engineers of the future.)

What should we say about the mental life of Cerberus if we actually met him? It is clear from the reaction of certain philosophers to the data of commissurotomy that they would say that Cerberus is possessed of "two consciousnesses," the events that constitute one consciousness occurring in one of his brains and the events that constitute the other consciousness occurring in the other. If this is the right conclusion to draw about Cerberus, then our answer to the Special Composition Question would seem to be wrong. 'Consciousness' is a mass term, and, therefore, to pluralize it must be to employ some sort of figure of speech—one might almost say a figure of grammar. To say that "two consciousnesses" are present in a certain situation can—or so one might argue—mean only that two conscious beings are present in that situation. At any rate, this is the only meaning that is relevant to questions about the composition of material things. If there were somehow two "consciousnesses" within Cerberus without there being two conscious beings within him, this state of affairs would create no difficulties for our thesis about composition. The case of Cerberus raises difficulties for our thesis about composition because it seems to force upon us the wrong number of beings; if "consciousnesses" are not conscious beings, however (and I suppose they are not *unconscious* beings), and if the presence of two of them does not entail the presence of two conscious beings, then Cerberus is, as far as we are concerned, a mere interesting oddity. Let us suppose, therefore, that it is the position of our opponents that there are two conscious beings within Cerberus.

This position seems to me to be based on a kind of picture-thinking. We could represent the picture that underlies this view by employing the device used by comic-strip artists to attach the propositional content of occurrent thoughts to their thinkers:

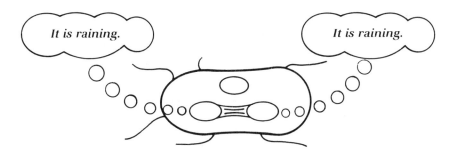

But why should we look at things in this way? Even if we leave aside my contention that, in the strict, philosophical sense, there are no brains, we should remember that, though thoughts are *located in* brains (as opposed to livers), it is not brains that think but rather the organisms whose brains they are. Why, then, should we not say that, in the case we have imagined, there is only one thinker, Cerberus, thinking one thought, though this thought is located in two places?

A thought, or the occurrence of a thought, is a certain event. Thoughts, in the relevant sense, are named by phrases like 'Cerberus' passing thought that it was raining'. (The count-noun 'thought' also has a quite different sense, one that corresponds to Frege's term *Gedanke*: in this sense, a "thought" is not an event but a proposition. I suppose that '*The Thoughts of Chairman Mao*' and 'two minds with but a single thought' are examples of the word used in that sense.) A thought is the thought of a certain thinker if it is a subevent of his life. If the thinker is a material being, then the thought will have a location in space. (It is not always possible to say exactly where an event occurs. In what *precise* region of space did World War II occur? But events can be approximately located, at least if they involve only spatially extended objects: World War II did not occur on Mars or in Antarctica. Approximate locations will do for our purposes.) Why should we not say, therefore, that Cerberus' single thought that it was raining occurred at two places—or in one spatially unconnected place, a place that was partly in one of his brains and partly in another? Why should we not repudiate the above cartoon and substitute this one?

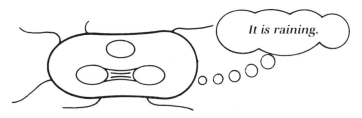

Objection

There may be some superficial plausibility to that suggestion as long as Cerberus' two brains remain synchronized. But suppose that the commissure connecting brain 1 and brain 2 is damaged. And suppose that the structure that "splits" Cerberus' sensory input begins to malfunction, with the consequence that different sensory information is sent to the two brains. Then it might be that the thought (= *Gedanke*) that it is raining is tokened in and only in one of Cerberus' brains, and the thought that it is not raining is tokened in and only in Cerberus' other brain. In such a case, surely, no one could deny that two thinkers thinking contradictory thoughts are to be found within Cerberus. No one could deny the correctness of this picture:

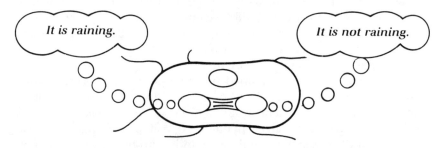

Reply

I do deny these things. In such a case there is one thinker thinking contradictory thoughts, a thinker who could be pictured this way:

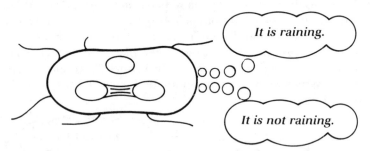

After all, it is certainly possible for one to have contradictory occurrent thoughts. Most of us who have them have them successively, of course, a fact that is at least partly due to the difficulty of thinking any two distinct thoughts, contradictory or not, simultaneously. But this sort of double-think should be easy enough for Cerberus, who has two brains. He is, in fact, ideally equipped for the task of thinking two things at once, just as a man with two mouths would be ideally equipped for the task of saying two things at once. I note in passing that our diagram lacks the capacity to represent a certain piece of information that its rival is capable of representing: It does not show us in which brain either of the two propositional contents it displays is tokened. But it would be easy to repair this minor deficiency by expanding our inventory of comic-strip-style representational devices. We might draw an arrow (for example) between each "thought-balloon" and the representation of the brain in which the content with which that balloon is labeled is supposed to be tokened. Such a device would be no more and no less conventional and arbitrary than the soap bubbles, if that is the correct technical term, that are such a prominent feature of the comic-strip artist's repertory of psychological representation.

Objection

I am laboring under the distinct disadvantage of being an imaginary creation of you, my opponent, the author of this book, and, since what I am saying is controlled by my opponent, I am probably not putting my case as well as it might be put. Even so, I have a hard time believing you're serious. I grant you that someone might, conceivably, simultaneously think two contradictory thoughts. But he would be *aware* that he was thinking them or had just thought them. But the two contradictory thoughts that figure in the present case—as *you* describe it anyway—are sealed off in separate consciousnesses. Cerberus, as you represent him, would be at once aware and unaware that he was thinking that it was raining, and at once aware and unaware that he was thinking that it was *not* raining. And that's a contradiction. Granted, there is no contradiction in saying that a thinker is thinking two contradictory thoughts, but a thinker cannot consistently be described as both aware and not aware of something.

Reply

That's true. But it doesn't apply to Cerberus as I've described him. He is aware that he is thinking that it is raining; he is aware that he is thinking that it is not raining; he is not unaware that he is thinking that it is raining; and he is not unaware that he is thinking that it is not raining. When he suddenly thinks that it is raining, he passes from not believing to believing that he is thinking that it is raining. This event occurs in one of his brains. When he suddenly thinks that it is not raining, he passes from not believing to believing that he is thinking that it is not raining. This event occurs in his other brain. We might sum this rather complicated state of affairs up by saying that his awareness that he is thinking that it is raining is located in one of his brains and his awareness that he is thinking that it is not raining is located in the other.

Objection

But these two awarenesses are not causally connected. Thus the consciousness of Cerberus is split. Or, better, we shouldn't talk of *the* consciousness of Cerberus at all. We should say that he has two consciousnesses.

Reply

Well, perhaps it is. I don't mind your saying that, as long as it's just shorthand for the description contained in the previous "Reply." But don't try to infer from this purely terminological concession the conclusion that two thinking beings are present in Cerberus. Only one thinking being is as close to Cerberus as any other: Cerberus himself.

Objection

What would happen if you asked the unsynchronized Cerberus whether it was raining? (Assume he is able to talk.)

Reply

Whatever happens when one tries simultaneously to say "Yes" and to say "No." (We, I think, are incapable of simultaneous contrary volitions of this sort, but Cerberus would be capable of them.) Paralysis of the vocal apparatus, followed by general panic, I should imagine.

Objection

Suppose you said to Cerberus, "Right now you are simultaneously thinking that it's raining and that it's not raining." He'd reply, "No, I'm not."

Reply

Well, he'd be wrong.

Objection

I hope you realize that Cerberus would be capable not only of simultaneously thinking (in the occurrent sense) that it was raining and that it was not raining, but of much more complex instances of the same phenomenon. Suppose we imagine sequences of thought that take an appreciable amount of time to get through; suppose we imagine two of them going on simultaneously. We should probably be tempted to talk of something like "parallel streams of thought." These streams of thought would be, for all practical purposes, causally independent. And we might so arrange matters that the causal independence of the two streams (and the internal causal interdependence of the parts of each stream) was reflected in the propositional content of each of the streams. Suppose, for example, that you were to say to Cerberus (under the conditions we are currently imagining), "At the present moment, you are having two contradictory thoughts: You are thinking that it is raining and you are also thinking that it is not raining. Before you contradict this assertion, do one small thing for me. Examine your memory carefully and see if I'm not right. Weren't you just now thinking that it was raining, and, at the same time, thinking that it was not raining?" If your description of Cerberus is correct, then each of the two following streams of thought (or something very much like them) will run through Cerberus' mind *pari passu*.

What can he be talking about? It doesn't make sense. How could I not know what I was thinking? Well, I'll humor him. Let's see . . . yes, I have a perfectly clear and indubitable memory of having thought, just a moment ago, that it was raining. And I have no memory whatever of having thought very recently that it wasn't raining. How *could* I have? It's coming down in buckets and has been all day.

What can he be talking about? It doesn't make sense. How could I not know what I was thinking? Well, I'll humor him. Let's see . . . yes, I have a perfectly clear and indubitable memory of having thought, just a moment ago, that it was not raining. And I have no memory whatever of having thought very recently that it was raining. How *could* I have? There isn't a cloud in the sky and there hasn't been one all day.

Isn't it hard to believe, when one reflects on these two streams of thought, that there aren't two independent thinkers within Cerberus, each the possessor of a mind within which one (and only one) of the streams proceeds? If the sheer obviousness of this doesn't move you, perhaps an awkward question will. What accounts for the internal coherency and unity of each of the two streams? If the thought *it's coming down in buckets* and the simultaneous thought *there isn't a cloud in the sky* are the thoughts of the same thinker, what accounts for or grounds the fact of their belonging to different sequences of thought? Why isn't there just one sequence with a few incoherent spots in it? Consider the possibility of superimposing one of the above two columns of print upon the other, thus producing a single column that looks a lot like both of them, but which contains a messy patch of overprinting at the end. Why wouldn't that be a better representation of Cerberus' thoughts (according to you) than two neat parallel columns?

Reply

The two columns of print and the single column with overprinting are each good representations of a certain aspect of Cerberus, though not of the same aspect. The two parallel columns represent the parallel (that is, simultaneous) activity of Cerberus' two brains by representing the *Gedanken* successively tokened in each and displaying the temporal relations between these two successions. (The word 'I' at each of its occurrences in both columns denotes the whole living organism that is Cerberus.) The overprinted column represents the course of Cerberus' thoughts, or it would if we adopted the convention that the thinking of two simultaneous thoughts was to be represented by printing two sentences in the same space. This convention would be of little use to us human beings, however, since it is very doubtful whether we are capable of thinking two thoughts at once, and since our alphabets and our perceptual apparatus are not well designed from the point of view of someone who wants to read overprinted sentences. But such a convention would be no more *arbitrary* than, say, the use of italicized sentences to represent unspoken thoughts.

Objection

If someone were thinking two thoughts simultaneously, he would be aware of this.

Reply

In one sense I accept this and in another sense I deny it. If someone is thinking that p, then—or so I am willing to concede—it follows that he is then aware that he is thinking that p. Hence, if someone is thinking that p and is simultaneously thinking that q, it follows that he is aware that he is thinking that p and aware that he is thinking that q. But it does not follow that he is aware that he is thinking that p and thinking that q. (If it followed from the premise that someone was thinking that p and thinking that q, that he was therefore thinking that p and q, it would follow that, if someone was thinking that p and thinking that q, then he was aware that he was thinking that p and q—and so, presumably, that he was aware that he was thinking that p and aware that he was thinking that q. But if Cerberus' thought that p is tokened in one of his brains and his thought that q in the other, he would be an example of someone who was thinking that p and thinking that q without thinking that p and q.)

Objection

What you are denying is a logical truth: If someone is aware that p and aware that q, then he is aware that p and q, and necessarily so.

Reply

I deny this. We might define a being with a "split consciousness" (or with "two consciousnesses") as one who is, or is possibly, such that, for some p and q, he is aware that p and aware that q but is not aware that p and q. And a being with two brains is just the sort of being of whom this might be a correct description.

Objection

But what would it be *like* to be such a being?

Reply

I don't suppose you want to be told that such a being would be aware that p and aware that q but not aware that p and q? Perhaps you want to know what it would be like for *you* to be such a being. If certain philosophers are right, you either already are such a being or could become one by undergoing a commissurotomy. In that case, you already know the answer, or at least know what to do to find it out. But if these philosophers are wrong, and your propositional thought and awareness are located in (are identical with physical changes in) only one of your cerebral hemispheres—the other hemisphere being a more computational instrument—then you are *essentially* not such a being. And I can see no sense in someone's asking what it would be like for him to be a being whose mental life is of a sort that is his in no possible world. What would it be like for me to be a being from Arcturus whose body chemistry was not based on the carbon atom? What would it be like for me to be a gaseous intelligence inhabiting intersiderial space? What would it be like for me to be God? These questions have no answer beyond "You *couldn't* be any of those things."

Objection

How very eloquent. Look, suppose that the thought that it is raining is tokened in one of Cerberus' brains and that neither this thought nor its denial is tokened in the other. Doesn't he both believe and not believe (not have the belief) that it is raining?

Reply

No. He simply believes that it's raining: a thought (*Gedanke*) that might have been tokened in a nonconnected location happens to be tokened in a connected one. The nonexistence or nonoccurrence of a thought (event) is not the sort of thing that can have a location. Of course the thought 'I have no opinion as to whether it's raining' might be tokened in the other brain, but that would not be essentially different from cases we have already considered.

Objection

Let me try an entirely different approach. Let us consider cases of fission. Let us redesign Cerberus in order to enable him to undergo fission. The most important difference between "Neocerberus" and Cerberus will be that Neocerberus has two "organs of maintenance" whereas

Cerberus had only one. Like Cerberus' brains, these organs will be so designed and connected that they mirror each other's operations. Like Cerberus' brains, neither will be more intimately connected with any part of Cerberus than the other. Thus, Cerberus' internal homeostatic activities—maintenance of body temperature, circulation of vital fluids, antisepsis, and so on—will be directed from two locations. But since the "orders" that proceed from these locations will be identical (or as nearly so as makes no matter) and received simultaneously by their addressees, these processes will be as well regulated and as integrated as they are in any organism. We can draw the following diagram of Neocerberus:

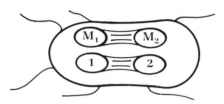

Now, suppose we surgically divide Neocerberus right down the middle. We suppose that his vital organs—pumps, glands, and so on—are symmetrically distributed, and that lesions in Neocerberus' outer integument heal almost instantly. When this is done, we shall obviously have two organisms. What is their relation to Neocerberus? You, I think, must say that neither is Neocerberus. You must hold that two new organisms have come into existence, and that Neocerberus ceased to exist at the moment it became true that the simples that had composed him began to compose two organisms. Call the two new organisms Alpha and Beta. Brain 1 is a part of Alpha—you, of course, would prefer to say certain simples that are caught up in the life of Alpha are arranged cerebrally, and that a moment ago they were caught up in the life of Neocerberus and were related to one another then in very nearly the same way they are related to one another now—and brain 2 is a part of Beta.

Now let me adapt a thought experiment you employed in Section 15. Let us suppose that Neocerberus was making a speech when the division began (unnoticed by him) and that Alpha and Beta spoke the closing words of this speech after the division and physical separation of Alpha from Beta was completed (unnoticed by them). In order to make our thought experiment coherent, we shall make two further suppositions. First, we shall suppose that Neocerberus had two mouths and, in fact, two complete sets of vocal apparatus. When Neocerberus' two brains are synchronized, the words spoken by mouth A are "overcaused": either the processes occurring in brain 1 or the descriptively identical processes occurring in brain 2 would have sufficed for the production of these same words. And, of course, the same thing is true of mouth B. When Neocerberus speaks, therefore, his two mouths speak in unison. When the division occurs, one mouth "goes" to Alpha, and the other to Beta. Secondly, we shall suppose that through some complicated arrangement of mirrors (and the application of a local anaesthetic), Neocerberus, Alpha, and Beta are kept unaware of, and are therefore not distracted by, the division until some time well after its completion. Let us imagine a film depicting the division. At the beginning of the film, mouth A and mouth B begin simultaneously to speak. They speak the same words throughout the film, one connected unit of discourse. We may as well borrow the speech you used in Section 15:

> The First Folio has 'and a table of green fields'. For a long time it was thought that it should be 'and 'a babbled of green fields'. But actually the correct reading is probably 'on a table of green frieze'; someone corrected a copy of the 1632 to read that way, and that doesn't seem to me to be a correction anyone would make as a guess. It's so uninspired and arbitrary that it's probably right. But most editions keep 'babbled' because it's a fine line.

This speech takes about thirty seconds to deliver. About five seconds into the speech an enormous scalpel begins the division of Neocerberus into two organisms. Twenty seconds later it has completely severed Neocerberus. Throughout the course of this operation, mouth A and mouth B have talked steadily away in unison. If *your* analysis of this case is correct, then the sounds the auditors of this speech hear are at first the words of a single speaker, Neocerberus, and then, at a certain moment, become the words of two speakers, Alpha and Beta. If you are right, then the referent of the word 'me' (which occurs just past the middle of the speech) depends upon the speed with which the scalpel cuts. If this word is spoken before the critical point, the point at which the organic unity of Neocerberus is destroyed, then this word refers to Neocerberus; if it is spoken after the critical point then (as spoken by mouth A) it refers to Alpha, and (as spoken by mouth B) it refers to Beta. But isn't this just absurd? Isn't it far more reasonable to say that there were two speakers all along, one speaking through mouth A and the other speaking through mouth B? Surely what we have here is two conscious, reasoning beings, the thoughts of one of them being tokened at one place in the organism, and the thoughts of the other of them being tokened elsewhere in that organism? But if that is right, then your answer to the Special Composition Question is wrong, since, before the division, there were two objects present in Neocerberus, neither of which was an organism.

Reply

Well, I agree that the truth about Neocerberus and the products of his fission is "absurd." That, I would say, is because Neocerberus is absurd—though I concede that he is logically possible. But many logically possible beings are absurd. I suppose I may play the absurdity game if you may. Consider the organism Alpha after the division. Suppose that shortly after his separation from Beta he speaks the words "I've just had a very strange experience." (Or, at any rate, suppose that these words issue from him.) If your analysis of the thought experiment you have constructed is correct, then the referent of the word 'I' that issues from Alpha is an object that existed before Alpha did. And isn't *that* absurd?

Objection

I seem to have turned into a reply. No, it's not absurd. But I have been speaking a bit loosely, and perhaps my words have misled you. Strictly speaking, the new organism is not Alpha but simply Alpha's (the speaker's) body. Before the division, either Alpha had a different body, or else he had the same body but it wasn't yet an independent organism.

Reply

Why do you want to say this? Why introduce other entities than the organisms?

Objection

Because it is obvious to one who reflects on the design of Neocerberus that the words and sentences that issue from mouth A, both before and after the division, are the productions of one continuous consciousness. (And, of course, the same goes for the words that issue from B.) There is something that it would be *like* to be the speaker of the words—*all* the words—that issue from A. And this speaker would notice no discontinuity in the course of his speech; much less would he cease to exist.

Reply

I deny this. No continuous consciousness would be present through-out the speech. You say that a "continuous consciousness" is present in a certain situation over a certain interval, and by that you mean that a certain conscious being is present and continuously conscious in that situation and over that interval. To find out whether a certain situation contains a "continuous consciousness," in your sense, therefore, we have first to find out whether that situation contains a continuously existent thinker. We can't do things the other way round. We can't find out whether that situation contains a continuously existent thinker by first finding out whether it contains a "continuous consciousness." According to the metaphysic of thinking beings that I accept, there was no thinker available to be the thinker whose thoughts are expressed in the words that issue from mouth A. And I have no contrary intuitive or preanalytical conviction that there must be such a thinker. You do have such a contrary conviction. I believe that you have this conviction because you take what I may call a "typically empiricist" view of mind. (Of course, I have no idea whether you are an empiricist.) You see a mind—better, you see a thinking being—as being made out of mental events. That is, in your view, the extended event or process that is the persistence or continued existence of a thinking being is composed entirely of mental events. (In *my* view, the continued existence of a thinking being is a life and thus is composed of both mental and nonmental events.) It is important to realize that I am not accusing you of being a dualist. Someone who takes a "typically empiricist" view of thinking beings may or may not be a dualist; if he is not a dualist, he will maintain that the mental events that compose the process that is the continued existence of a thinking being are also material events. Now, why do I call your view "typically empiricist"? Because of what must be your view of what ties a sequence of mental events together into an event of the type *continued existence of a thinker*. Consider a temporal sequence of mental events, XYZ—thoughts, say, though the point I am making applies to any sort of mental event. Are these thoughts the thoughts of a single thinker, or are they the thoughts of more than one thinker, or even the thoughts of no thinkers at all? According to your view, the answer to this question is determined entirely by the causal relations that hold among X, Y, and Z. (If you subscribe to a typically empiricist theory of causation, then you are faced with the famous "bundle" problem; but perhaps you do not subscribe to a typically empiricist theory of causation.) It is a consequence of your view that if X, Y, and Z are the thoughts of a single thinker, then any three events having the same intrinsic mental properties as X, Y, and Z and bearing the same temporal and causal relations to one another as X, Y, and Z must also be the thoughts of some one thinker. And it is the causal continuity within a sequence of mental events that you identify with the continuity of consciousness that you appeal to in drawing your moral from the story of Neocerberus. You believe that if a certain succession of thoughts or other mental events constitutes a continuous consciousness—a thing that will be possible only if a thread of causation runs through the succession like a string through a necklace of beads—then any other succession of mental events having the same intrinsic mental properties, and bearing the same temporal and causal relations to one another, will be a case of continuous consciousness.

I, on the other hand, take a "typically rationalist" view of thinking beings. I think of a sequence of thoughts as being thoughts of the same thinker just in virtue of their being modifications of one, continuing substance: the understander that stands under them. (A rationalist whose picture of the continuity of thought was not only typical but paradigmatic would hold that the whole being of this one continuing substance consisted in its mental activity. I hold, of course, that the whole being of the continuing substance is biological.) Because I take this view, I see no difficulty in the assertion that the succession of thoughts that underlies the words that issue from mouth A are not thoughts that belong to one continuous consciousness, even though they exhibit as high a degree of causal continuity as any empiricist could wish for. An initial segment of this series of thoughts comprises the thoughts of Neocerberus; the remainder comprises the thoughts of Alpha. I find it plausible to suppose that if Neocerberus had not been partitioned, then the very occurrent thoughts that were thoughts of Alpha would have been occurrent thoughts of Neocerberus. (But whether this is the case depends on what the correct principle of "counterfactual event-identity" is. This result follows from a principle of event identity which I in fact accept,[68] but which is not a premise of the present book.) Thus, in my view, a certain sequence of mental events might be the content of "a single continuous consciousness" in one possible world, and be partly the content of one "consciousness" and partly the content of a second "consciousness" in another world; and the events in this sequence might have the same mental properties and bear the same causal relations to one another in both worlds.

Objection

Suppose we destroyed one of the brains in the undivided Neocerberus—say, the one that would have gone to Beta. According to you, Neocerberus would survive the destruction of one of his brains, just as a human being might survive the destruction of one of his kidneys. We should then have (according to you) Neocerberus with his thoughts tokened in only one brain and his actions caused by events in that brain alone. Suppose we now destroy all of Neocerberus' cells but those that became parts of Alpha in the "division story." This obviously would not destroy Neocerberus—if it indeed was Neocerberus we did this to (that is, this action would not destroy whatever organism was there). But, equally obviously, the resulting organism would be Alpha. Hence the destruction of the "Beta brain" must have left us with Alpha, and not with Neocerberus.

Reply

No, the destruction of the Beta brain leaves us with Neocerberus. But the subsequent destruction of all of Neocerberus' cells except those that became parts of Alpha in the division story ends Neocerberus' life, and hence ends Neocerberus. This action ends Neocerberus' life because it destroys one of the two "organs of maintenance" that had been directing that life. The resulting life is a new event, distinct from Neocerberus' life because it had different causes from Neocerberus' life. It is in fact Alpha's life, and the resulting organism is, as you say, Alpha.

Objection

Well, what would happen if we surgically removed from Neocerberus the organ of maintenance that "went to" Beta in the division story, and did nothing else to him?

Reply

The remaining organism would be Alpha, with his thoughts tokened in two brains instead of one.

Objection

Suppose we surgically removed both brains from Neocerberus but left the two organs of maintenance undisturbed. Wouldn't that destroy Neocerberus?

Reply

No, he'd still be there, although he'd now be incapable of thought and sensation.

Objection

Well, look. Suppose we surgically remove one of his brains and supplied it with a mechanical life-support system. Who would *that* be?

Reply

No one. There'd be only a lot of cells that did not compose anything (and hence did not compose any*one*).

Objection

But there would still be *thoughts*, since there would be all of the right physical processes. And if there were thoughts, there would be someone who was aware of himself as the "I think" that accompanies all perceptions. You couldn't tell him that he was under an illusion as regards his own existence, or he'll reply *Fallor, ergo sum.*

Reply

None of what you say is true if there's no one there. And, I, with my typically rationalist view of thinking, say there's no one there because I can't locate an object to have the thoughts. You with your typically empiricist view of thought say that, because there are events of the right sort to be thoughts that are causally connected in the right way, there therefore must be thinking going on, and you are so deeply convinced that thinking is going on that you are willing to regard the problem of the metaphysical nature of the thinker as a detail that can be left unresolved. (Other "empiricists" might be content to say that there were thoughts there but no thinker.) I, however, continue to distrust these intuitions that tell us (on the basis of the presence of a connected series of events of the right sort) that there must be thinking. Here is a case devised by José Benardete that, I think, militates against the trustworthiness of such intuitions. Suppose that every thousandth of a second or so Alice were to vanish for (say) a hundred-millionth of a second. More exactly, suppose that Alice were annihilated, and that a hundred-millionth of a second later a perfect duplicate of her (as she had been when she vanished) was created; and suppose that this cycle of annihilation and creation occurred every thousandth of a second for an indefinite period. No one, of course, would notice this. (If someone protests that in this situation it would look as if Alice had become slightly transparent, we could adjust the ratio of the intervals involved; but we must keep the interval between "disappearances" short in comparison with the smallest interval that can be noted by the conscious mind.) Is there any conscious experience associated with the region of space that appears to contain Alice? (Never mind for the moment whether there would be a continuing conscious *being* in that space, or whether, if there were, it would be Alice.) Empiricist intuitions, I think, say yes: there is a continuous consciousness there, the very slight tincture of psychic blankness that the intervals of nonexistence have introduced being too small to make any perceptible difference to consciousness. After all, if a super-cinema-film displayed a hundred million frames per second, no one in the theater would notice a thing if every hundred-thousandth frame were painted out. Reason, however, says no: there is no continuous being, and hence no continuous conscious being, and hence no conscious being, and hence no consciousness. A world of "Alices" would be a world without consciousness. And (to return to the case you asked about) no mass of cells, however arranged and connected, can be the locus of conscious experience unless those cells compose something. Of course, you may want to say that the brain cells excised from Neocerberus (arranged cerebrally and kept individually alive by a life-support system) *do* compose something. But then I shall ask you what answer to the Special Composition Question it is that generates that "something." My general point is that one can't first decide with respect to some real or imaginary situation whether consciousness is "present in" that situation and then go on to inquire about the existence and nature of a being that is the bearer of that consciousness. That's doing things the wrong way round. To find out whether consciousness is present in a given situation, you must first find out whether that situation contains a being of a sort that can be conscious. And if the existence of such a being entails that certain objects that are known to be present in that situation (brain cells, say) compose something, you are committed to the existence of an answer to the Special Composition Question that entails that those objects, arranged as they are, compose something. You may, of course, go on to say that you do not know what that answer is. But then why do you suppose there is one? Only because there is obviously conscious experience going on there? But how can it be obvious that conscious experience is going on there if conscious experience requires a subject and it is not obvious whether there is any subject there?

Objection

There's no reasoning with you. Let me change my tack one more time. Suppose you were to find out that you were a being like Neocerberus (internally, at least; we know you don't have two mouths). That is, suppose you were to discover that all the anatomy texts were part of a cosmic hoax and that all human organisms contained two brains that mirrored each other's activities, and so on. Or, if you like, suppose you were to discover that you were a freak and that you alone had these features. Now, suppose you were told that you were going to be partitioned, like Neocerberus. What should you expect to happen to you? What experiences should you anticipate?

Reply

I should expect to die. Whether one expects to have any experiences after one's death is, of course, a matter of one's religious beliefs. I take it you're not asking me about my religious beliefs.

Objection

Wouldn't the two thinking organisms who resulted from partitioning you remember your present experiences?

Reply

They would perhaps "remember" them. They would not remember them. The case is similar to the case of the philosopher's duplicating machine, which produces atom-for-atom duplicates of existing objects. A duplicate made of me by such a machine would "remember" my present experiences but not remember them, just as a duplicate of a photograph made by such a machine would be a "photograph" but not a photograph.

Objection

Suppose you were given a choice between being partitioned and being totally destroyed. Which would you choose, supposing that you care only about yourself and have no preference whatever about what happens after your death?

Reply

I'd choose to be partitioned. After all, my metaphysic might be wrong. I accept this metaphysic, but I do not assign to it as high a subjective probability as I assign to, say, the proposition that I require food to live or the proposition that I speak a language called 'English'. What have I got to lose? But suppose I did have something to lose. Suppose I were given a choice between being totally destroyed a year from now and being partitioned now. Then, I think, I would choose to be destroyed in a year.

Objection

But wouldn't you in some important sense *survive* the partition, even if neither of the organisms that it produced was you?

Reply

I don't understand that. When I say that someone has survived a certain adventure, what I say entails that this person existed both before and after the adventure. We can, of course, talk about someone's "surviving" in his work or in the memory of those who knew him. ("He became his admirers," as Auden wrote on the occasion of Yeats's death.) But this sort of survival is of no metaphysical interest.[69]

17. The Problem of the Many and the Vagueness of Composition

I have proposed the following answer to the Special Composition Question:

($\exists y$ the xs compose y) if and only if
the activity of the xs constitutes a life.

If this answer is correct, then there are living organisms: They are the objects whose lives are constituted by the activities of simples, and, perhaps, by the activities of subordinate organisms such as cells; they are the objects that have proper parts. Therefore, if there are no organisms, then, since there *are* lives, the Proposed Answer is wrong. In Section 12 I gave reasons for supposing that there were living organisms. That is, I gave reasons that I intended to be available to the philosopher who, like me, thinks that there are no visible inanimate objects. (Most philosophers, unless they are Nihilists or general skeptics, will scarcely want reasons for believing in organisms.) I have argued that situations apparently involving tables and chairs and all the other inanimate furniture of the world are to be understood as involving only simples. There are no chairs, I maintain, but only simples arranged chairwise. My "reasons for believing in organisms," therefore, are reasons for stopping where I do and not going on to maintain that there are no organisms but are only simples arranged organically. My argument for the existence of organisms, it will be remembered, involved in an essential way the proposition that I exist. In Section 12 I presented various reasons for thinking that I exist—that is, for thinking that I am a real and not a virtual object. (The question at issue was the nature of the facts expressed by those ordinary-language sentences like 'Van Inwagen was born in 1942' that would ordinarily be supposed to express facts. It was not the question whether this ordinary supposition was, as I suppose it to be, correct.) These reasons ranged from certain rather pedestrian "Cartesian" considerations to more subtle points about the possibility of understanding assertions that are, prima facie, ascriptions of mental predicates to unified subjects, as being really the ascriptions of multigrade relations to pluralities of simples. I will now take up a question I laid aside in Section 12 and examine a powerful and subtle argument for the conclusion that neither I nor anyone else exists. This examination will serve the double purpose of filling a lacuna in the reasoning of Section 12 and of leading us into a topic I have on several occasions rather abruptly avoided confronting: the vagueness of living organisms.

Peter Unger has recently presented arguments for the conclusion that he does not exist, and he has presented more general arguments against the existence of people and other visible things that, if cogent, would show that I (among many other things) do not exist. In the present section I shall attempt to reply to one of Unger's arguments. In this reply I shall presuppose my own answer to the Special Composition Question. There is nothing dialectically improper in this. In fact, I regard the present section as a part of my defense of my answer. Unger's "nihilistic" arguments are much harder to deal with than many philosophers have supposed. I think that at least some of them can be met only if what I have called a Moderate answer to the Special Composition Question is correct. If that is the case, then only a Moderate answer to the Special Composition Question is consistent with there being such things as you and I. If this is so, it is an argument in favor of the Proposed Answer, which is the only Moderate answer I know of that can withstand much dialectical pressure. (I repeat a warning about terminology that was given in Section 8: Unger describes his position as "nihilistic." But in the system of classification employed in the present work, he is, as we shall see, a Universalist. He calls himself a nihilist because, in his view, none of the many objects generated by Universalism—none of the objects that, as he sees it, there are—is suitable for identification with any person or any of the other objects we unreflectively suppose to exist. He therefore differs from a "non-nihilistic Universalist" who proposes to identify people and chairs and so on with a few among the many objects generated by Universalism.)

I cannot discuss all of Unger's arguments, for they are many and the issues they raise are many and subtle. I shall discuss only an argument that depends on the alleged impossibility of finding a solution to what Unger calls 'the problem of the many'.[70] Even with this restriction of the scope of my discussion, however, I shall be forced to concentrate on a sort of skeletal reconstruction of his argument, a reconstruction that will not do justice to its psychological force and will leave out many important details. But I think that my reconstruction will do justice to its *logical* force and that if I succeed in refuting the reconstruction, I shall have succeeded in untying the very complicated knot that lies at its center. I shall, accordingly, proceed by assuming that my answer to the Special Composition Question is correct and showing that, on that assumption, Unger does not succeed in demonstrating (or at least not by posing the problem of the many) that I do not exist. I am reasonably sure that the proponent of any answer to the Special Composition Question that identified cases of composition with cases of the instantiation of some multigrade causal relation could easily adapt the following arguments to the peculiarities of his own view of composition; that is, he could easily transform the following arguments into arguments for the conclusion that, if *his* view is correct, Unger's demonstration fails.

Unger's argument may be compactly formulated as a *reductio*. Assume I exist. Then certain simples compose me. Call them 'M'. Now, a single simple is a negligible item indeed. Let x be one of these negligible parts of me—one that is somewhere in my right arm, say. Now, consider the simples that compose me *other than* x ('M $-$ x'). Since x is so very negligible, M $-$ x could compose a human being just as well as M could. We may say that M and M $-$ x are "equally well suited" to compose human beings. And, of course, for *any* simple y, "M $-$ y" will be as well suited to compose a human being as M are. Moreover, it would be surprising indeed if there were not a simple z such that "M $+$ z" were as well suited to compose a human being as M are. It would, in fact (if I may once more use this phrase), be intolerably arbitrary to say that M composed a human being although M $-$ x didn't and M $-$ y didn't and M $+$ z didn't. Suppose, therefore, that M $-$ x et al. do compose human beings. Then there are present, in pretty much the same place, the "M $-$ x man," the "M $-$ y man," and the "M $+$ z man." And, of course, simples being so numerous, in any situation in which we should ordinarily say that I was alone in a room, there will be present in that room an enormous, albeit finite, number of men. Some of these will be practically indistinguishable from me and some will be noticeably smaller. There will, for example, be legions of men who are composed entirely of simples that are among the simples we have already mentioned but who lack a right arm. It is, however, perfectly ridiculous to suppose that there are that many men about. But the only alternative is to say that neither M nor any other simples compose a man, and, therefore, to say that I do not exist. Suppose, however, that someone replies by saying that it's even more ridiculous to say that there are no men at all, and that we must therefore suppose that there are many more men than we thought. We respond as follows: anyone who does bite the bullet and who concedes that there are "all these men" and who also wishes to say that *he* exists will need a "selection principle," a principle that selects one man out of an enormous class of overlapping men to be himself. But because there is no significant difference between, say, the M man and the M − χ man, any principle that identifies me with one of them must be intolerably arbitrary.

This completes my reconstruction of Unger's argument. The argument seems to presuppose the following four propositions. (1) In every situation of which we should ordinarily say that it contained just one man, there are many sets of simples whose members are as suitably arranged to compose men as any simples could be. (2) The members of each of these sets compose something. (3) Each of these "somethings" is a man, provided there are any men at all. (4) If I exist, there is a man. It would be possible to view the problem of the many (as it touches one's own existence) in a slightly different way: One might reject (3) and contend that, in a situation of which we should ordinarily say that it contained just one man, there *is* just one man, provided there are any men in that situation at all; the other "somethings," one might say, are not men but "man-candidates," things in many respects suitable for being men but which aren't men because some other thing of their type has bested them in a competition whose prize is the privilege of being the only man in that situation. I call this a "slightly" different view of the problem of the many (conceived as primarily a problem about one's own existence) because, like Unger's view, it demands a solution in the form of a selection principle. Unger's view of the problem demands that I discover a way of selecting one man among many to be myself; the alternative view demands that I discover a way of selecting one man-candidate among many to be a man. (Once *this* selection has been made, of course, there is no problem about which man is myself, there being only one man "there." One might, of course, raise the question why I should suppose that *I* am the man, and not merely one of the also-rans.)

Now, both of these views of the problem seem to me to rest upon Universalism. It is difficult to see what other basis one could have for accepting proposition (2) of the preceding paragraph. But I reject Universalism. I therefore deny that in a situation of which we should ordinarily say that I was the only man present in it, there are an enormous number of things—sums, collections, clouds, or aggregates of atoms, "cohesions of particles of matter anyhow united," men, man-candidates, categorize them as you will—which are pretty much alike and which are all candidates for the office of being myself. In my view, I am present in that situation, and none of the other things present—simples, cells, the cat in my lap—is even remotely like me. In particular, there are no things that are almost as large as or minutely larger than I. Suppose, for example, that Celia is one of my cells. The cells that compose me, of course, compose me. But "the cells that compose me other than Celia" do not compose anything whatever, and the same goes for "the simples that compose me other than Simon."

"Your rejection of 'Universalism' is a red herring. You still face a problem of the many. You haven't dealt with the fact that M and M $-$ x and M $-$ y and M $+$ z are equally well suited to compose a man, and, in fact, equally well suited to compose *you*. You may protest that if M compose something, then M $-$ x don't and M $-$ y don't, and so on. You may say that there are simples that compose you, and that any simples that compose you are exactly those simples. But what's so special about *those* simples? If the xs compose you, after all, there are ys which are not (quite) those xs but which are equally well suited to compose you. Why don't they? To state this problem in its full generality, I shall have to make use of some sort of abstract object such that, for any xs, the xs define or pick out a unique object of that type. Sets would seem to be admirably adapted to this purpose. We pose the problem thus. Suppose for the moment that you exist. Consider the set of simples S whose members compose you. Now consider all the sets of simples that have 'nearly the same members' as S (it will make no difference to the force of our argument how we spell out this rather vague requirement) and whose members and the members of S are equally well suited to compose a man. Having got these sets before your mind's eye, forget our momentary supposition that you exist. (There obviously exist sets having the properties of the sets we are considering, whether or not you exist.) Now, which of these sets is such that its members compose something? What principle of selection will you apply to them to determine which of them is the set the members of which compose something?"

None. There is no such set. No set is the set that contains just the simples that compose me or the set that contains just the simples that compose anything having proper parts. This is because parthood and composition are vague notions. Consider again the carbon atom we discussed in Section 9, or, since a chemical atom is a virtual object, consider the simples that virtually compose it. There can be no right answer to the question 'When, exactly, did they begin to be parts of Alice?' And, therefore, there are moments such that there is no right answer to the question whether they were parts of Alice at those moments. If I am right about parthood and composition, there is no way round this. Being caught up in the life of an organism is, like being rich or being tall, a matter of degree, and is in that sense a vague condition. Set membership, however, is not vague. Being a member of a set is not a matter of degree. And, therefore, there cannot be a set of simples the members of which are just exactly the simples that compose me, any more than there can be a set that contains just exactly the men who are tall. For let x be any simple such that there is no answer (that is to say, *yes* or *no*) to the question whether x is a part of me. If there were such a thing as the set of simples whose members composed me, than either yes or no *would* be the right answer to 'Is x a part of me?' since x must either be a member, without qualification, of any given set, or else a nonmember, without qualification, of that set. I therefore cannot legitimately be asked to produce a selection principle that picks out the set of simples whose members compose me, for no set of simples has this feature.

"If you say that about sets, what will you say about plural quantification? Consider the proposition that for some xs, those xs now compose you. Is that proposition true? You will remember that in Section 2 you laid it down that a sentence of the form 'For some xs, those xs F' expresses a truth just in the case that for some set, the members of that set F."

I will accept the obvious implication of what I laid down. And that implication seems right. Just as, for any set, an object must either be or not be, without qualification, a member of that set, so, for any xs, an object must either be or not be, without qualification, one of the xs. For example, any object must either be or not be, without qualification, one of Tom, Dick, and Harry. (This thesis is true provided that *identity* is not vague. In Section 18 we shall consider the implications of supposing that there may be cases of "vague identity." For the present, we shall continue to suppose that identity, in Quine's words, "knows no gradations."[71] This would certainly seem to be justified in the present context; here we are concerned only with plural quantification over simples, and the only plausible candidates for cases of "vague identity"—we shall examine them in Section 18—involve composite objects.)

"But that doesn't seem right. Consider the rich. It is simply not true that every person can be said either to be or not to be, without qualification, one of the rich. Similar examples abound. In fact, such an example could be constructed on the basis of at least nine out of ten of the plural referring expressions we use in the ordinary business of life."

This shows only that substituting a referring expression (singular or plural) for a variable (singular or plural) can be a tricky business if that expression contains vague terms. The phrase 'the distance from Chicago to Salt Lake City' is, I suppose, a vague singular term. And the quantifier-variable sentence 'For all x, if x is a distance, then x is less than, equal to, or greater than 1,400 miles' would seem to express a truth. But we might hesitate to say that the distance from Chicago to Salt Lake City was less than, equal to, or greater than 1,400 miles—that is, 2,253,090,000 millimeters—particularly if 'or' were understood in its exclusive sense. (Textbooks of formal logic advise us to substitute English predicates for the schematic predicate-letters of formal logic only when we are, in the context in which we are applying formal logic, willing to regard these predicates as having perfectly precise extensions. Textbook writers seldom if ever tender any corresponding advice about the substitution of singular terms for variables, but only, I think, because it hasn't occurred to them. Since singular terms can contain predicates, and since vague predicates are common, vague singular terms are common. Consider, for example, 'the tallest man Sally knows', given that lots of men are such that there is no definite answer to the question whether Sally knows them.[72]) Someone might respond to this example by saying that, strictly speaking, there is no such thing as the distance from Chicago to Salt Lake City, and that our disjunctive predication is therefore simply false; but this person would have to account for our unhesitating assent to the sentence 'The distance from Chicago to Salt Lake City is less than the distance from Chicago to Tokyo'. This is, as I have said, a tricky business. But whatever tricks one may employ in the transaction of this business, they may be applied *mutatis mutandis* with equal success and equal plausibility to the problem of substituting vague plural referring expressions for plural variables. Whatever accounts for our hesitation over the Chicago–Salt Lake City sentence (despite our assent to the universal quantification of which it appears to be an instance) should, with suitable modification, account for our hesitation over 'The rich number more than, or fewer than, or just exactly, one million', despite our assent to 'For any xs, the xs number more than, or fewer than, or just exactly one million'. And whatever accounts for our assent to the Chicago–Salt Lake City–Tokyo sentence should with suitable modification account for our assent to 'The rich are a minority'. Therefore, I am not troubled by the fact that all the following sentences seem to me to express truths:

For any xs, those xs are not the simples that compose me.

The simples that compose me collectively weigh about 68 kilograms.

The simples that compose me are more numerous than the simples that compose my cat.

We have been talking about the difficulties that vague terms raise in connection with the logical operation commonly called instantiation. There will obviously be exactly parallel difficulties about generalization.

Though I accept the second and third of the displayed sentences, I do not, of course, accept 'For some xs, those xs are simples and compose me'.

"But throughout the course of this book you have been employing just such quantificational sentences. For example, it would seem to be obviously a presupposition of almost everything you have said about the metaphysics of organisms that, for any organism and any time, there are certain simples such that they and they alone compose that organism at that time. Why, the Special Composition Question, which is supposed to be the central question of this book, is the question 'When do the xs compose something?' Now you seem to be saying that the answer is 'Never'."

That is because the earlier parts of this book (Sections 1 through 16) were written within the scope of a certain simplifying assumption, an idealization of the way things really are: That parthood and composition are not matters of degree. One cannot say everything at once. Just as it is permissible for a study of the statistical mechanics of gasses to begin with the idealizing assumption that a gas consists of tiny spheres that interact with one another and their container only in the transfer of impulse in elastic collisions, and only after the meat has been extracted from this idealization to proceed to closer approximations to the real nature of gasses, so it is permissible for a study of the metaphysics of organisms to begin with the idealizing assumption that parthood and composition are perfectly precise conditions, and only later to confront the facts of vagueness.

"It is all very well to talk of idealizations. But idealizations must not be indispensable, or it is cheating to call them idealizations; if they are indispensable, then they are only difficulties in your theory that you have given a Greek name to but have not otherwise dealt with. How will you dispense with the idealizing assumption of vagueness? More precisely, what are you going to do about quantifiers that bind plural variables in mereological contexts? Such quantification was, it would seem, an indispensable part of the metaphysical apparatus of the earlier parts of this book. Now, you tell us, it is proper only when it occurs within the scope of a certain idealizing assumption. Well, let us relax that assumption. Then what happens? More precisely still, consider this sentence, which is suggested by something you said in Section 14:

Any organism could, at any time at which it existed, have been composed of completely different simples at that time.

You obviously regard this sentence as expressing what is in some sense a truth. But how will you express this truth if you are not allowed to make your idealizing assumption, and, therefore, are not allowed to say that for any organism and any time, there are xs such that those xs compose that organism at that time?"

When you first raised the problem of the many in a way that did not presuppose Universalism, you said that to state the problem in its full generality, you would have to make use of ordinary quantification over certain abstract objects (sets of simples), plural quantification over simples having insufficient expressive powers for your purposes. In order to solve the problem you have posed, I too shall have to resort to quantification over abstract objects: fuzzy sets.

The notion of a fuzzy set is a generalization of the classical notion of a set. Fuzzy sets differ from classical sets in that, although membership in a classical set is, as we have noted, not a matter of degree, membership in a fuzzy set *is* a matter of degree. To specify a classical set is to specify its membership. Or, equivalently, to specify a classical set is to specify for each object *whether* that object is a member of that set. Similarly, to specify a fuzzy set is to specify for each object *to what degree* that object is a member of that fuzzy set. (From now on, I shall abbreviate 'fuzzy set' as 'f-set'.) The membership relation of classical set theory is a two-term relation. The analogue in f-set theory of the classical membership relation is a three-term relation whose terms are objects, f-sets, and special objects called 'degrees'. Thus, a typical "membership" statement of f-set theory would be of the form 'x is a member of the f-set y to the degree z'. If we assume that there are only two degrees—the truth-values, say—then f-set theory reduces to classical set theory. (F-set theory is therefore, as I have said, a generalization of classical set theory.) If there are three degrees of membership—call them *Definitely*, *Definitely Not*, and *Up to a Point*—then we have a rudimentary theory of sets with "borderline membership." But borderline membership is rarely perfectly homogeneous. Typically, we shall want to be able to say of two borderline cases of something-or-other that, although both are borderline cases, one is closer to being a definite case of whatever-it-is than the other. And if we have an f-set theory based on only three degrees of membership, this theory will not provide us with the resources we need to say that. If we assume that nature is continuous—a common enough assumption in science, though it is not beyond criticism—we had better have as many degrees as there are points in a continuum, and we had better provide them with an order that mirrors the order of the continuum. (To apply such a theory to the real world will involve idealization just as surely as will the application of classical set theory or plural quantification to the real world. For such application assumes that there is always a single dimension along which objects approach or depart from being absolutely definite cases of something-or-other. But in the real world there is often a manifold of dimensions of approach-to-and-departure-from its various sorts and conditions. I have no interesting thoughts about how to eliminate the "unilinear" feature of our idealization—though in a certain trivial sense this would present no formal difficulties.) Let us, therefore, choose the real numbers from 0 to 1 as our "degrees," 0 and 1 corresponding respectively to the definite nonmembership and definite membership of classical set theory, and the intermediate numbers standing for intermediate degrees of membership: The greater the degree to which an object is a member of an f-set, the "closer" it is to being fully or definitely a member of that set. And we assume that the *size* of the numbers in this interval has meaning, as well as their order: if x is a member of F_1 to the degree y and z is a member of F_2 to the degree $y/2$, then z is only "half as much" a member of F_2 as x is of F. To specify an f-set, one specifies the degree to which each object is a member of that set. Thus we may specify an f-set by saying that Napoleon belongs to it to the degree 1, Caesar to the degree ½, the number 43 to the degree $\pi/7$, and everything else to the degree 0. (Or we may call those objects that are members of an f-set to a degree greater than 0 its "members" and say that to specify an f-set is to specify the degree to which each of its members belongs to it.)

We shall make some use of f-sets and the three-term membership relation of f-set theory in the remainder of this section, but we shall not have to appeal to any facts or theorems of f-set *theory*, beyond those immediately evident from the definitions of its basic concepts. But there is such a thing as f-set theory. This is shown by the fact that f-sets have an obvious classical model. An f-set may be identified with any classical function F that takes as values only real numbers greater than 0 and less than or equal to 1. If $F(x) = y$, then x is a "member of F to the degree y." If x is not a member of the domain of F, then x is a member of F to the degree 0. We may call the members of the domain of the classical function F the "members" of its *Doppelganger*, the f-set F. But if we adopt this way of talking, we must remember that two f-sets may have the same members. For example, the f-set that has Caesar as a member to the degree ½ and no other members is not identical with the f-set that has Caesar as a member to the degree ¼ and no other members. We may call two f-sets *coextensive* if they have the same members. (Obviously, at most one member of any class of coextensive f-sets can be identified with the classical set of their members.)

Since there are distinct but coextensive f-sets, we cannot speak of the f-set "whose members" compose me or compose any other object. Or, at any rate, we must explain what we mean by these words. I will propose a definition. (Since we are at present interested only in composition by simples, I shall define only 'the f-set of simples whose members compose x'. This reduces the task of definition essentially to the task of defining 'the f-set of simples whose members are parts of x' since every physical object is composed entirely of simples—that is, every part of every physical object overlaps a simple—and since simples do not overlap other simples.)

The f-set of simples whose members compose x = df.

The f-set of simples whose members are parts of x = df.

The f-set y of simples such that $\forall z$ a simple is a member of y to the degree z if and only if that simple is a part of x to the degree z.

We assume that (at any given moment) any given simple is a part of x to some precisely specifiable degree, a "degree" being a real number greater than or equal to 0 and less than or equal to 1. We assume that "parthood to degree 0" is definite nonparthood, "parthood to degree 1" is definite parthood, and that the intermediate numbers stand for intermediate degrees of parthood (as was the case with membership). We assume that the size of degrees of parthood is significant (compare our earlier remarks about the size of degrees of membership), and that "degree of membership" and "degree of parthood" are in some intuitive sense comparable notions: that it makes sense to say that the degree to which x is a member of F *is* the degree to which z is a part of y. It is evident from our definition that at any given moment of my career the members of exactly one f-set of simples will compose me. There is, therefore, no "problem of the many" for the f-sets. No selection principle is needed to pick out the one f-set among many equally suitable candidates to be the one whose members compose me, for only one is suitable. Once the concept of the composition of an object by the members of an f-set of simples has been introduced, it is a more or less trivial task to paraphrase sentences involving plural quantification into mereological contexts into sentences involving singular quantification over f-sets. Here, for example, is the paraphrase you have asked for:

For any organism x and any time t, if the members of an f-set of simples y compose x at t, then, possibly, the members of an f-set of simples z such that no simple is a member of both y and z compose x at t.

Or consider the Proposed Answer. Suppose we are willing to accept the following four theses: that, for each life and each simple, that simple is caught up in that life to a certain *degree*; that such "degrees of involvement in a life" may be identified with the real numbers from 0 to 1; that the degrees of involvement 0 and 1 and the size of the intermediate degrees of involvement have meanings analogous to the meanings we postulated for degrees of f-set membership and degrees of parthood and their sizes; that it makes sense to say that the degree to which a simple is caught up in a life *is* the degree to which a simple is a member of a given f-set, and *is* the degree to which a simple is a part of a given organism. Suppose we say that the activity of the members of the f-set of simples x constitutes a life just in the case that there is a life such that, for every simple, that simple is a member of that f-set to just the degree to which it is caught up in that life. Then we may represent our answer to a restricted version of the Special Composition Question (When do the members of an f-set of simples compose an object?) as follows:

($\exists y$ the members of the f-set of simples x compose y) if and only if

the activity of the members of x constitutes a life.[73]

"You say that there is no problem of the many for f-sets since exactly one of them is, at any moment, such that its members are suited to compose you. But your argument for this conclusion presupposes that there is such a thing as you, which is just the point at issue."

But I am not trying to prove that I exist. My intention is rather to show that I can use 'I' and 'me' without falling into a certain alleged incoherency. I therefore feel free to refer to myself whenever I find it convenient. It's up to my adversaries to show that I fall into incoherency by doing so—or to show that I *should* fall into incoherency if I existed and did so.

"Well, what about all the other f-sets? I mean, what about the f-sets that are coextensive, or very nearly coextensive, with the f-set whose members compose you (supposing for the sake of argument that one of them does have members that compose you)? The members of all these sets are, at present, suitably arranged for composing a man. Consider an f-set F that differs from the f-set G that is supposed to be the one whose members compose you only in that a certain simple x that is definitely a member of G is definitely a nonmember of F. If God were to annihilate x without altering the disposition of and causal relations among the other members of G, then, you will concede, the members of F would compose a man and, in fact, would compose *you*. There is therefore nothing in the disposition of, or the causal relations that hold among, the members of F that prevents them from composing a man.[74] But then why *don't* they compose a man? According to you, this must be because a certain simple, x, is in the general vicinity of the members of F. But how could a single simple have the power to prevent the members of a perfectly *enormous* f-set of simples, which are suitably arranged to compose a man, from composing a man? How could it acquire this power simply by being in their neighborhood?"

The members of F do not compose a man owing to the fact that their activity does not constitute a life. Their activity does not constitute a life because there is only one life that *any* of them is caught up in, and there is a certain simple—x—that is a member of F to degree 0 and is caught up in that human life to a degree greater than 0 (to the degree 1, as you have stated the case, but my reply would be the same for any degree greater than 0).

So I reply from the perspective on the metaphysics of composition that is afforded me by the Proposed Answer. And so, I think, could the proponent of any causal answer to the Special Composition Question reply from the perspective that is afforded him by *his* theory. You, of course, must have some other answer to the Special Composition Question. You don't say what it is, but what you say strongly suggests that you accept "Fuzzy Universalism." Fuzzy Universalism (restricted to simples) is the thesis that the members of every f-set of simples compose something. This thesis seems to have little to recommend it. Let us look at a case that does not involve so many simples as to overwhelm our powers of visualization. Consider, in fact, a single simple. This simple will be the sole member of as many fuzzy sets of simples as there are degrees of membership other than 0. If the number of degrees of membership is the power of the continuum, then there will be such f-sets of simples as the one that has this single simple as a member to the degree 1, the one that has it as a member to the degree $\pi/4$, the one that has it as a member to the degree ½, and so on. If Fuzzy Universalism is correct, then to each of these f-sets there will correspond a distinct object. (I say 'distinct' because I assume that for no x and y can x be a part of y to two or more degrees.) Presumably the simple itself would correspond to the first of these f-sets. But what objects would correspond to the others? Fuzzy Universalism would seem to be best avoided.

"You have said that there is only one human life that any of the simples that are parts of you to any degree are caught up in. Your whole case, really, rests on your assertion that there is only one such life. If we grant you this unique life, then you can use its uniqueness to show that a certain f-set of simples is unique in being the one f-set such that every simple is a member of that f-set to just the degree to which it is caught up in that unique life; and that f-set, you contend, is the f-set whose members compose you. But why should the friends of the many grant you this unique life? Why should one not suppose that any life is more or less conterminous with an enormous number of more or less similar events, each of which is a life? Consider the event that you say is your life. This event is constituted by the activity of the members of the f-set we have called G. But why should we not suppose that there is an event that is constituted by the activity of the members of F, and why should we not suppose that this event is a life? If God were to annihilate x without altering the disposition of and causal relations among the other members of G, then, you will concede, the activity of the members of F *would* constitute a human life, and would, in fact, constitute *your* life. There is, therefore, nothing in the disposition of, or the causal relations that hold among, the members of F that prevents their activity from constituting a human life. But then why *doesn't* the activity of the members of F constitute a human life? According to you, this must be because the activity of a certain simple, x, is going on in the vicinity of the activity of the members of F. But how could the activity of a single simple have the power to prevent the activity of the members of an enormous f-set of simples from constituting a human life when it is intrinsically suited for doing so? If, however, the activity of the members of F constitutes a human life, so will the activity of the members of each of many, many other f-sets. And then, according to your own theory of human composition, there will be many, many men present in any situation in which we should normally say there was just one man present. In short, you haven't evaded the problem of the many; you have merely turned it into a problem about lives. What selection principle will you apply to choose among all these lives?"

This strikes me as a desperate move. Consider a certain riot. (A riot, I suppose, is a concrete event.) There will be some people who are perfectly definite cases of people who took part in this riot: people who were near its geometrical center and who assaulted police officers and smashed things and who did these things in large part because everyone else was doing them, and who, in doing them, were giving some sort of inarticulate expression to widespead discontents. There will be some people who are perfectly definite cases of people who did *not* take part in the riot. And there will be borderline cases. Consider, for example, Alice, who stood about on the outskirts of the mob and who shouted a few slogans and made a few inflammatory remarks and left as soon as she heard sirens. Consider the people other than Alice who took part (to whatever degree) in the riot. Had they a special riot of their own, one that differed from the "larger" riot in this respect alone: that Alice was not even a borderline participant in it? It seems to me that we should require some very good reason to believe that there was any event of that description. I think that we have no such reason. And neither have we any reason to believe that there are very many more human lives than the census-takers say there are human beings. But if that is right, then there are about as many human beings in any given situation as we normally think there are.

18. The Vagueness of Identity

We have seen in the preceding section that if our answer to the Special Composition Question is correct, then the part-whole relation is vague: there are cases in which it is indeterminate whether x is a part of y. But the Proposed Answer and our thesis about the persistence of organisms (*Life*) have further implications about vagueness. If parthood is vague, composition is vague. Thus, there could be a case in which, owing to its being indeterminate whether the activity of certain objects constituted a life, it was indeterminate whether a composite object was present. And there could be a case in which, owing to its being indeterminate whether a life now going on was the same event as a life that had been going on at an earlier time, it was indeterminate whether a currently existing composite object was the same object as one that had existed at an earlier time. A metaphysic that has these implications places its defenders in rather a difficult position.

In order better to appreciate their difficulties, let us examine the difficulties faced by those who believe in heaps. A heap, as we all know, has the following disturbing feature: If you set yourself the task of removing from it its constituents one by one, you will have a heap, that very heap, before you in the early stages of your task, and you will have *no* heap—that or any other—before you in the final stages of your task. Moreover, you will be wrong if you say of any of the objects you removed from the heap, "Before I removed *this*, the heap existed; when I removed it, the heap ceased to exist." Heaps, therefore, are puzzling things indeed. Fortunately for the metaphysical peace of mind of those who accept the Proposed Answer, there are no heaps. That is to say: If you have various solid, movable objects at your disposal and if you heap them, they will not compose anything just in virtue of being heaped. In fact, since the activity of objects that are heaped cannot constitute a life—at least, it's hard to see how it could—they will simply *not* compose

228

anything. Therefore, a laborer who is removing bricks one by one from a pile does not present us with the problem of determining when the pile before him will cease to exist, for there is not and never was any pile of bricks to pose that problem. The only problem even remotely resembling a *Sorites* (*Sorites* is derived from *soros*, heap) problem that our laborer's efforts might pose is this: At what point does it cease to be true that there are bricks before him that are piled or piled up or "arranged pilewise"? And we may say without falling into any obvious incoherency that there is no answer to this question: just as 'is bald' and 'is rich' are vague monadic predicates, 'are bricks arranged pilewise' is a vague, variably polyadic predicate.

Now, someone might want to know why a similar tactic could not be employed by the friends of the heaps. Why shouldn't a philosopher take the position that, while there are objects that are definitely heaps and objects that are definitely not heaps, there are also objects such that there is no answer to the question whether they are heaps, owing to the fact that 'is a heap' is a vague monadic predicate? I have said that 'are bricks arranged pilewise' is like 'is rich': Each is a vague predicate, its vagueness, one would suppose, reflecting no vagueness in the world (whatever that might mean), but only the fact that people have not bothered to set forth rules for applying it that cover every possible case. But then why can't exactly the same thing be said about 'is a pile of bricks'?

Suppose we have *n* bricks, each of which we shall treat as an honorary simple (see our discussion of the Ship of Theseus in Section 13). We shall pretend that none of the bricks by itself raises any problem about vagueness. That is, we shall pretend that each of the bricks has the following feature: For every (nonrelational) property, the brick either definitely has that property or else definitely lacks it. Our hesitation about applying 'are bricks arranged pilewise' to these bricks in various possible circumstances must, therefore, be traceable to our lacking precise rules for applying this predicate. To what else could it be traced? The case is otherwise with 'is a pile of bricks', however. If this predicate ever applies to anything, it does not apply to any of the *n* bricks, but to an *n* + 1st object. And this "new" object is a potential new source of vagueness. If we think that the bricks compose no larger object, we can raise questions of this form:

Suppose we rearranged the bricks in this way: [insert here any description of a rearrangement of the bricks, such as 'remove brick 23 to Kiev and leave the others just where they are' or 'exchange the positions of brick 6 and brick 7 and leave the others just where they are', or 'rotate brick 16 forty degrees clockwise']; would the bricks still be arranged pilewise?

But if we think that the bricks compose a larger object x, we can ask *two* questions:

Suppose we rearranged the bricks this way: [description]; would x still exist? Given that x still existed, would x still be a pile of bricks?

The second of these questions is very much like the question 'would the bricks still be arranged pilewise?' since x is a pile of bricks if and only if some bricks compose x and those bricks are arranged pilewise. The first question, however, the existence question, corresponds to nothing we who deny the existence of sums of bricks can ask since we think that there was no sum of bricks, no n + 1st object, there in the first place.

Those who believe in piles of bricks will find that piles of bricks are indeed an additional source of vagueness, unless they are willing to accept the following metaphysical principle: For any xs, if the xs compose a pile of bricks y, then, for any possible way of rearranging the xs, if the xs were rearranged in that way, then it is either definitely true or definitely false that y would exist after the rearrangement. Let us call this principle *Definitude*. *Definitude* calls for three comments. First, it does *not* commit its adherents to the thesis that, for any possible rearrangement of the xs, if y exists after that rearrangement, it is either definitely true or definitely false that y is then a pile of bricks. Perhaps a pile of bricks is only accidentally a pile of bricks; perhaps an object that is in fact a pile of bricks might alter in such a way that it was no longer a pile of bricks. And perhaps, in the course of this alteration, it might pass through a stage in which it was neither definitely true nor definitely false that it was a pile of bricks. Secondly, the range of the plural variable in this principle is not restricted to bricks, for other objects than bricks—simples if nothing else—compose piles of bricks if there are any piles of bricks. Thirdly, I am letting the friends of piles of bricks off lightly in saying that they will not find piles of bricks to be sources of vagueness if they accept *Definitude*. Actually, they will need to accept a rather more comprehensive principle, one that "covers" not only cases of the rearrangement of the bricks and the simples composing a pile but cases of the admixture of new bricks and simples—and perhaps other objects—with the old, as well. But let that difficulty go.

It is easy to see why piles will raise their own problems about vagueness if *Definitude* is false. Suppose that there are piles of bricks and that *Definitude* is false. Then there is, or could be, a pile of bricks x that has this feature: There are certain ways of rearranging the bricks that compose x such that if those bricks were arranged in any of those ways, then it is not definitely true or definitely false that x would exist (just as there are certain amounts of money such that, if someone possessed money in any of those amounts, then it is not definitely true or definitely false that he would be rich).

But why should anyone object to this additional source of vagueness? Why should anyone mind a little more vagueness, if he—like the rest of us—must in any case put up with vague terms like 'are piled' and 'rich'? The answer is that an object of which it is not definitely true or definitely false that it exists presents a philosophical problem of an entirely different order from the problem presented by an object of which it is not definitely true or definitely false that it is rich. Let us see why.

There is a comfortable and sensible view of vagueness that could be expressed metaphorically by saying that vagueness resides in language and not in the world. Let us call this view the Linguistic Theory of Vagueness. According to the Linguistic Theory, *words* can be vague, but objects, properties, and relations cannot be vague. Moreover, not just any words can be vague. It is only words, or strings of words, whose extensions are established by some sort of boundary drawing—typical predicates, adjectives, adverbs, and prepositions—that can be vague. Logical constants such as (unrestricted) quantifiers, the copula, and the identity sign cannot be vague. (Here 'can' and 'cannot' have the force they have in 'Names of people can be misspelled, but the people they name cannot be misspelled.') For example, the predicate 'is rich' is vague, but this is not because it expresses the vague property *being rich*. There is in fact no such property as *being rich*. There may be such properties as *having an annual income after taxes of at least one hundred thousand 1980 U.S. dollars* and *having more money than 99.6 percent of the people in the world*. But *being rich*, if there is such a property, is none of these properties, and these properties are the only competitors there are for the position supposedly occupied by the property *being rich*. The fact is, we English-speakers have just not bothered to tie 'is rich' to any particular property. There are properties the possession of which is wholly irrelevant to the problem of deciding whether to call their possessors rich. There are properties the possession of which compels us to call their possessors rich. There are properties the possession of which compels us to deny that their possessors are rich. And there are properties that fall into none of these three categories, properties the possession of which will cause us to *hesitate over* the question whether their possessors are rich, even if we know all the other properties of these people. And that, detail aside, is what there is to be said about the relations between 'is rich' and the properties of objects. 'Rich' is a type of vagueness; all vagueness is a phenomenon of language. Vagueness arises when and only when (and because and only because) the rules that govern the application of certain general terms are insufficiently specific to compel us in every case either to apply those terms to, or withhold them from, a given object. Or objects: For some objects we shall (even if we are omniscient) hesitate over the question whether those objects are clustered, or arranged in a circle, or marching in step, or piled.

David Lewis has stated this thesis about vagueness, and the intuitions that support it, with his usual succinct elegance:

> The only intelligible account of vagueness locates it in our thought and language. The reason it's vague where the outback begins is not that there's this thing, the outback, with imprecise borders; rather there are many things, with different borders, and nobody has been fool enough to try to enforce a choice of one of them as the official referent of the word 'outback'. Vagueness is semantic indecision. But not all of language is vague. The truth-functional connectives aren't, for instance. Nor are the words for identity and difference, and for the partial identity of overlap. Nor are the idioms of quantification, so long as they are unrestricted. How could any of these be vague? What would be the alternatives between which we haven't chosen?[75]

This is the comfortable and sensible Linguistic Theory of Vagueness. (Or perhaps, since quantifiers et al. are no less linguistic items than predicates or adverbs are, it would be better to call it—taking our cue from Lewis—the Semantical Indecision Theory of Vagueness.) As I said above, an object of which it is not definitely true or definitely false that it exists presents a philosophical problem of an entirely different order from the problem presented by an object of which it is not definitely true or definitely false that it is rich. Now we may say why: Objects of the latter sort are easily accounted for by the Linguistic Theory of Vagueness and objects of the former sort are not. If it is not definitely true or definitely false that John is rich, this is simply because—so the Linguistic Theorist says—even perfect knowledge of all John's properties (and there is no such property as *being rich*) would leave a speaker in doubt about whether to apply the predicate 'is rich' to John. But suppose it is not definitely true or false that James *exists*. Shall we say that this is simply because even perfect knowledge of James's properties (and there is no such property as existence) would leave a speaker in doubt about whether to apply the predicate 'exists' to James? Although the parenthesis about existence is an extremely popular thesis in modern philosophy, the remainder of this statement will very likely strike the reader as bizarre. Many philosophers will be tempted to reply to it by saying something like "Look, either James is *there* for you to hesitate over, or he isn't. If he *is* there, he exists; if he isn't, he doesn't." Or one might say, "You have mentioned 'perfect knowledge of James's properties'. Perfect knowledge of *whose* properties? Perfect knowledge of the properties possessed by *what*? If certain properties are possessed, then there is something that possesses them, and if that thing *is*, then it exists." (There are, of course, philosophers who, for reasons unrelated to the sort of problem we have been discussing, will not find this reply tempting. I have in mind those philosophers who believe in nonexistent objects. These philosophers do think that there are things which are there to be hesitated over, which possess properties, and which, nevertheless, do not exist. We may for example—they allege—hesitate about whether to call Mr. Pickwick a fool, and we may correctly predicate *being human* of him, and yet Mr. Pickwick does not exist. But even these philosophers do not suppose—at least, I know of none of them that does—that the borderline between existent and nonexistent objects is vague.)

Indeed, it would seem that the philosopher who believes in objects that stand to 'exists' as people with medium-sized fortunes stand to 'is rich' is going to have trouble even stating his general position coherently. Suppose we call these objects 'borderline-existent'. Shall he say, "In my view, there are borderline-existent objects"? But if there are such objects, then they exist, and if they exist, then they are existent and not borderline-existent. We shall return to these difficulties presently. For the moment, let us simply note that if a philosopher thinks that there are piles of bricks, and if he declines to accept the metaphysical principle *Definitude* (for any xs, if the xs compose a pile of bricks y, then, for any possible way of rearranging the xs, if the xs were rearranged in that way, then it is either definitely true or definitely false that y would exist after the rearrangement), then he will be faced with another source of vagueness than the word 'pile'. And the vagueness that proceeds from this other source cannot be accounted for by the comfortable and sensible Linguistic Theory—or, at least, it is very hard to see how it could be. This philosopher who believes in piles of bricks and rejects *Definitude* must concede that vagueness is not entirely a matter of language; he must concede that there are, or could be, objects that are vague "in themselves," quite independently of the terms that are used to describe them.

How reasonable is *Definitude*? I think that it would be a rather unsatisfactory procedure to accept it but to say nothing in its defense, for it does have a certain air of implausibility about it. (Compare: For any possible program for the redistribution of wealth, if that program were carried out, then it is either definitely true or definitely false that x would be rich after the redistribution.) The only way I can think of to defend *Definitude* would be to exhibit some general and plausible position of which it is a consequence—one that is consistent with the existence of piles of bricks, for we are not interested in vacuous truth. For example, the thesis called *positional essentialism* in Section 8 entails *Definitude*. But I know of no one who holds that thesis, and it does seem rather extreme. A more plausible, or at least more widely held, thesis that entails Definitude is Universalism. (More exactly, *Definitude* is entailed by the proposition that, necessarily, for any nonoverlapping xs, those xs compose something whenever they all exist and always compose the same thing. This proposition entails but is not entailed by Universalism. But I have attempted to show, in Section 8, that the Universalist ought to accept this stronger proposition; note that the stronger proposition is the conjunction of Universalism with the consequent of premise (F) on p. 75. I will speak loosely and call the stronger proposition Universalism in the sequel.) Universalism, like positional essentialism, is a very strong thesis. I know of no general thesis that entails *Definitude* that is not a very strong thesis. (Perhaps I am not sure what I mean by 'general'; I would not count the thesis got by deleting the words 'pile of bricks' from *Definitude* as "general" in the required sense.) *Contact*, for example, does not entail *Definitude*, nor does the conjunction of *Contact*, *Uniqueness* (p. 39), and Strengthened Mereological Essentialism (p. 144). This conjunction is a strong thesis indeed, but it does not tell us that, if we shift a brick from one place in a pile to another, the resulting composite object will be identical with the pile we began with; and it does not tell us that the resulting object will not be identical with the pile we began with. Therefore, this conjunction could be accepted by one who held that if the bricks in a pile were rearranged in a certain way, it would not be definitely true or false that the original pile still existed.

Universalism entails *Definitude* because Universalism entails that being a pile of bricks is not part of anything's essence but is merely a status that certain very nearly indestructible objects achieve when their constituents are arranged in certain ways. (I say 'very nearly indestructible' because, according to Universalism, if God wished to destroy an object that was currently a pile of bricks, He could do this by, but only by, annihilating one or more of its parts.) According to Universalism, therefore, for any rearrangement x of simples whatever—and, a fortiori, for any rearrangement of objects composed of simples—the answer to the question 'Will (the object that is) this pile of bricks survive x?' is definitely either yes or no since it is definitely yes. A weaker principle than Universalism also gives this result: necessarily, for any nonoverlapping xs, either those xs compose something whenever they all exist and always compose the same thing, or else those xs never compose anything. This principle is obviously entailed by Universalism (and by Nihilism). It does not seem to me very plausible to suppose that Universalism might be false and this principle true: If it were revealed to me that this principle was true, I should suppose that it was true because Universalism was true. But I do not know how to defend this conviction.

It seems, therefore, that the philosopher who believes in piles of bricks must either (1) accept the prima facie rather implausible and arbitrary principle *Definitude* without defending it, or (2) defend *Definitude* by deriving it from some very strong metaphysical principle like positional essentialism or Universalism (he cannot defend it by an appeal to Nihilism; Nihilism entails *Definitude* but is incompatible with the existence of piles of bricks), or (3) accept the existence of vagueness which is a real, inherent feature of objects and which does not derive from the indeterminacy of the rules governing talk about these objects. And, of course, what goes for piles of bricks goes for heaps of sand and anything else of that sort. How nice to have an answer to the Special Composition Question that does not present us with such a choice!

But let us not be complacent. Heaps confront those who believe in them with this choice. And our answer to the Special Composition Question does not permit the existence of heaps. (We may define a heap as any object x that has this feature: for some ys, and for some way of heaping those ys, necessarily, if those ys are heaped in that way, then they compose x. If our answer to the Special Composition Question is correct, then nothing has this feature.) But it does not follow that only heaps confront those who believe in them with this choice.

I am afraid that composite objects over a very wide range are going to embarrass those non-Universalists who believe in them with problems about vagueness. That is to say, Moderate answers to the Special Composition Question that purport to generate such objects are going to embarrass their advocates with problems about vagueness. Consider *Contact*. Are the advocates of *Contact*—if there are any—really willing to say that, even given *Uniqueness*, for any xs and any ys and any arrangement of the xs that entails their being in contact and any arrangement of the ys that entails their being in contact, if the xs were arranged in the former way and the ys in the latter, then it is either definitely true or definitely false that the thing the xs compose is the thing the ys compose? Moreover, the advocates of *Contact* are not faced only with problems about the persistence of composite objects through rearrangement; they are faced with problems about whether, on a given occasion, the xs compose any object at all. There will, of course, be no problem about whether the χs compose something at a given moment if we restrict the application of *Contact* to objects with mathematically sharp boundaries; but, unfortunately, there are no such objects. If we remember that actual material objects are composed of molecules and attend to the fact that interaction among molecules is, at bottom, a matter of the interaction of continuous electromagnetic fields, we must concede that contact is as much a relation with vague boundaries as are friendship and mutual admiration. What goes for *Contact* goes for *Fastening, Cohesion,* and *Fusion.* (In fact, to partition impingement—itself a vague notion—into contact, fastening, cohesion, and fusion is to make a set of vague distinctions. As I have remarked, these four types of impingement are distinguishable only if the size of the impinging objects falls within something like nine or ten orders of magnitude of the size of the medium-sized, solid objects—real or virtual—of our everyday experience. We cannot make these distinctions if we are talking about nucleons or stars. And if we are talking about macromolecules or large planetoids, we may be of two minds about distinguishing contact from cohesion or fastening from fusion.)

Nihilism and Universalism, however, raise no problems about vagueness. (They *raise* no problems, but the Nihilist and the Universalist may *face* problems about vagueness if individual simples raise problems about vagueness.) If one's only metaphysical goal were a metaphysic that presented as few problems about vagueness as possible, one could hardly do better than to become a Nihilist or a Universalist.

What about our own answer to the Special Composition Question? In our discussion of the problem of the many, we saw that vagueness is involved in our answer, since the relation x *is caught up in the life of* y is a vague relation. As a consequence of this fact, x *is a part of* y is, if our answer is correct, a vague relation: There are cases in which it is not either definitely true or definitely false that x is a part of y. But this is not so very unsettling, for the Linguistic Theory of Vagueness is adequate to deal with *this* sort of vagueness: we may say that although the *word* 'part' is vague, there is nothing vague either about organisms or their relations to simples (or to any other objects that might be vaguely described as the parts of organisms). Every simple, after all, is caught up in the life of any organism to some degree or other, and the three-term relation x *is caught up in the life of* y *to the degree* z is not vague. (Someone might object that it is not at all evident that this relation is not vague. We have said little about what degrees are—we have at certain places identified them with the real numbers x, $0 \leq x \leq 1$, but this was no more than a convenient idealization—and one might protest that if this relation between constituent, organism, and degree is not vague, our discussion of it at any rate was. There is probably something to this objection. But even if I could deal with it, I should face a more immediate and profound problem about vagueness: "life" and "organism" are themselves vague notions.)

There are simples such that it is neither definitely true nor definitely false that the activity of those simples constitutes a life. And, therefore, if our answer to the Special Composition Question is correct, there are simples such that it is neither definitely true nor definitely false that they compose an object; more exactly (taking into account the elaborations of our original theses on composition that we were forced to make in the course of our discussion of the problem of the many), there are fuzzy sets of simples of which we may say the following: If x is one of these f-sets, it is neither definitely true nor definitely false that there is something that the members of x compose. The conditional that concludes the preceding sentence may be expanded as follows: If x is one of these f-sets, it is neither definitely true nor definitely false that there is a y such that a given simple is a member of x to just the degree to which it is a part of y. Our answer to the Special Composition Question (the elaborated answer of Section 17) tells us that this conditional is equivalent to: If x is one of these f-sets, it is neither definitely true nor definitely false that there is a life z such that a given simple is a member of x to just the degree to which it is caught up in z.

It would be hard to avoid supposing that there are f-sets that satisfy this condition. Suppose we make the following assumption: for any x and any y and any z, if x is an f-set of simples and y is a simple and z is an event, it is either definitely true or definitely false that (at any given time) y is a member of x to just the degree to which y is caught up in z. Or, if you like, suppose we assume that for any simple and any event, there is at any given time a definite degree to which that simple is caught up in that event. This assumption might be questioned, but even if we accept it, it does not follow that there is always a definite answer to the question whether a given simple is caught up in a life to a given degree, for the notion of a life is vague: There are events of which it is neither definitely true nor definitely false that those events are lives. I do not see how we can deny this. If we held that every event was, at any given time, either definitely a life or definitely not a life, then we should be faced with all sorts of questions that have the same sort of "feel" as the questions that would attend an intransigent assertion that every human being is either definitely rich or definitely not rich, or either definitely tall or definitely not tall.

We have said that a human embryo, at least in the early stages of "its" development, is a mere virtual object, a mere cohesive mass of cells. The activity of these cells, therefore, does not in the early stages of embryonic development constitute a life, just as the activity of the soldiers sorting themselves out on a drill field shortly before a parade is to begin does not yet constitute a parade. But, if all goes well, there will be a time at which the activity of these cells (or of some of these cells and some of their descendants) does constitute a life. Must there be an intermediate mathematical instant that is either the last instant at which the activity of these cells does not constitute a life or the first instant at which it does? *Could* there be? This seems very doubtful. In fact, it seems incomprehensible to suppose that there could be such an instant. Mathematical instants aside, it seems incomprehensible to suppose that there could be a first hundred-millionth of a second during which a given human life is going on: Life is essentially a chemical phenomenon, and the coming to be and passing away of molecular bonds cannot typically be dated to within the nearest hundred-millionth of a second. One might as well date the beginning of the Wisconsin Glaciation to the nearest hour as date the beginning of my life to the nearest hundred-millionth of a second. One might as well insist that at every mathematical instant in the past it was then either definitely true or definitely false that the Wisconsin Glaciation had begun as insist that at every instant in the past it was either definitely true or definitely false that my life had begun. And if at a given instant it is neither definitely true or definitely false that the activity of certain cells then constitutes my life, this will not be because their activity constitutes *some* life but one that is a borderline case of being *my* life; it will be because their activity constitutes an event that is a borderline case of a life.

As it is with generation, so it is with corruption. John has a heart attack and dies and is turned into corruption. Is there a last instant at which his life is going on or a first instant at which it is not going on? No, there is probably not even a last *second* during which it is definitely true that his life is going on. And if it is neither definitely true nor definitely false that his life is going on at a certain instant, this is not because some life is going on at that instant of which it is neither definitely true nor definitely false that that life is *his*; it is because there is a certain event of which it is not then definitely true or definitely false that it is a life.

Individual human lives, therefore, are infected with vagueness at both ends. (Even if a person is "instantly" volatilized by the explosion of a hydrogen bomb, the end of his life is a *bit* vague. Nothing happens instantly in nature.) Could there be a life that was vague "all the way through"? More exactly, could there be an event that is never definitely a life and sometimes not definitely a nonlife? (Let us call an event that satisfies this condition a *borderline life.*) There could, of course, be

lives—say, the lives of radically genetically defective offspring of men
and women—of which it is not definitely true or false that they are ever
human lives, and for any species there could be events of which it is not
definitely true or definitely false that they are ever lives of members of
that species, and of which it is definitely false that they are ever lives of
the members of any other species. Still, they could be, and, I should
think, would be, lives: If there is an event of which it is sometimes not
definitely false that it is a human (or canine or feline) life, then it will
sometimes be definitely true of this event that it is a life. If we wish to find
examples of borderline lives, we should not beat about the borders of the
class of lives of large, complex organisms like human beings and oysters;
we should instead examine the frontier that separates macro-molecules
from micro-organisms. It is with reference to the inhabitants of just this
region, after all, that we find biologists saying things like 'whether an x is
a living thing is a matter of definition'.[76] (For x substitute 'virus', 'viroid',
'mitochondrion', 'plasmid'. . . .) Now, the phrase 'a matter of definition' is
used in connection with ambiguity as well as vagueness. If you ask me
how many deans were at the chancellor's dinner, I may be unsure
whether you mean only academic deans or whether I should count the
dean of the cathedral. If I am determined to be mysterious, I may say,
"Well, that's a matter of definition." And the biologist who says that
whether a virus is a living thing is a matter of definition could mean
either (1) that there are several meanings that might be assigned to
'living', according to some of which a virus is living and according to
some of which it is not, or (2) that, although 'life' has only one meaning,
that meaning is vague. (Compare 'How many deans were present?' with
'How many rich men were present?') Probably the biologist means a bit
of both: There is more than one way in which 'life' could be defined, and
each of the possible *definientia* is vague. However this may be, it is simply
not possible to suppose that there are no borderline lives. I should like to
say that there were none; it would make things much simpler for me if
the concept of a life were a perfectly sharp concept, but it is not. As I
remarked in an earlier section, the lives of the lower links of the Great
Chain of Being trail off into vague, temporary episodes of molecular
interaction.

If life is vague, composition is vague. Consider the embryo that was in
my mother's womb five or six days after my conception. This embryo was
composed, either actually or virtually, of a few hundred cells. Let us
suppose that a certain event, which was then occurring, was either a
homeodynamic event or a borderline case of a homeodynamic event,
and that those hundreds of cells—call them 'the embryonic cells'—were
all caught up in it to some degree greater than 0, and that everything

caught up in it to any degree greater than 0 was either one of the embryonic cells or something caught up in the life of one of the embryonic cells. And let us suppose that it is not definitely true or definitely false that that event was a life. Then, if our answer to the Special Composition Question is correct, it is not definitely true or definitely false that the embryonic cells then composed anything. But if composition is vague, existence is vague: If it is not definitely true or definitely false that the embryonic cells compose something, then it is not definitely true or definitely false that there exists an object that the embryonic cells compose; and it is not definitely true or definitely false that there exists an object that just exactly fills the region of space that the embryonic cells jointly fill.

What does it mean to say that existence is vague? As we saw in our discussion of heaps, whatever it means, it cannot mean that there are certain objects that fall into a vague frontier between existence and nonexistence. For suppose x to be one of these objects. If x is there to be talked about in the first place, then x exists, and in fact definitely exists. (Again, those who believe in nonexistent objects will not accept the presuppositions of this statement. But, as I said, I think that even these philosophers would agree with me that there is no vague frontier between existence and nonexistence. I will leave it to them to explain in their own terms why there are no borderline cases of existent objects.) And, therefore, anyone who accepts our answer to the Special Composition Question cannot accept the comforting and sensible Linguistic Theory of Vagueness as fully adequate to explain all cases of vagueness. Consider these words. "I've come across an object with a puzzling feature; despite the fact that I have perfect knowledge of its intrinsic, qualitative properties, I don't seem to be able to decide whether to say that it 'exists'. I was in a similar situation last week. I met a man whom I couldn't decide whether to describe as 'rich', despite the fact that I knew every detail of his financial situation." Anyone who spoke these words would be speaking nonsense. Of course, one could say without speaking nonsense, "Despite my perfect knowledge of the properties of the individual xs and of the relations they bear to one another, I don't seem to be able to decide whether to apply the variably polyadic predicate 'compose something' to them," or "Despite my perfect knowledge of what is going on in this situation, I don't seem to be able to decide whether to apply the predicate 'contains a composite object' to it." And it is just things of this sort that someone who accepts our answer to the Special Composition Question will have to say about certain objects and certain situations. Moreover, he will have to account for his indecision by maintaining that it is not definitely true or definitely false of those objects that they compose something and not definitely true or definitely false of that situation that it contains a composite object. Well, why shouldn't someone in this situation simply say that this indefiniteness arises wholly from the fact that 'compose something' is a vague predicate like 'are marching in step' or 'are arranged in a circle'? He may not *simply* say that. If the xs are arranged in a circle, this fact entails nothing much about any other objects. But if the xs compose something (and are two or more), then there exists another object that the xs, one that has them as parts and whose properties are presumably determined by their properties. What *about* this other object? we want to ask. Is it there or isn't it? Surely there is an incoherency here?

The Proposed Answer, therefore, appears to entail that existence is vague. In a similar way the principle *Life*, which purports to describe the persistence of composite objects, appears to entail that identity is vague. Suppose that a person, Alpha, enters a certain infernal philosophical engine called the Cabinet. Suppose that a person later emerges from the Cabinet and we immediately name him 'Omega'. *Is* Alpha Omega? Was it Alpha who emerged from the Cabinet, now bearing (owing to our timely baptism) the name 'Omega' as well as the name 'Alpha'? According to *Life*, Alpha and Omega are the same organism if and only if their lives are the same life. But, surely, the question whether the life that was going on at a certain place and time and the life that was going on at a later place and time are the same is a question that does not automatically have a right answer. One's life may be disrupted in various ways. If a pin is stuck into one's finger, one's life goes on. If one is blown to bits by a bomb, then—even if God immediately puts the bits together again—one's life has ended. The life of the organism that God has made by putting the bits of the old organism together is a new life. (Or so it seems to me.) If, at the extremes of a spectrum along the length of which are arranged more and more radical disruptions of lives, we can find definite cases of the end of a life and definite cases of the continuation of a life, then it seems reasonable to suppose that somewhere between the extremes will be found disruptions of which it is not definitely true or definitely false that they constitute the end of a life. And if this is so, then there are possible adventures of which it is not definitely true or definitely false that one would survive them. Let us call such episodes 'indeterminate adventures'. Not everyone—perhaps hardly anyone— will agree with my contention that one survives an adventure if and only if one's life persists through that adventure. But anyone who thinks that people are complex material organisms will be hard put to it to deny the possibility of indeterminate adventures. Suppose someone thinks that if Alice were cut into two pieces of about the same size and the two pieces were then reunited (having remained uncorrupted while they were apart, and their reunion or healing being perfect even at the molecular level), Alice would definitely survive this adventure. Suppose he also thinks that if Alice were divided into her component atoms and these atoms were then reunited—here we must appeal once more to the God of the Philosophers—she would definitely *not* survive *that* adventure. It is very hard to see how this person could suppose that every adventure that is a mean between these extremes is such that either Alice would definitely survive it or definitely not survive it. Only a dualist—presumably no one thinks that Alice is a *material* simple—would think that, and a dualist, of course, does not think that such adventures really happen to *persons*; or, at least, dualists think that persons participate in such adventures only vicariously: According to dualists, the direct participants in such adventures are the "bodies" of persons.

Let us suppose that the dials on the Cabinet have been set to provide its inmates with indeterminate adventures. (We need not agree on what would constitute an indeterminate adventure to suppose this. Let each philosopher fill in for himself the part of the story that tells how the dials are set.) Alpha has entered and Omega has emerged. It is, therefore, not definitely true or definitely false that Alpha is Omega.[77] Is this a coherent idea? Two sorts of philosophers other than dualists (and other than Nihilists, who will reject the possibility of the story, since they hold that neither Alpha or Omega ever exists) will not be deeply troubled by this consequence of the story of the Cabinet. They will hold that the "indefinite identity" of Alpha and Omega is easily accounted for by the Linguistic Theory of Vagueness and that, therefore, "indefinite identity" is no more a source of incoherency than (say) indefinite equality of financial resources.

Universalists will hold that (unless simples are annihilated) exactly the same objects always exist—and *definitely* so—and, therefore, that the only question that is raised by the story of the Cabinet is the question whether the redistribution of simples effected by its operations has left 'Alpha' with a bearer. (Remember that, according to the Universalist, 'W. V. O. Quine' had a different bearer in 1950 and 1960. In 1960, they will say, the thing that had borne 'W. V. O. Quine' in 1950 was a rarefied object shaped much like the terrestrial biosphere. And so it had been for millions of years and so it will be for millions of years. In 1950, however, it momentarily contracted into a Quine-shaped thing.) The Universalist will tell us that it would be surprising indeed if our rules for applying a proper name yielded definite instructions in every possible case as to what to apply a name to or whether to apply it at all. And, of course, the Cabinet is by definition set to produce one of the puzzle-cases.

Those who believe that people are a certain special type of four-dimensional object will hold that 'Alpha' is a name for a segment of a four-dimensional object and that 'Omega' is also a name for a segment of this object. Whether 'Alpha' and 'Omega' are names for the same segment—namely, the whole thing—will depend on whether the predicate 'is an enduring object' applies to the whole thing or not. This predicate (they will say) is vague, like the predicate of three-dimensional objects, 'is a spatially continuous object'. 'Is an enduring object' definitely applies to Caesar and definitely does not apply to the sum of the first half of Caesar and the second half of Napoleon. But there are cases in which it neither definitely applies nor definitely fails to apply. The Cabinet is designed to disrupt a four-dimensional object locally in just such a way as to cause the application to it of 'is an enduring object' to be of indefinite correctness. The case of 'Alpha' and 'Omega' is therefore analogous to the following case in three dimensions. Columbus says, "I name this land Columbia." Vespucci says, "I name this land America." The places at which they speak are connected by a marshy and frequently inundated isthmus that is not definitely either land or sea. Our rules for the naming of new lands stipulate (let's suppose) that the "spread" of an act of geographical naming from the point at which it was performed is halted by the sea. Is America Columbia? There is no answer to this question, not because of any vagueness in reality but owing to purely linguistic considerations. (I have assumed in this explanation that the proponent of people-as-four-dimensional-objects accepts a metaphysic of composition for four-dimensional objects that is strong enough to "give" him an object of which Alpha and Omega are segments, one that is definitely "there" even if it is not definitely an enduring thing.)

But what of the rest of us? What of those of us who are neither Universalists nor "four-dimensionalists" and who believe that human beings are composite material objects and who therefore think that it is not definitely true or definitely false that Alpha is Omega? The Linguistic Theory will be of no help to us, or it's hard to see how it could be. What, exactly, is the object that is "there" to be considered, and what is the term that neither definitely applies to it nor definitely fails to apply to it? In our discussion of the vagueness of existence we saw that we faced the following question: "You say that the xs are such that it is not definitely either true or false of them that they compose an object? Well, what about that object; is it there or isn't it?" Our position on the vagueness of identity forces us to face this question: "Alpha and Omega are such that it is neither definitely true nor definitely false of them that they are identical? Look, how many of them are there? One or two? The answer can't be one-and-a-half, can it?" Surely there is an incoherency here?

Our answer to the Special Composition Question and our principle about the persistence of composite objects (*Life*) appear to commit us to incoherent theses: that existence is vague and that identity is vague. I shall argue, however, that it is not clear that either of these theses is incoherent. I shall first examine the thesis that identity is vague. Although it may seem to be in some sense the less fundamental of the two, I shall begin with it simply because someone actually has attempted to demonstrate that vague or indefinite identity is an incoherent notion. Our discussion of this attempt will touch at some point or other on all of the conceptual and logical problems that confront the friends of vague identity. When we return to the problem of vague existence in Section 19, we shall find some of the ideas and techniques employed in our discussion of vague identity to be very useful.

The alleged demonstration, as the police might call it, of the incoherency of vague identity is to be found in a one-page article by the late Gareth Evans.[78] For a while I saw Evans's disturbing paper as a little cloud, like a man's hand. On reflection, however, I think I know what to say about it. The reader must judge.

Here is an informal representation of Evans's argument. Consider Omega, who is supposed to be "indefinitely identical" with Alpha. If Omega is indefinitely identical with Alpha, then Omega has the property: being indefinitely identical with Alpha. But it is false that *Alpha* is indefinitely identical with Alpha, and, therefore, Alpha *lacks* this property. Therefore, by the Principle of the Nonidentity of Discernibles, Alpha and Omega are not identical, *contra hyp.*

Let us begin our evaluation of this argument by restating it. The restated argument will be both closer to Evans's statement of it and, more importantly, will be clearer. It will be clearer because it will not contain the slippery form of words 'is indefinitely identical with'. Instead of talking of "indefinite identity," we shall introduce a sentence-operator 'indef', which may be prefixed to sentences of any sort—including, of course, identity sentences. 'Indef' may be regarded as an abbreviation for 'it is neither definitely true nor definitely false that' or 'there is no fact of the matter as to whether' or 'the question whether . . . has no definite answer'. Now the revised argument. According to the friends of vague identity, it is neither definitely true nor definitely false that Alpha (the man who entered the Cabinet) is identical with Omega (the man who has emerged from the Cabinet). For short:

(1)   indef $\alpha = \omega$.

We refute them by *reductio*. From (1) there follows by the principle of property abstraction

(2)   α has $\hat{x}$ indef x = ω.

(The symbol '$\hat{x}$' is pronounced "the property of being an x such that.") Sentence (2) is simply a somewhat stilted expression of the proposition that Alpha has the property (or quality, attribute, feature, or characteristic) of being a thing of which it is neither definitely true nor definitely false that it is identical with Omega. Some philosophers, on grounds that are not very clear, deny that names as complicated as this could name properties. Real properties, they say, have short names ending in '-ness' or '-hood'. These philosophers may read (2) as saying: One of the things that is true of Alpha is that it is neither definitely true nor definitely false of him that he is identical with Omega.

Now it is obviously true that

(3)   ~indef ω = ω,

which entails, by property abstraction again, and by the principle that any subsentence of a sentence may be replaced by a sentence equivalent to that subsentence,

(4)   ~ω has $\hat{x}$ indef x = ω.

And from (2) and (4) there follows by the Principle of the Nonidentity of Discernibles

(5)   ~α = ω,

"contradicting," Evans says, "the assumption with which we began, that the identity statement 'α = ω' is of indeterminate truth value." Well, perhaps there is a contradiction here, but there is no *formal* contradiction: no line in our deduction is the result of prefixing some other line with a negation sign. (Evans gives instructions for turning his argument into one that yields a formal contradiction, but they are far from clear.)[79] Never mind. Evans's argument is trouble enough for the friends of vague identity just as it stands. The friends of vague identity wish to assert (1) without qualification, and they most definitely do not wish to assert (5)— not without the qualification 'indef'. But, if Evans is right, (5) follows logically from (1); that is, (5) *simpliciter* follows from (1). And, it would seem, one is committed to the assertibility of anything one recognizes as a logical consequence of that which one holds to be assertible.

What shall the friends of vague identity say is wrong with Evans's argument? It might occur to them to be suspicious of the two inferences involving property abstraction. Property abstraction is not universally valid, as the "property" version of Russell's Paradox shows. Suspicions are one thing, however, and proof is another. Can we show that the use made of property abstraction in Evans's deduction of '~α = ω' from 'indef α = ω' is invalid? Or if we cannot *show* that this use is invalid, can we at least show that it would be reasonable for the friends of vague identity—those philosophers who, antecedently to their exposure to Evans's argument, had what they regarded as good reasons for believing in cases of vague identity—to regard it as invalid? Can we at least provide a candidate for the office of "incorrect use of property abstraction by Evans," a candidate that is a reasonable one on the assumption that it is antecedently reasonable to believe in cases of vague identity, and hence reasonable to suppose that there is *some* flaw in Evans's reasoning? (I think that the "Cabinet" case does make it reasonable to suppose— though it does not prove—that there are such cases and hence that there is such a flaw.)

There would seem to be no way to investigate this question other than by giving a precise codification of the rules of inference that should apply in pieces of reasoning involving 'indef', '=', and property abstraction. I shall do this by providing a semantics for the language of first-order logic with identity and property abstraction, supplemented by the constant 'indef'. Or, rather, I shall provide a fragment of such a semantics. (A full semantics even for first-order logic is a lengthy business.) But what I provide will be sufficient to show that Evans's reasoning is invalid according to that fragment. It is also possible to provide a semantics for such a language that confers validity upon Evans's reasoning; the friends of vague identity will, of course, do well not to accept any such semantics.

The semantics I present will be based on two root ideas. First, since certain of the sentences of the language we shall be treating are to be thought of as neither definitely true nor definitely false, we shall need more than two truth-values. (We shall in fact employ three.) Secondly, if identity is indeed vague, then the semantic relation between name and thing named must also be vague. If, for example, 'Alpha' definitely names x and it is neither definitely true nor definitely false that $x = y$, then it seems inevitable to suppose that it is neither definitely true nor definitely false that 'Alpha' names y. Our semantics must somehow reflect this consequence of vague identity for the naming relation.

A note on what a formal semantics is. A formal semantics is a systematic statement of which sentences and inferences in a given formal language are to count as 'valid' and which as 'invalid'. A formal semantics does not, as some philosophers seem to suppose, explain the meanings of the items peculiar to the vocabulary of the formal language to which it is applied. You already know everything about the meaning of 'indef' that you will learn from me. I am simply going to tell you what in my opinion is valid and invalid when one reasons with 'indef', '=', 'has', and '^ ', and tell you this systematically. You can agree with me or not. If you do not agree with me, at least you will be able to predict what steps I shall reject in the proofs you construct to show the incoherency of vague identity. In telling you what the valid rules for manipulating 'indef' et al. are, I shall not presuppose that there is any vagueness in the world: I will employ classical set theory, and I will talk in the normal way about "objects" and informally apply the rules that usually govern counting, identity, and so on. This might be an improper procedure if I thought that there were *no* cases in which the "usual" rules applied (though I think that even then I could defend my procedure ad hominem), but of course I don't think that. Consider this analogy. A nominalist claims to be able to show that a platonistic belief in properties is incoherent; perhaps he claims to be able to deduce '~a is a property' from 'a is a property'. A platonist constructs a semantics for property-talk and, in doing so, asserts the existence only of things that satisfy the nominalist's ontological scruples (individuals and their sums, it may be) and shows that, according to this semantics, the nominalist's reasoning is invalid. There would seem to be nothing exceptionable in this procedure, at least provided that the platonist himself accepts the existence of individuals and sums of individuals (and even if he didn't, his strategy might be defensible ad hominem). Let us begin.

First, we have a formal language. Its primitives are: *individual constants*, 'a', 'b', 'c', ...; *variables*, 'x', 'y', 'z', ...; *circumflexed variables*, '$\hat{x}$', '$\hat{y}$', '$\hat{z}$', ...; two sentential operators, '~' and 'indef'; and two two-place predicates, '=' and 'has'.

It will be noted that our primitive vocabulary is extremely sparse. We have no predicate letters, not even zero-place ones (that is, we have no sentence letters); we have no binary sentential connectives; we have no variable-binding operators other than the abstraction operator (in particular, we have no quantifiers). Moreover, we shall count fewer strings of the items of our sparse vocabulary as well-formed sentences than one might, intuitively, expect. The reason for this minimalism is simple: only a very few symbols and constructions figure in Evans's argument, the evaluation of which is our present concern. Why load ourselves down with semantical apparatus that is irrelevant to the task at hand? It would be a trivial exercise to embed the semantics of the sequel in a semantics for a more powerful language, one that did contain quantifiers and the rest. That is, this would be a trivial exercise provided that a coherent semantics for the more powerful language could be constructed at all. If it could not, that fact would constitute a cogent argument against the coherence of the notion of vague identity. But this cogent argument would not be Evans's argument. I call the problem of embedding the semantics that follows in a semantics for a more powerful language "trivial" because it could be done ad hoc: that is, if we could devise any semantics for the more powerful language, we could always combine that semantics with our semantics for the sparse language simply by stipulating that in the case of any sentence to which the "general" and the "special" semantics assign different values, the special semantics prevails. In theory, combining one semantics with another in this way—the "brute force" method, one might call it—could produce some totally unacceptable results: say, a true disjunction both of whose disjuncts are false. Doubtless, however, such embarrassments could be purged from the combined semantics at the cost of a little tinkering. Whether our "special" semantics could be embedded in a "general" semantics for vagueness—assuming that one exists—in a neat, pleasing, and intuitive way is a question I am not logician enough to investigate. If the only possible embeddings were ad hoc, piecemeal, scissors-and-paste jobs, that would certainly count against my treatment of Evans's argument.

From our primitive vocabulary, we construct (one-place) predicates, (property) abstracts, and (closed) sentences.

Predicates

—The result of flanking the identity sign with a constant and a variable is a predicate (an "identity predicate"; the constant is its *term*).

—The result of prefixing a predicate with '~' or 'indef' is a predicate.

—Nothing else is a predicate.

Abstracts

The result of prefixing '$\hat{x}$' to a predicate containing 'x', '$\hat{y}$' to a predicate containing 'y', and so on, is an abstract (the abstract *formed on* that predicate); nothing else is.

Sentences

—The result of flanking the identity sign with (occurrences of) one or two constants is a sentence (an "identity sentence"; the constants are its *terms*).

—The result of writing a constant followed by 'has' followed by an abstract is a sentence (an "ascription sentence"; the constant is its *subject*).

—The result of prefixing a sentence with '~' or 'indef' is a sentence.

—Nothing else is a sentence.

With an eye to defining *validity* (of inference) within this language, we specify *models*. A model determines an *extension* and a *frontier* for each abstract, and a *value* for each sentence.

Roughly speaking, a model assigns to each constant an object to be its referent and specifies what objects that referent is "indefinitely identical" with. Because our language is so very simple, such an assignment suffices to determine an extension and frontier for each abstract (and a value for each sentence). We are to think intuitively of each abstract as denoting (relatively to a model) a property; the extension of an abstract is, intuitively, the class of objects that definitely have that property, and the frontier of an abstract is the class of objects that neither definitely have nor definitely lack that property. We proceed as follows.

A *universe* is a nonempty set of objects. A *pairing on* a universe is a (possibly empty) set of two-membered sets (pairs) of members of that universe. (These are to be "genuinely" two-membered: $\{x, x\}$ [= $\{x\}$] cannot be a member of a pairing.) If x and y, $x \neq y$, are members of a pair (belonging to a certain pairing), they are said to be *paired* (in that pairing).

A *model* consists of a universe, a pairing on that universe, and an assignment of one object in that universe to each individual constant (the constant's *referent* in that model). It will occasionally be useful to call the objects with which the referent of a constant is paired the *fringe referents* of that constant. (The objects with which an object is paired are to be thought of as the objects such that it is indefinite whether that object is identical with them, and the *fringe referents* of a constant are to be thought of as the objects such that it is indefinite whether that constant denotes them.)

The extensions and frontiers of abstracts (in a given model) are determined as follows (as a preliminary step, extensions and frontiers are assigned to predicates):

The extension of an identity-predicate contains just the referent of its term; the frontier of an identity predicate contains just the fringe-referents of its term.

The result of prefixing '~' to a predicate having extension e and frontier f is a predicate having extension $\mathbf{U}$-$(e \cup f)$—where $\mathbf{U}$ is the universe of the model—and frontier f.

The result of prefixing 'indef' to a predicate having frontier f is a predicate having extension f and an empty frontier.

The extension and frontier of an *abstract* are the extension and frontier of the predicate on which it is formed.

A model also assigns a value to each sentence. A value is one of the three numbers 1, ½, and 0—intuitively, (definite) truth, neither definite truth nor definite falsity, and (definite) falsity:

The value of an identity sentence is

—1 iff something is the referent of both its terms;

—½ iff nothing is the referent of both its terms and the referents of its terms are paired;

—0   otherwise; that is, if and only if nothing is the referent of both its terms and their referents are not paired.

Intuitively, an identity sentence has the value 1 if the referents of its terms are identical, ½ if the referents of its terms are indefinitely identical, and 0 otherwise.

The value of an ascription sentence is
—1 iff the referent of its subject belongs to the extension of its abstract;

—½ iff the referent of its subject does not belong to the extension of its abstract, and either (a) the referent of its subject belongs to the frontier of its abstract, or (b) a fringe referent of its subject belongs either to the extension or to the frontier of its abstract;

—0   otherwise; that is, if and only if neither the referent nor a fringe referent of its subject belongs either to the extension or to the frontier of its abstract.

The values of sentences starting with '~' and 'indef' are determined by the table:

ϕ	$\sim\phi$	indef ϕ
1	0	0
½	½	1
0	1	0

An *inference form* is a finite, nonempty sequence of sentences; the final sentence of an inference form is its *conclusion* and the earlier sentences are its *premises.*

A *counterexample* to an inference form is a model that assigns a value to its conclusion that is less than the least value that that model assigns to any of its premises. A *valid* inference form is one that has no counterexample: A valid inference form is 1-preserving and cannot lead from ½ to 0.

Let us now return to Evans's argument. If we consider only its premise and its conclusion, we can regard it as an instance of the inference form.

$$I_0 \qquad \text{indef } a = b \vdash {\sim}a = b$$

We should, of course, expect this inference form to be invalid; any model whose structure is intuitively that of the "Cabinet" example should be a counterexample to it. Consider the (partial) model.

$$\{A, B\}, \{\{A, B\}\}, \text{`}a\text{' ref A, `}b\text{' ref B,}[80]$$

which is so structured. This model—let us call it M—is a counterexample to I_0: it assigns the value ½ to '$a = b$' (since the referents of 'a' and 'b' on M are paired) and hence assigns a value of 1 to 'indef $a = b$' and a value of ½ to '$\sim a = b$'.

Since M is a counterexample to I_0, it must be a counterexample to at least one of the four inference forms that Evans's reasoning comprises:

$$I_1 \qquad\qquad\qquad \vdash {\sim}\text{indef } b = b$$
$$I_2 \qquad\qquad \text{indef } a = b \vdash a \text{ has } \hat{x} \text{ indef } x = b$$
$$I_3 \qquad\qquad {\sim}\text{indef } b = b \vdash {\sim}b \text{ has } \hat{x} \text{ indef } x = b$$
$$I_4 \qquad a \text{ has } \hat{x} \text{ indef } x = b, \quad {\sim}b \text{ has } \hat{x} \text{ indef } x = b \vdash {\sim}a = b.$$

The model M is not a counterexample to I_1, which is obviously valid: '$b = b$' will have the value 1 on any model, and hence 'indef $b = b$' the value 0, and '$\sim$indef $b = b$' the value 1.

The model M is not a counterexample to I_2. M assigns to '$x = b$' the extension $\{B\}$ and the frontier $\{A\}$; hence it assigns to '$\hat{x}$ indef $x = b$' the extension $\{A\}$; the referent of 'a' on M is A, and hence the value of 'a has $\hat{x}$

indef $x = b$' on M is 1. In fact, it is easy to see that I_2 is valid. If a model assigns 1 to 'indef $a = b$', it must assign distinct referents to 'a' and 'b' and must pair them. But the extension of '$\hat{x}$ indef $x = b$' in any model comprises just the things that model pairs with the referent of 'b'.

The model M is, however, a counterexample to I_3. As we saw in our examination of I_2, the extension of '$\hat{x}$ indef $x = b$' on M is $\{A\}$; the referent of 'b' is B, which does not belong to this extension; but A *is* a fringe referent of 'b' on M, since M pairs A and the referent of 'b'; hence, 'b has $\hat{x}$ indef $x = b$' has the value ½ on M, as does its negation; but, as we saw in our examination of I_1, the value of the premise of I_3 on M is 1; hence I_3 is invalid.

It follows from the values established in the examinations of I_0, I_2, and I_3 that M is not a counterexample to I_4. But I_4 does have counter-examples. I shall consider them in due course. They are, in a sense I shall briefly outline, of far less importance than our counterexample to I_3. This is because all of the counterexamples to I_4 assign a value of ½ to its premises and a value of 0 to its conclusion. Thus, although I_4 can lead from ½ to 0, it is 1-preserving. Since the friends of indefinite identity assign a value of 1 to 'indef $\alpha = \omega$', Evans's argument will constitute a *reductio* of their position unless it employs some inference form that is not 1-preserving. But it is just this feature that our semantical fragment ascribes to I_3 and denies to I_2, I_3, and (as we shall see) to I_4. The only real interest in the fact that I_4 (unlike I_1 or I_2) can lead from ½ to 0, therefore, is contained in this question: Does that fact tend to render our semantical fragment implausible? I shall take up this question later, and I postpone consideration of the counterexamples to I_4 till then.

Evans's argument, therefore, employs an inference form which is not only invalid on the semantical fragment I have proposed but which fails to preserve "definite truth." I would make these observations.

(i) One could, of course, construct a semantics that confers formal validity on Evans's reasoning. (It would suffice to replace our rule for determining the value of an ascription sentence with the following rule: $\ulcorner a$ has $\hat{x}Fx\urcorner$ has the same value as $\ulcorner Fa\urcorner$.) The friends of vague identity will, of course, be understandably hostile to the proposal that they adopt such a semantics. Insofar as there is such a thing as "the burden of proof," it would seem to weigh on the enemies of vague identity: *they* are the ones trying to prove something, *viz.* that the notion of vague identity is incoherent. The friends of vague identity are not trying to prove that vague identity *is* coherent, but only to undermine the appeal of Evans's argument; to do that (I should think) they need only construct a reason-ably plausible semantics according to which Evans's reasoning is for-mally invalid. They need not show that the semantics they have constructed is "superior" (in any sense) to a semantics that endorses his argument, much less "correct."

(ii) The individual components of the semantics I have presented seem to me to be very plausible. And each of them was chosen for its intrinsic plausibility. These components were not chosen, either individually or collectively, with any end in view. The invalidity of the inference form I_3 and the consequent formal invalidity of the move from step (3) to step (4) in Evans's argument was in no way "engineered." This is simply what popped out of the semantical engine when Evans's argument was dropped into the hopper. I was rather surprised. I should not have been surprised if *both* of the inferences involving property abstraction had turned out to be formally invalid. That one of the inferences should be valid and the other invalid, however, was a quite unanticipated result.

(iii) The only component of our semantics that could reasonably be called into question is, I think, the rule for determining the values of ascription sentences. Let me, therefore, say something to provide some intuitive motivation for this rule.

Suppose that it really is indefinite whether x is identical with y. Suppose that y definitely has the property F. Can it really be definitely false that x has the property F? In order to focus our intuitions about this matter, let us consider two cases of indefinite identity, a "diachronic" case and a "synchronic" case.

We already have a diachronic case of indefinite identity at our disposal: the case of Alpha, Omega, and the Cabinet. (We may say that we have a diachronic case of indefinite identity when we have an x and a y such that it is indefinite whether $x = y$ and there is a time such that it is definitely true that x exists at that time, and another time such that it is definitely true that y exists at *that* time, and there is no *one* time such that it is definitely true that x exists at that time and definitely true that y exists at that time.) Now, suppose that soon after Omega emerges from the Cabinet, we hang him; that is, we hang *him*: it is quite definitely true of Omega that *he* dies by hanging. Could it be definitely false of Alpha that *he* dies by hanging? It is hard to see how this could be, given that it is not definitely false that Alpha is numerically distinct from Omega.

We shall say that we have a synchronic case of indefinite identity if it is indefinite whether $x = y$ and there is a time such that x and y both definitely exist at that time. To construct such a case, we might imagine that we take two people and (by delicate and sustained application of our supernatural powers) establish increasingly elaborate and intimate vital and neural connections among their virtual parts till we reach a point at which we have, definitely, *one* person—or one thinking organism. It seems plausible to suppose that at *some* point in the establishment of this sequence of connections, there is a person x and a person y such that it is indefinite whether x is y. Suppose that this is the case and that y definitely has a certain property—wisdom, say. Could it be that x definitely lacks wisdom? It is hard to see how this could be, given that it is not definitely false that x is numerically distinct from y.

These examples suggest that if a constant k definitely denotes something x, and there is a y such that it is indefinite whether $x = y$, and y definitely has the property denoted by the abstract F, then $\ulcorner k$ has F$\urcorner$ should receive a value of at least ½. (It should obviously receive the value 1 if x definitely has—"in its own right," so to speak—the property denoted by F.) Or, at any rate, this seems plausible in cases in which F denotes a reasonably "ordinary" property like wisdom or ending on the gallows. Should matters be different if F contains the symbols '=' and 'indef'? I do not see why they should. These reflections seem to me strongly to support the rule our semantical fragment follows for assigning values to ascription sentences.

Interestingly enough, there is a sense in which one could regard the argument of the preceding several paragraphs as a rather weak one and still find it convincing. More exactly, suppose that one were not thinking in terms of three values, but only in terms of truth and falsity. And suppose that one were wondering whether to call 'Tom has wisdom' true or false, given that Tom is foolish but is indefinitely identical with Tim, who is wise. Suppose that one regarded the sort of considerations raised in the preceding paragraphs as providing a *very weak* reason for saying that 'Tom has wisdom' was true; a reason that was, perhaps, plainly overridden by the fact that Tom is foolish, but still a reason that was there to be overridden. Having made these suppositions, consider the following general strategy for distributing the *three* values "definitely true, "definitely false," and "neither" among the members of some class of sentences:

> Assign "definitely true" to a sentence only if there is *no* reason, however weak, that militates against calling that sentence "true"; and similarly for "definitely false" and "false"; in all other cases, assign the value "neither." In other words: assign the value "neither" to a sentence if there is the least excuse for doing so.

(This "strategy" is to be looked upon as a rule of thumb or heuristic to be kept in mind by one who is formulating a three-valued semantics—a semantics that assigns *only one* value besides definite truth and definite falsity—whatever sort of sentences that semantics applies to.) Now, one who accepts the thesis that the considerations adduced in the preceding paragraphs provide a reason (however weak) for assigning truth to 'Tom has wisdom' if the foolish Tom is indefinitely identical with the wise Tim and who accepts the proposed strategy will obviously be moved to accept our "ascription" rule. It seems to me that both the thesis and the strategy are quite plausible.

If we find these reflections congenial, we shall not find it counterintuitive to suppose that Omega does not *definitely* lack the property of being a thing such that it is indefinite whether that thing is Omega. Omega, of course, does not definitely *have* that property; but Omega is *sort of* identical with someone who *does* definitely have that property; and, therefore, Omega *sort of* has the property of being a thing such that it is indefinite whether that thing is Omega. And, therefore, it does not follow from the truth of 'It is not indefinite whether Omega is Omega'—*or* from the truth of 'It is not indefinite whether Omega has the property of being identical with Omega'—that Omega lacks the property of being indefinitely identical with Omega.

If Omega sort of lacks the property of being indefinitely identical with Omega, it follows that Omega sort of *has* the property of being indefinitely identical with Omega. That is, Omega sort of has the property of being a thing such that it is neither definitely true nor definitely false that that thing is Omega. Does it follow that Omega sort of has the property of being such that it is neither definitely true nor definitely false that it is identical with *itself*? One would hope not, for it is plausible to suppose that this property is flatly self-contradictory and, therefore, is quite definitely not possessed by any object whatever. Now, the question whether this does follow can't really be raised in connection with our semantical fragment because we have no way of representing the property we are worrying about in our simple language. But that is easily enough remedied. Let us simply add to the recursive definition of "predicate" in our formal language a codicil that says that the result of flanking the identity-sign with two occurrences of the same variable is a predicate (a "self-identity predicate"). Then our language will contain the abstract '$\hat{x}$ indef $x = x$', which, intuitively, should denote the property we are interested in. What sort of addition to our semantics should we make to accommodate the items we have added to our language by adding self-identity predicates to our basic stock of one-place predicates? What we need to do is to stipulate an extension and frontier (relative to each model) for every self-identity predicate. And only one stipulation seems even remotely plausible: the extension of a self-identity predicate in a model is the universe of the model; the frontier of a self-identity predicate is empty in every model. This stipulation has the obvious consequence that '$\hat{x}$ indef $x = x$', and its alphabetic variants have an empty extension and frontier in every model, which entails that every ascription sentence containing any of these abstracts has the value 0. Therefore, the inference form

indef a has $\hat{x}$ indef $x = a$ ⊢ indef a has $\hat{x}$ indef $x = x$

is invalid. Any model in which the referent of 'a' is paired with something will be a counterexample: the value of the premise will be 1 in such a model, and the value of the conclusion is 0 in every model.

I leave open the question whether a similar result could be achieved in a "natural" way by a properly general semantics for a language containing '$=$', 'indef', and property abstraction. By a properly general semantics for such a language, I mean one that begins in the usual way by constructing models that provide extensions for two-place predicates formed by flanking the identity sign with variables, and which, as a consequence, generates "automatically," as special cases, extensions for the two kinds of one-place predicates containing the identity sign that have in this paper been treated separately, *viz.* identity predicates and self-identity predicates.

It is reasonably evident from the foregoing that the friends of vague identity need not be troubled by Evans's argument, considered simply as a piece of formal reasoning. They need only adopt a system of rules for reasoning about vague identities that is consistent with the semantical fragment I have presented and declare that (in their opinion) Evans's reasoning is invalid. If they are wise, they will not claim to have *shown* that Evans's reasoning is invalid.[81] But there is no reason for them to make so strong a claim. Suppose A says to B, "Your position is incoherent" and backs up this charge by the formal deduction of some sort of incoherency from B's position, a deduction that employs plausible but not wholly uncontroversial principles of reasoning. B need not defend himself by *showing* that A's reasoning is invalid. He need do nothing more than present a system of reasoning that *he* accepts, according to which A's reasoning is invalid. Since A is the one who announced that he was going to prove something, it is up to him to show that his system of reasoning is right and B's alternative system wrong. Or, at any rate, the next move is A's. If A doesn't believe that he can *prove* that his own system is correct, he may try to cast philosophical doubts of one sort or another on B's proposed alternative; if A can do this—and if no corresponding doubts can be raised about his own system—this will constitute a dialectically acceptable reply on A's part. What would certainly be dialectically improper would be for A to insist that B present some sort of *proof* that B's system is the correct one.

I shall now consider four philosophical objections that might be brought against the semantical fragment that I have proposed—and, derivatively, against the judgments it makes about the validity of various inference forms.

Objection One

You employ a three-valued logic. But how are we to interpret the value '½'? The answer is: We can't. The idea of a *tertium datur* makes no sense.

Reply

For any sentence φ, the truth-value of indef φ must be a function of some feature of φ (or of the proposition that φ expresses; important as this distinction is, I will ignore it): if indef φ and indef ψ are both true, this must be because of some feature common to φ and ψ, just as is the case with ~φ and ~ψ (common feature falsity) and □φ and □ψ (common feature necessity). The feature of φ in virtue of which indef φ is true is incompatible with the truth *and* with the falsity of φ, since indef φ is false if φ is either true or false. Therefore, this feature may reasonably be called a 'truth-value' since it "competes with" truth and falsity. And, therefore, if indef φ makes sense at all, there must be a third truth-value, which I designate '½'.

But if it seems just too paradoxical to posit a *tertium datur*, we are not forced to do so. We can read '1' as expressing a feature of sentences called "definite truth" and '0' as expressing "definite falsity" and '½' as expressing a *tertium* in addition to definite truth and definite falsity. And we could say that these three values are the appropriate ones to employ in investigating validity in a language that contains 'indef'. In the matter of the relation between these three values and the two classical truth-values, there are two positions whose consequences might be investigated: it might be said that definite truth implies truth and definite falsity implies falsity, but not vice versa; or it might be said that, strictly speaking, classical truth and falsity do not exist but are idealizations that it is convenient to employ in cases in which indefiniteness is absent (as in mathematics) or can safely be ignored.

An investigation of these alternatives would take us far afield. The important thesis for present purposes is this: '½' makes just as much sense as 'indef', owing to the fact that it represents that feature of a sentence φ in virtue of which indef φ is true (or definitely true). The possibility remains, of course, that 'indef' does *not* make sense. But, if I understand Evans, he is willing to grant for the sake of argument that 'indef' makes sense in order to show that the sense it makes is incompatible with its application to identity sentences. We might compare his strategy with the strategy of Quine, who (in one place) is willing to grant for the sake of argument that 'necessarily' makes sense in order to show that the sense it makes is incompatible with its application to open sentences. (We might, in fact, distinguish two "grades of indefinitional involvement," the first represented by 'indef John is rich'—or 'indef John = the tallest man Sally knows'—and the second by 'indef John = James'. The first can be accounted for by the Linguistic Theory of Vagueness and the second cannot, just as the first and second grades of modal involvement can be accounted for by the Linguistic Theory of Necessity and the third cannot.) I have not undertaken the task of showing that 'indef' makes sense, but only the task of showing that Evans has not succeeded in forcing the friends of indefinite identity to admit that their position faces a special sort of incoherency that they do not face as friends of indefiniteness *simpliciter*.

Objection Two

Either 'Omega' denotes the man who entered the Cabinet or else it does not. That is, in performing your act of naming, you either succeeded in giving the name 'Omega' to the man who entered the Cabinet or you didn't. Moreover, the man who entered and the man who emerged both exist. They're *there* (timelessly speaking). And either 'they' are identical or they are not.

Reply

This would seem to be either a simple denial of the possibility of vague identity, or else an argument whose premise is the Law of the Excluded Middle. In the former case (I suppose), one could counter it with a simple *assertion* of the possibility of vague identity. As to the Law of the Excluded Middle, this "law" has no legal force at all in conversations in which 'indef' figures. It is natural to suppose that a disjunction has the value that is the greatest value of any of its disjuncts. On that natural assumption, if 'John is rich' has the value ½, so will

John is rich $\bigvee$ ~John is rich.

And the same goes for

Alpha = Omega $\bigvee$ ~Alpha = Omega.

Since, one would suppose, to accept a proposition is to accept it as true (or as definitely true, if a distinction is made between truth and definite truth), one who holds that 'Alpha = Omega' has the value ½ is thereby debarred from accepting the proposition that Alpha = Omega $\lor$ ~Alpha = Omega. (Exercise for the reader: show that ~indef $\phi \vdash \phi \lor$ ~ϕ.) I am aware that it is possible to construct a three-valued logic according to which the alternation of a sentence with its negation always has the value 1. Here is how to do it. Rename what we have been calling the 'value' of a sentence the "supervalue" of a sentence.[82] Say that the supervalue of a disjunction is equal to the greatest supervalue had by any of its disjuncts. And say that the *value* of a sentence is the supervalue had by that sentence "under all resolutions of vagueness" if there is such a unique supervalue, and is otherwise its actual supervalue. For example, the value of 'John is rich $\lor$ ~John is rich' is 1 according to this proposal, because no matter what *precise* term replaced 'rich' in this sentence, the resulting sentence would have the supervalue 1. On the other hand, 'John is rich' and '~John is rich' both have the value ½, since each has the supervalue ½ and neither has the same supervalue under all resolutions of vagueness. This clever device seems to me to answer to no philosophical need.[83] The word 'rich' *is* vague, and the sentence 'John is rich $\lor$ ~John is rich' does not mean 'If one were arbitrarily to fix a precise boundary between being rich and not being rich, John would fall on one side or the other of it'. If it is neither definitely true nor definitely false that John is rich, then it is not definitely true that John is either rich or not rich. If this *were* definitely true, then it would be definitely true, true without qualification, that either Tom (who contends that John is rich) or Tim (who contends that John is not rich) was right. But it is not definitely true that either Tom or Tim is right. It is, of course, definitely true that *if* there were a sharp boundary between the possession and the nonpossession of riches, then it *would be* definitely true that one or the other of them was right. But there isn't and it's not. Or so *I* think. But suppose I'm wrong. This will be cold comfort for the enemies of vague identity. It will not suffice for their purposes that the sentence '$\alpha = \omega \lor$ ~$\alpha = \omega$' express a definite truth—not unless one can infer from the definite truth of this disjunction that if Tom says "$\alpha = \omega$" and Tim says "~$\alpha = \omega$", then, definitely, one of them is right. If the Law of the Excluded Middle does not warrant this inference, that law is of no use whatever to the enemies of vague identity.

Objection Three

But how many people *are* there in the Alpha-Omega story? How many members has the set {Alpha, Omega}? You have no coherent way of answering this question.

Reply

That this set is empty is definitely false. That it has one member is not definitely true or definitely false. That it has two members is not definitely true or definitely false. That it has one member *or* has two members is not definitely true or definitely false. That it has one member *and* has two members is not definitely true or definitely false. That it has three or more members is definitely false.

["That's crazy. A set has to have a definite number of members, a definite cardinality. That's essential to the idea of a set."]

I'm not sure of that. I concede that it's a theorem of set theory. But perhaps set theory is an idealization. I am enough of a platonist about mathematical objects to take seriously the idea that although there really are sets, they don't have precisely the properties that set theory ascribes to them—just as, although there really are gasses, they don't have precisely the properties that the kinetic theory of gasses (an idealization) ascribes to them. But if you insist that every "set" has a definite number of members, then I shall say that there is no such set as {Alpha, Omega}.

["There has to be such a set, since there are such *individuals* as Alpha and Omega."]

Alpha and Omega are individuals in the metaphysical sense, I suppose. But 'individual' is a technical term in set theory: individuals are nonsets that are capable of being members of sets. If "being a set" entails "being an object that perfectly conforms to the requirements imposed upon 'sets' by what is called 'set theory'," then it is clear that if x and y are such that it is neither definitely true nor definitely false that they are identical, then x and y are not "individuals" in the required sense, owing to the fact that every set that perfectly conforms to the requirements of set theory has a definite number of members. If set-theorists sometimes define individuals as nonsets (or nonclasses, if "class" is distinguished from "set"), that is only because they either reject or have not considered the thesis that there is such a thing as vague identity.[84]

["You yourself, in constructing your semantics, have employed set-theoretical notions. Universes, pairings, extensions, and frontiers are all sets."]

I have employed these notions only in giving a formal semantics. Recall my analogy of a formal semantics for a platonistic language whose universe of discourse consisted entirely of objects acceptable to the nominalist. There is no reason that a pure, formal semantics for a language containing 'indef', '=', and ' ^ ' cannot be constructed whose universe of discourse comprises only objects among which no indefinite identities hold (numbers, say, or men who have not got involved with the Cabinet). Suppose that the fragment of a semantics I have offered does have a universe of discourse comprising only "definite" objects. It never-theless succeeds in distinguishing "valid" from "invalid" inferences, and its use of classical set-theoretic notions is unobjectionable. If we move from a "pure" to what Plantinga has called a "depraved" seman-tics, however, we shall have to be more careful about our use of set-theoretic notions. If we really do propose, in our semantics, "in the meta-language" as they say, to quantify over objects among which indefinite identities hold, then we shall have to take one of two courses. If we want it to be literally true that there are such *objects* as universes and pairings and frontiers and so on, then we shall have to resort to a set theory that allows sets of indefinite cardinality. (An example of a set of indefinite cardinality would be a set of which it is definitely false that it is empty, neither definitely true nor definitely false that it has one member, neither definitely true nor definitely false that it has two members, and definitely false it has more than two members.) As far as I know, no such theory has actually been constructed. (Fuzzy sets are not sets of indefi-nite cardinality. In fuzzy-set theory, one has various "degrees" of set membership—perhaps as many degrees as there are real numbers be-tween 0 and 1—and to specify a set is to specify, for each object, what its degree of membership in that set is. Classical set theory is a special case of fuzzy-set theory, the case in which there are just two degrees of membership: 'Yes' and 'No', one might call them. A fuzzy set—unless it is also a classical set—does not really have such a thing as *a* cardinality at all; rather, each fuzzy set has n cardinalities, where n is the number of possible degrees of membership other than "definite nonmembership.")

In the absence of a theory of sets of indefinite cardinality, it might be better for the depraved semanticist investigating languages in which vague identity is expressible to try to get along without such *objects* as universes, pairings, and frontiers. I am not sure whether this could be done. There are, as we have seen, various devices for making statements about things collectively that do not require quantification over collec-tions of things: plural referring expressions and plural quantification. Languages embodying such devices fall far short of the expressive power of set theory, but they may contain sufficient resources for talking about things collectively to meet the needs of the depraved semanticist inves-tigating vague identity. I have not tried to construct a semantics for vague identity using only these resources for collective reference. It would be interesting to see whether this was possible.

Objection Four

Various *truths of reason* fail in your system. That is, your semantics fails to confer validity on inference forms that have always been accepted. We have already seen that the Law of the Excluded Middle fails on the only plausible extension of your system to include disjunction. The same point could be made about the Law of Noncontradiction (given the obvious definition of conjunction: a conjunction has the least value had by any of its conjuncts). Even if we stick with what is strictly speaking expressible in your sparse language, the Principle of the Transitivity of Identity fails. That is, the model

$$\{A, B, C\}, \{\{A, B\}, \{B, C\}\}, \text{ '}a\text{' ref } A, \text{ '}b\text{' ref } B, \text{ '}c\text{' ref } C$$

is a counterexample to

$$a = b, b = c \vdash a = c;$$

it assigns ½ to the premises and 0 to the conclusion. Moreover, the Principle of the Nonidentity of Discernibles fails in your system—or, rather, since the general principle is not expressible in your sparse language, instances of it do. For example, as you have noted, I_4 is invalid. The model

$$\{A, C\}, \{\{A, C\}\}, \text{ '}a\text{' ref } A, \text{ '}b\text{' ref } A$$

assigns ½ to its premises and 0 to its conclusion.

Reply

I have already remarked on the Law of the Excluded Middle. I think that the validity of this "law" depends on the assumption that every proposition is definitely true or definitely false. But if anyone *must* have it, he can secure it by the "supervalue" trick outlined above. A similar remark applies to the Law of Noncontradiction. I think that the validity of this law, too, depends on the assumption that every proposition is definitely true or definitely false. (Suppose it is neither definitely true nor definitely false that John is rich. Suppose Tim says "John is rich" and Tom says "John is not rich." Is it definitely false that they're both right? Remember, it's definitely true that they're both *sort of* right.) Again, however, anyone who insists on having this "law" can have it by employing the "supervalue" trick. Since Evans's argument employs no binary connectives, *no* way of assigning values to sentences involving binary connectives will affect the implications of our semantical fragment for his argument.

As to the failure of transitivity of identity, isn't that just what we should want? Suppose that *Omega* enters the Cabinet, and that Aleph (who is only indefinitely identical with Omega) emerges, and that Aleph then reenters the Cabinet, from which Beth subsequently emerges. Suppose that this process continues till Tav emerges from the Cabinet. *Must* we say that it is neither definitely true nor definitely false that Alpha is identical with Tav? Couldn't the twenty-four operations of the Cabinet have so diluted whatever factor is the ground of personal identity that Alpha and Tav are definitely *not* identical? Must *logic* rule this out? Must we allow logic to dictate to us that if all members of the chain: indef Alpha = Omega, indef Omega = Aleph, indef Aleph = Beth, . . . , indef Sin = Shin, indef Shin = Tav are true, then it can't be that Alpha and Tav are definitely two distinct objects? If we accept the transitivity of identity as a logical truth, we are accepting this consequence as a decree of logic.

Well, *isn't* the transitivity of identity a truth of reason? Can't my own words be quoted against me? (I once wrote, "Anyone who denies the transitivity of identity simply does not understand the difference between the number 1 and the number 2.")[85] No and no. What is a truth of reason—and what I was *calling* 'the transitivity of identity'—is the principle that should in the present context be called 'the transitivity of *definite* identity': if it is definitely true that $a = b$, and it is definitely true that $b = c$, then it is definitely true that $a = c$. And this principle *is* endorsed by our semantical fragment: any model that assigns 1 to '$a = b$' and to '$b = c$' will also assign 1 to '$a = c$'. We may note that this fact constrains anyone who accepts our fragment in the following important way: if he accepts '$a = b$' and '$b = c$', he must also accept '$a = c$'. (In Section 14, I appealed to "the Principle of the Transitivity of Identity" in the course of a discussion of the question whether a given life could have been going on in other circumstances. And in Section 15, I appealed to "the Principle of the Transitivity of Identity" to establish the conclusion that an object could not become a preexistent object. In both cases the principle appealed to was the Principle of the Transitivity of Definite Identity.)

But suppose someone insists that identity have *this* feature: if it is indefinite whether $a = b$ and indefinite whether $b = c$, then it cannot be definitely false that $a = c$; we can give this person what he wants easily enough. We simply impose the following condition on pairing: For any model, if three objects x, y, and z belong to the universe of that model, and if that model pairs x with y and y with z, it must also pair x with z. We may note that the model M, our counterexample to I_3, satisfies this condition. Therefore, adopting this restriction on pairing would not affect our discussion of Evans's argument.[86]

Let us finally examine the invalidity of the Principle of the Nonidentity of Discernibles. I will make three points.

(i) What we normally call 'the Nonidentity of Discernibles' certainly has the aspect of a truth of reason. But perhaps what we normally think of under the description 'the Nonidentity of Discernibles' is a principle that would be better described in the present context as 'the *definite* nonidentity of *definite* discernibles'. And this principle is valid according to the semantical fragment I have proposed. (Compare our remarks about the transitivity of *definite* identity.) Consider any inference form

a has F, $\sim b$ has F $\vdash \sim a = b,$

where F is an abstract. Any model that assigns 1 to both premises must include the referent of 'a' in the extension of F and exclude the referent of 'b' and anything paired with it from both the extension and the frontier of F. Thus, the referents of the two constants in that model must be distinct and not paired, and the model will assign 1 to the conclusion.

(ii) Is it so very implausible that (if there is such a thing as the indefinite possession of a property at all) the Principle of the Nonidentity of Discernibles can take us from ½ to 0? Suppose it is not definitely true and not definitely false that x has the property F. Then the proposition that x has F and its denial will both have the value ½; but the proposition that x is not identical with x should, it seems, nevertheless receive the value 0. Consider a formal instance of the Nonidentity of Discernibles that contains only *one* constant, 'a'; let the abstract it contains be that of I_4:

a has $\hat{x}$ indef $x = a$, $\sim a$ has $\hat{x}$ indef $x = a \vdash \sim a = a.$

Any model that pairs the referent of 'a' with something will assign ½ to each of the premises of this inference form, and any model at all will assign 0 to its conclusion. Perhaps it is implausible to assign ½ to either of these premises. We have already considered that question. Given that we do that, however, we should certainly want the conclusion to have the value 0. And should matters really be different if we assigned a second constant 'b' the same referent as 'a' and replaced the first occurrence of 'a' in the second premise and one of the occurrences of 'a' in the conclusion with 'b'?

It is important to note that the failure of the Nonidentity of Discernibles in our semantical fragment does not turn on our "controversial" rule for assigning values to ascription sentences. It will arise in any semantics that allows a sentence of the form 'a has F' to take the value ½. And that, surely, must be a feature of any plausible semantics that applies to a language that attempts to represent the possession of properties that have vague extensions. Suppose, for example, that a certain man is a borderline case of a wise man, and that he bears the names 'Tom' and 'Tim'. It is hard to see how to avoid the conclusion that both of the following arguments have "sort of true" premises and a definitely false conclusion:

Tom has wisdom, ~Tom has wisdom ⊢ ~Tom = Tom

Tom has wisdom, ~Tim has wisdom ⊢ ~Tom = Tim.

(iii) Our adherence to the Principle of Nonidentity of Discernibles is based on our adherence to an even more fundamental truth of reason, Leibniz's Law or the Principle of the Indiscernibility of Identicals, which we may represent schematically as follows:

$a = b$, a has F ⊢ b has F.

The counterexamples to the Nonidentity of Discernibles that assign ½ to the premises of that inference form and 0 to its conclusion will not be counterexamples to Leibniz's Law: they will assign 1 to the identity premise, ½ to the other premise, and ½ to the conclusion. (In two-valued logic the two principles are equivalent; in three-valued logic—as the present case shows—it does not follow from the fact that p, q ⊢ r is valid that p, $\sim r$, ⊢ $\sim q$ is valid.)[87]

Nevertheless, Leibniz's Law is not valid in our semantical fragment. It would become valid, however, if we adopted the condition on pairing that secures the transitivity of identity. (The proof is left as an exercise.) Therefore, any philosopher who wishes to have Leibniz's Law can have it at the same price as the Transitivity of Identity.

This concludes my examination of possible philosophical objections to the semantical fragment I have presented. I know of no others. Though I should not want to say that these objections, taken collectively, have no force whatever, they seem to me to be very far indeed from being decisive. I conclude that the friends of vague identity can take Evans's argument in their stride.

It might, however, be argued that the modification of standard logic entailed by this semantical fragment weakens the case for the central thesis of this book.

"A very powerful motivation for your adherence to an answer to the Special Composition Question, which allows no composite objects but living organisms, was that to admit the existence of other composite objects would seem to lead to logical paradoxes or intractable meta-physical puzzles. Witness the case of the Ship of Theseus. But if you have rejected the Principle of the Transitivity of (vague) Identity, it is hard to see how the problem of the Ship of Theseus could arise. In the story of the Ship of Theseus, we have the Original Ship, the Reconstructed Ship, and the Continuous Ship. Why not simply say that although the Reconstructed Ship and the Continuous Ship are definitely nonidentical (being definitely in different places at the same time), it is not definitely true or definitely false of the Original Ship that it is identical with the Continuous Ship, and it is not definitely true or definitely false of the Original Ship that it is identical with the Reconstructed Ship? You have devised a logic to make the world safe for Moderate answers to the Special Composition Question, but this logic undercuts a very powerful argument, perhaps your most powerful argument, for your *own* rather extreme Moderate answer. To reject the transitivity of identity is to make the world safe for more moderate Moderate answers than yours."[88]

This, of course, is correct. (I would point out, however, that I have not rejected the Principle of the Transitivity of Identity in order to solve any particular philosophical problem. Rejection of this principle "does" nothing for me; I have rejected it simply because it seems implausible to me that vague identity should be transitive. If I changed my mind about this, I could incorporate the transitivity of vague identity into my "system" without having to make any adjustments.) But I have not adopted the answer to the Special Composition Question that I have been defending in this book in order to avoid confronting paradoxes about any particular kinds of material object (such as ships or shoes or bits of sealing wax). I have adopted it because I am looking for a systematic account of material objects (an account, of course, that is free from paradox).

One *could* raise the question whether the proposition that ships et al. exist entailed any logical paradoxes or intractable metaphysical puzzles, but a much more interesting and fruitful question would be whether an answer to the Special Composition Question that allowed the existence of ships et al. (an answer such as *Contact* or Universalism) entailed any paradoxes or puzzles. An adherent of *Contact* and a Universalist will each of them say that his own theory allows the existence of "ships," and each will make the same ostensive gestures when asked to point some of these objects out. But each will attribute very different metaphysical properties to the things he is pointing at. The Universalist will say that "ships" are indestructible, barring the annihilation of a simple (though they can easily be turned into nonships). The adherent of *Contact* will probably not say this; he must say that if a "ship" is cut in half and the halves separated, then the simples that formerly composed the ship now compose nothing, and he will presumably want to say that the ship has ceased to exist (but *Contact* alone does not entail that the ship has ceased to exist). The lesson is: If one wishes to know whether a metaphysician of the material world faces logical paradoxes or metaphysical puzzles, one should concentrate one's attention not so much on the range of material objects that this metaphysician believes in, as on the metaphysical principle that (as he sees it) these objects he believes in owe their existence to. A mere list of the material objects in the metaphysician's universe of discourse is unlikely to convey sufficient information about the metaphysician's position to enable one to tell what paradoxes and puzzles, if any, he faces. And this will be particularly true of lists that are written in the language of everyday life.

Of course, a metaphysician may be content simply to present us with a list of objects; the famous opening remarks of Moore's *Some Main Problems of Philosophy* suggest that this is the primary task of the metaphysician. But, to my mind, the philosopher who does only this (however cogently he may argue for the correctness and completeness of his list) is hardly a metaphysician at all. It is my view that the answer I have given to the Special Composition Question provides us with a metaphysic of composite material objects that faces fewer paradoxes and puzzles than does any other metaphysic of composite material objects that is as fully explicit as mine. (A metaphysic of composite material objects is *inexplicit* just insofar as it is a mere list of the kinds of composite material objects. An inexplicit metaphysic avoids paradoxes and puzzles—if it does avoid them—in the way that a witness who persistently invokes the Fifth Amendment avoids perjury.) I would go so far as to say that if my answer to the Special Composition Question is correct, no paradoxes or intractable puzzles can be deduced *by standard logic* from any *actual* episode of change and persistence. The nonstandard logic that I have introduced for reasoning about indefinite identity is needed to block paradoxical inferences only from science-fictional episodes like the passage of a man through the Cabinet. In my view, any very explicit Moderate ontology of physical objects, if it were very different from my own—in particular, if it allowed the real existence of "ordinary" nonbiological objects—would not have that property: Either very ordinary episodes of endurance and persistence would confront it with insoluble problems, or, at least, very ordinary episodes would confront it with problems that could be solved only by the employment of a nonstandard logic. Evans's argument shows that *something* needs to be done to prevent sentences of the form 'indef $a = b$' from leading to paradox. This "something" is not just automatically a revision of standard logic, since it is no part of standard logic that the operation of property abstraction can be applied to just any sentence. But the only "something" I know of does count as a revision of standard logic. Nevertheless, I think it is worth pointing out that, if my ontology is correct, then there probably *are* no truths of the form 'It is neither definitely true nor definitely false that John is identical with James', where 'John' and 'James' get their semantical properties in virtue of someone's dubbing an object 'John' at one time and someone's dubbing an object 'James' at another time. There are none, but there could be; the apparent possibility of a device like the Cabinet establishes this thesis to my satisfaction. But there is in fact no Cabinet and never has been one. I feel fairly confident, however, that if any Moderate answer to the Special Composition Question that allowed the existence of "ordinary" nonbiological objects were correct, then there would actually be truths of this form. (But this cannot be shown in the absence of an actual example of such answers.) Why is this important? Well, it is important to me to think that standard logic, the logic of the transitivity of identity and the Law of the Excluded Middle, is, if it is not strictly correct, at least a good approximation to a correct logic. I should like to think that I can unhesitantly apply standard logic in ordinary circumstances. Just as it would be a defect in a (physically interpreted) geometry if it did not "reduce to" Euclidean geometry under ordinary conditions, so, I take it, it would be a defect in a logic if it did not reduce to standard logic under ordinary conditions. I should like it if standard logic applied in all thinkable episodes of alteration. I shall have to be content with the supposition that it applies in all (as yet) actual episodes of alteration.

Before leaving the topic of identity and vagueness, I will make a few remarks about the logical problems raised by counterfactual identity. As we observed in Section 14, there are perfectly mundane states of affairs—not science-fictional at all—having this feature: If they had obtained, then it would have been neither definitely true nor definitely false that I existed. (I do not mean: In some of the closest worlds in which these states of affairs obtain I exist and in others of them I do not exist. I mean: *Each* of the closest worlds in which these states of affairs obtain is such that it is not definitely true or definitely false of that world that I exist in it.) Suppose, for example, that an energetic cosmic ray had slightly rearranged the genetic material in that one particular spermatozoon to which I am so intimately related, and that this sperm united with the egg it actually united with and produced a viable human being with two hearts and a photographic memory. Would he have been I? Or suppose that monozygotic twins had developed from the zygote that, in actuality, only I developed from. Should I have been one of them? Or consider two monozygotic murine embryos; a biologist takes some cells from one and places them against the other (where they adhere and are right at home) and vice versa; two perfectly normal mice develop from these modified embryos. Are they the two mice that would have developed from the unmodified embryos? It seems a plausible speculation that these questions have no definite answers. (These are questions about the counterfactual identity of organisms. As we saw in Section 14, there would seem to be questions about the counterfactual identity of simples that cannot be said to have definite answers.) Suppose this were true. What would follow? Let A be a state of affairs such that, if it had obtained, it would not have been definitely true or definitely false that I existed. Suppose someone were to say, "I hereby name the person who would have been Peter van Inwagen if A had obtained 'Paul'." (I am assuming in this example what seems to me to be true: that one can give a proper name to an object via a proper definite description. For example, given this assumption, there is nothing a priori wrong with saying "I hereby name the tallest Albanian 'George'," though this attempt at naming might fail if, as a matter of contingent fact, 'the tallest Albanian' had the wrong semantical properties—if, say, two equally tall Albanians were taller than all other Albanians.) It seems to me that if the name 'Paul' were introduced into our discourse in the way I have imagined, 'indef Peter = Paul' would express a truth. (The story of the introduction of the name 'Paul' is fiction but not science fiction. It would be easy to turn it from fiction into truth: For *some* replacement for 'A' in the formula I have constructed for conferring the name 'Paul', the story would be true if someone simply pronounced this formula under felicitous conditions.) Does our semantics for 'indef' block the deduction of a contradiction from this sentence, as it does in the case of 'indef Alpha = Omega'? It would seem not, for the semantical properties of the name 'Paul' are not represented in our formal semantics. 'Peter' may be represented as a constant having a referent and no fringe referents (since everyone is either definitely identical with me or definitely not identical with me: The Cabinet is no part of *my* life or of the life of any other person). 'Paul', on the other hand, would seem to be a phrase having no referent but having a fringe referent: *I* am its fringe referent. Some philosophers will protest that 'Paul' does have a referent: It definitely denotes a certain man who exists in the closest possible worlds in which the state of affairs A obtains. I say it definitely denotes no such thing, for there is no such thing for it definitely to denote. There are, in my view, men who exist in other possible worlds, but they are just the men who exist in the actual world. (There are of course worlds in which there exist just the men who exist in actuality and in which there also exist other men. But there are no men who exist in those worlds who do not exist in actuality. This is an extraordinarily simple point that many philosophers have a great deal of trouble grasping. I recommend they read Plantinga.)[89] The semantical properties of 'Paul' are exhausted by this assertion: 'Paul' definitely denotes nothing and indefinitely denotes me. Therefore, if we wish to investigate the consequences of 'indef Peter = Paul', we must relax our requirement that every individual constant have a referent. This will lead to a proliferation of the types of cases that must be treated semantically, and some of these cases will be philosophically problematical. (For example: Suppose 'a' and 'b' are constants without referents but with the same fringe referents; should '$a = b$' be assigned 1 or ½? For that matter, what about '$a = a$'?) I believe that a consistent and plausible semantics for 'indef' can be constructed that does not require constants to have referents (though it would require every constant without a referent to have at least one fringe referent), a semantics, moreover, that would render invalid an Evans-style deduction of a contradiction from 'indef Peter = Paul'. But that is a project for another time. Perhaps the example provided by our treatment of vagueness and diachronic identity makes it at least plausible to suppose that similar if more elaborate techniques can be used to deal with vagueness and counterfactual identity.

19. The Vagueness of Existence

We saw in Section 18 that composition is vague: There are xs such that it is not definitely true and not definitely false that the activity of the xs constitutes a life; there are, therefore—given our answer to the Special Composition Question—xs such that it is not definitely true and not definitely false that those xs compose anything. An obvious consequence of this fact is that there will be truths of the form 'indef $\exists x\ Fx$'. Now this consequence is not itself puzzling, for the indisputable fact that there are vague predicates has the same consequence. Consider, for example, the vague predicate 'is wise'. If Socrates is wiser than anyone else but is, nevertheless, only a borderline case of a wise man, then, obviously, 'indef $\exists x\ x$ is wise' should count as true. But the vagueness of composition presents us with instances of 'indef $\exists x\ Fx$' that are radically different from this one. We briefly considered such a case early in Section 18: the case of the embryo that was in my mother's womb five or six days after my conception. Let us look at a simpler case.

Suppose that the activity of certain simples, which are ten in number, constitutes a borderline case of a life. Call these simples P. And suppose that *no* simples are such that their activity constitutes an event that is *definitely* a life. And suppose that no event other than the activity of P constitutes a borderline case of a life. Then—given our answer to the Special Composition Question—it is indefinite whether P compose anything, and, for any simples that are not identical with P (including any nine of P and any eleven simples that P are among), it is definite that they compose nothing. Finally, suppose that each simple weighs exactly one ounce. What value $(1, \frac{1}{2}, \text{ or } 0)$ should we then assign to the sentence '$\exists x\ x$ weighs more than four ounces'? It seems clear that this sentence should receive the value $\frac{1}{2}$; equivalently, the sentence 'indef $\exists x\ x$ weighs more than four ounces' should receive the value 1. But why, exactly? The case is not like the case of Socrates and his imperfect wisdom. In that case 'indef $\exists x$ x is wise' "comes out true" because no object definitely satisfies the predicate 'x is wise' and a certain object does not definitely fail to satisfy it. Or, in the language of Section 18, because no object belongs to the "extension" of 'x is wise' and a certain object belongs to the "frontier" of this predicate. In the case we have imagined, however, we cannot say that any object belongs to the frontier of 'x weighs more than four ounces'. Each of the simples weighs exactly one ounce and is, therefore, not a borderline case of a thing that weighs more than four ounces. And we cannot say that the thing that P compose is a borderline case of a thing that weighs more than four ounces, and this for two reasons. First, it is indefinite whether there is anything that P compose, and, therefore, we who know this cannot make assertions having 'the thing that P compose' as their subject. Secondly, if P *did* compose something, it would not be a borderline case of a thing weighing more than four ounces, for it would weigh exactly ten ounces.

This sort of result is by no means peculiar to the Proposed Answer. It will be a consequence of any answer to the Special Composition Question according to which objects compose something just in the case that they stand to one another in a certain multigrade causal relation—for, it would seem, any *causal* relation must be vague, in the sense that it will be possible for there to be objects that constitute a borderline case of objects standing in that relation. Consider, for example, the thesis we have called *Contact*. Since contact among material objects is, ultimately, a matter of the interaction among continuous electromagnetic fields, it is possible to imagine cases in which there is no fact of the matter as to whether x is in contact with y, and, therefore, for any number of zs, it is possible to imagine cases in which there is no fact of the matter as to whether the zs are in contact. Now, suppose that *Contact* is right. Imagine the following situation: there are just ten simples, each weighing exactly one ounce, and they are neither definitely in contact nor definitely not in contact. Then it will be indefinite whether there is something that weighs more than four ounces, despite the fact that it cannot be said of this imaginary situation that it contains a borderline case of a thing weighing more than four ounces. David Lewis has seen this consequence of adopting a causal answer to the Special Composition Question and has argued that it entails that no answer to that question more moderate than Universalism can be tolerated. In *On the Plurality of Worlds* he says:

> The question whether composition takes place in a given case, whether a given class does or does not have a mereological sum, can be stated in a part of language where nothing is vague. Therefore, it

cannot have a vague answer. There is such a thing as the sum, or there isn't. It cannot be said that because the *desiderata* for composition are satisfied to a borderline degree, there sort of is and sort of isn't. What is this thing such that it sort of is so, and sort of isn't, that there is any such thing? No restriction on composition can be vague. But unless it is vague, it cannot fit the intuitive *desiderata*. So no restriction on composition can serve the intuitions that motivate it. So restriction would be gratuitous.[90]

The fact that our answer—or any causal answer—to the Special Composition Question generates possible cases in which 'index $\exists x\ Fx$' is true, even though there is nothing (or, at any rate, cases in which it is not definitely true that there is anything) that belongs to the frontier of F, has implications for the logic of indefinite existence.

The statement that something belongs to the frontier of F is mirrored in the object language by the sentence '$\exists x$ indef Fx'. It follows that there are cases in which we should want to assign definite truth to 'indef $\exists x\ Fx$' but not to '$\exists x$ indef Fx'. "Ordinary" cases of indefiniteness, cases in which indefiniteness arises from an object's falling within the frontier of a predicate, are not of this type. For example, in the "Socrates/Wisdom" case, 'indef $\exists x\ x$ is wise' and '$\exists x$ indef x is wise' would seem both to be definitely true. (The reader may be reminded of puzzles about the Barcan formula in the philosophy of quantified modal logic and may begin to wonder whether one must distinguish between *de dicto* and *de re* vagueness. Recall our parenthetical remark about "grades of indefinitional involvement" in Section 18. Presumably, the question whether one must distinguish *de dicto* from *de re* vagueness is closely connected with the question whether it is proper for one to employ sentences exhibiting the second grade of indefinitional involvement; and, presumably, this close connection is very strongly analogous to the close connection between the question whether one must distinguish *de dicto* from *de re* modality and the question whether it is proper for one to employ sentences exhibiting the third grade of modal involvement.) Therefore, it would seem, a logic whose vocabulary includes both 'indef' and quantifiers ought not to endorse the inference form

indef $\exists x\ Fx \vdash \exists x$ indef Fx.

Is it possible to construct a coherent semantics that will enable us to evaluate inferences containing both '$\exists$' and 'indef'; and is it possible to do this in a way that does not confer validity on the inference form displayed above? (If this inference form is invalid, then we may note—in connection with the passage quoted from Lewis—that from the fact that it is indefinite whether anything is the sum of the xs, it does not follow that something is such that it is indefinite whether it is the sum of the xs.) I shall sketch a semantics that has the required features. I shall consider only the simple case in which quantifiers bind monadic predicates.

Let us consider a very simple formal language. Its vocabulary consists of '∃', 'indef', (singular) variables, and a stock of monadic predicate-letters. The formation rules are the obvious ones. Suppose that G is a predicate—we allow predicates containing 'indef' to be among the predicates that are represented by G—and let ∃G be the existential quantification of G on the variable that is free in G. How shall we assign the values 0, ½, and 1 to ∃G? There would seem to be two relevant factors. First, G will have both an extension and a frontier, and the value of ∃G will obviously depend partly upon whether the extension and the frontier of G are empty or nonempty. But, as we have seen, there would seem to be cases in which ∃G should have the value ½ even though both the extension and the frontier of G are empty. We can provide a foothold for cases of this type in our semantics by dividing the objects in our universe of discourse into two kinds: "full objects" and "borderline" objects. Intuitively, a full object is definitely there or definitely exists, and a borderline object dwells in the twilight between the full daylight of Being and the night of Nonbeing. Now, we have already said several times that the idea of such an object makes no sense at all, but, by a familiar paradox, ideas that make no sense at all can have enormous heuristic value, a value that justifies using them to give intuitive force to elements of a formal semantics. The most famous case of this sort in recent philosophical logic would probably be the use of the notion of a "merely possible object," both in informal modal heuristics and in giving intuitive force to certain elements in the standard formal semantics for quantified modal logic. In my view, the notion of a merely possible object is an even more defective notion than the notion of a borderline object; after all, a merely possible object is an object that *definitely* isn't there. Not all philosophers, of course, take such a jaundiced view of merely possible objects, and many would protest that my characterization of them in the preceding sentence is a travesty. But that characterization seems right to me, and yet, despite this fact, I am willing to talk of merely possible objects at a certain informal level of modal discourse. When I do this, of course, I issue a promissory note that I am committed eventually to redeem. I hereby promise eventually to redeem the promissory note that I have issued by calling certain objects in my universe of discourse "borderline objects." Let us by all means be conceptual puritans at the end of our inquiries; but if everyone were a conceptual puritan *ab initio*, we should never have had the arithmetic of negative numbers or the infinitesimal calculus.

We have both full and borderline objects. How shall we use them in determining the value of $\exists$G? There are four possibilities about the membership of the extension of a predicate G that would seem to be relevant to determining the value of an existential quantification on its free variable: The extension of G may contain full objects and no border-line objects (designate this possibility by F); the extension of G may contain both full and borderline objects (FB); the extension of G may contain borderline objects but no full objects (B); the extension of G may be empty (E). And, of course, the same four possibilities exist for the frontier of G, making sixteen possibilities in all. I suggest that the value of $\exists$G should be determined according to this table:

the extension of G	the frontier of G	the value of $\exists$G
F	F	1
F	FB	1
F	B	1
F	E	1
FB	F	1
FB	FB	1
FB	B	1
FB	E	1
B	F	½
B	FB	½
B	B	½
B	E	½
E	F	½
E	FB	½
E	B	½
E	E	0

(This table may be summarized as follows: The presence of a full object in the extension of G is necessary and sufficient for the definite truth of $\exists$G; if the value of $\exists$G is not 1, we assign it the value ½ if there is the least excuse for doing so.) Let us stipulate that—as in Section 18—indef G has the frontier of G as its extension and an empty frontier; and let us retain the value table for 'indef' that was given in Section 18. One may then mechanically continue this table to provide values for $\exists$ indef G and indef $\exists$G.

Now, what about the inference we wish to avoid, 'indef $\exists x$ Fx ⊢ $\exists x$ indef Fx'? Inspection of the table shows that there are two sorts of counterexample to the validity of this inference. First, if the extension of

F contains no full objects and the frontier of F contains only borderline objects, then 'indef $\exists x\, Fx$' has the value 1, and '$\exists x$ indef Fx' has the value ½. Secondly, if the frontier of F is empty and its extension contains only borderline objects, then 'indef $\exists x\, Fx$' has the value 1 and '$\exists x$ indef Fx' has the value 0.

Let us leave aside for the moment the question of the intuitive meaning of these formal results and take up the question of the promissory note I have issued by talking of borderline objects. Have I not in some way involved myself in paradox? When I am speaking the metalanguage— there is a good example of this in the preceding paragraph—I am perfectly willing to say things of the general form "Suppose there are borderline objects that. . . ." And isn't the assertion that there are border-line objects just the metalinguistic "version" of the assertion that there are objects of which it is not definitely true and not definitely false that they exist? The paradox is merely apparent. It is very strongly analogous to the following apparent paradox. '$\sim\exists x \sim x = x$', and, indeed, '$\Box\sim\exists x \sim x = x$', are theorems in standard systems of quantified modal logic. The sentence '$x = x$' may be read 'x exists'. (This assertion seems to trouble some people. I can only point out that it is very natural to read '$\exists y\, x = y$' as 'x exists' and that this sentence and '$x = x$' are logically equivalent.) And yet, when one is speaking the standard metalanguage for quantified modal logic, one will be perfectly willing to say things of the general form "Suppose there are merely possible objects that . . ."; but isn't the assertion that there are merely possible objects just the metalinguistic version of the assertion that there are possible objects of which it is false that they exist?

This second paradox is a familiar one. It is, in fact, so familiar that most philosophers are no longer troubled by it. There are various ways of resolving it. The question that should interest us at the moment is, How do these philosophers resolve it who deny that there are merely possible objects and who nevertheless employ a Kripke-style semantics for quantified modal logic? The usual way is this: to treat the so-called merely possible objects as objects which are not literally nonexistent but which mimic in some semantically useful way some of the behavior that, on the intuitive level, one expects of nonexistent objects. For example, one might treat so-called merely possible objects as being, in the final analysis, uninstantiated maximally consistent sets of properties. Or one might treat them as uninstantiated individual essences or haecceities. Such objects, of course, may be regarded without paradox as existing: If there exist any properties at all, some of them are uninstantiated, just as, if there exist any propositions at all, some of them are false. But, despite their being existent objects, these items can be made to mimic certain aspects of the behavior we expect of the nonexistent. Such objects, so employed, may be called proxy objects. To employ proxy objects is to have one's cake and eat it; or, better, to have one's words without having to eat them.

Let us now redeem our promissory note. We shall redeem this note in proxy objects. There are no borderline objects. Not *really*. There are really no objects that "dwell in the twilight between the full daylight of Being and the night of Non-being"—just as there are really no wholly nocturnal, Meinongian objects. If there really were borderline objects, one might focus one's attention upon one of them and say, "It is neither definitely true nor definitely false of *that* that it exists." And that is nonsense. What there really are, however, are sets such it is not definitely true and not definitely false of their members that they compose anything. (Or, if parthood is vague, there are fuzzy sets of which it is not definitely true and not definitely false that their members compose anything: There is a fuzzy set S of which it is not definitely true and not definitely false that there is an object x such that, for every y, y is a part of x to just the degree to which y is a member of S.) And these sets can be made to mimic some of the behavior that, on the intuitive level, we expect of borderline objects. We may offer a definition of "proxy borderline objects" as sets, or rather (since we are interested primarily in objects that gain and lose parts), as functions from moments of time to sets. The definition I shall give will presuppose the answer to the Special Composition Question and the account of persistence through mereological change that it has been the central purpose of this book to defend. I have had a stab at a more general answer, but I have found my attempt to be very messy and to contain some rather dubious notions, and I will not reproduce it. I think I am perfectly well justified in declining to produce an account of "proxy borderline objects" that is independent of my beliefs about composition and persistence, just as someone who produces an account of proxy *possibilia* is in no way required to produce an account that can accommodate beliefs about existence and actuality that are not his own. The definition is

x is a proxy borderline object if and only if

x is a function from moments of time to sets of simples and there is a borderline life y such that for all times t and all simples z, z belongs to the set that x assigns to t if and only if z is caught up in y at t.

A "borderline life," of course, is an event that is a borderline case of a life, an event of which it is neither definitely true nor definitely false that it is a life. Consider a region of space of which we should ordinarily say that at *t* it was "occupied by a virus." The simples within that space at *t* are then caught up in a certain homeodynamic event. In the case of a virus (or a mitochondrion or a plasmid) it seems plausible to say that this event is a borderline case of a life.

We must keep clearly in mind that two types of vagueness can enter into discussions of composition. A borderline life is, by definition, an event of which it is not definitely true and not definitely false that it is a life; but, quite independently of this, there will (no doubt) be simples of which it is not definitely true and not definitely false that they are caught up in that event. The above definition of a proxy borderline object does not take account of this second type of vagueness, but we may take account of it by replacing the reference to sets in the *definiens* with reference to fuzzy sets:

> *x* is a function from moments of time to fuzzy sets of simples, and there is a borderline life *y* such that for every time *t* and every simple *z* and every degree *w*, *z* belongs to the degree *w* to the fuzzy set that *x* assigns to *t* if and only if *z* is caught up in *y* to the degree *w* at *t*.

Now that we have our proxy borderline objects, we must explain what it means to say that they belong to the extensions and frontiers of predicates. For example, what does it mean to assign the case FB to the extension of the predicate G?

To explain this, we need the notion of the *associated properties* of a proxy borderline object. These are, loosely speaking, the properties that a thing *would* have if the simples that figure in the set-theoretic borderline object did (definitely) compose something and it was the thing they composed. We may think that there is no definite answer to the question whether viruses are alive, and that (speaking strictly and philosophically) there is therefore no definite answer to the question whether there are viruses. Still, it is quite plain what properties a given virus would have if it definitely existed (that is: for certain simples arranged virally, it is quite plain what properties a thing they composed *would* have if they did definitely compose something). Or, at least, this is true for many properties. For example, it is easy to say what the weight and shape of a virus composed of certain simples arranged virally would be if only those simples did definitely compose something. (For that matter, it is easy to say what the weight and shape of a given table would be if only the simples that virtually composed it actually composed something.) These counterfactuals—or counterindefinites—rest fairly securely on certain "principles of composition," as we called them in Section 4. For a very large range of intrinsic properties capable of being possessed by a material object, perhaps all of them, the possession of properties in this range by a composite material object supervenes upon the intrinsic properties and the arrangement of the simples of which it is composed. "Principles of composition" are the rules that codify this supervenience: The mass of a composite object is the sum of the masses of the simples that compose it; the region of space occupied by a composite object is the union of the regions of space occupied by the simples that compose it; and so on. (Some principles of composition will have logical forms that are far more complicated than the logical forms of these two examples, the principles governing solidity or electrical conductivity, for example.) These principles of composition tell us what properties would be possessed by an object composed by certain simples if those simples (arranged as they are and having the intrinsic properties they do) did definitely compose an object. They tell us, for example, that the xs, of which it is not definitely true or definitely false that they compose anything, are such that, if they did definitely compose something, its mass would be the sum of the masses of the xs. This may be regarded as a definition, if you like: this is what it *means* to say of certain simples that if they did definitely compose an object, it would have such-and-such properties: It would have the properties that the correct principles of composition (whatever they may be) say it would have on the basis of the properties of and arrangement of those simples.

We may now answer the question 'What does it mean to assign the case FB to the extension of the predicate G?' It means that certain objects satisfy G and that certain proxy borderline objects have associated properties such that anything that had these associated properties would, necessarily, satisfy G. Other questions, such as 'What does it mean to assign the case B to the frontier of G?' may be answered by using this answer as a model. (As regards this case, think of some complicated shape-predicate which is satisfied by certain viruses alone, if by anything, and which is satisfied even by those viruses only very imperfectly. That is, suppose that the correct principles of composition, when applied to certain simples arranged virally, yield the result that an object composed of those simples would be a borderline case of something that satisfied that shape-predicate.) I think that we have now redeemed our promissory note.

Let us now return to the question, What is the intuitive sense of our two kinds of formal counterexample to the inference form 'indef ∃F ⊢ ∃ indef F'?

We first have the case in which the extension of F contains no full objects and the frontier of F contains only borderline objects. Let us take viruses as our example of borderline objects—that is, let us assume that simples arranged virally constitute a borderline case of composition. Let our predicate be 'wedge-shaped', whatever that may mean. Now suppose that for any xs such that those xs definitely compose something, what they compose is neither a definite nor a borderline case of a wedge-shaped thing; and suppose that some viruses are borderline-wedge-shaped (that is, suppose that the correct principles of composition yield the result that, for some xs arranged virally, a thing composed of those xs would be a borderline case of a wedge-shaped thing). Then the statement that it is indefinite whether there is anything wedge-shaped is definitely true; but the statement that there is something such that it is indefinite whether it is wedge-shaped is only "sort of true." (This result is independent of the question whether there are, in addition to the borderline-wedge-shaped viruses, also some that are definitely wedge-shaped.)

Our second case is this: the frontier of F is empty and its extension contains only borderline objects. Suppose that for no xs do those xs definitely compose an object that is either definitely wedge-shaped or borderline-wedge-shaped, and that some viruses are definitely wedge-shaped and that no viruses or other borderline objects are borderline wedge-shaped. (It should by now be clear how to translate these loose statements into statements about principles of composition and borderline cases of composition.) Then the statement that it is indefinite whether anything is wedge-shaped is definitely true, and the statement that there is something that is borderline wedge-shaped is definitely false.

We noted earlier that David Lewis's argument for the incoherency of vague composition employed the inference form 'indef $\exists x\, x$ is the sum of P ⊢ $\exists x$ indef x is the sum of P'. This inference form is open to counterexamples of the second kind. For suppose that it is indefinite whether P compose anything. Then the predicate 'x is the sum of P' will have a borderline object in its extension (and no full object) and an empty frontier. (That is to say, if P *did* definitely compose something, it would be the sum of P, and nothing would be a borderline case of something that was the sum of P. The relevant "principle of composition" is a tautology: Anything the xs compose has the property of being the sum of the xs.)[91] It follows that 'indef $\exists x\, x$ is the sum of P' has the value 1. And it follows—via the step that 'indef x is the sum of P' has an empty extension (has as its extension the frontier of 'x is the sum of P') and an empty frontier—that '$\exists x$ indef x is the sum of P' has the value 0.

There is generally more than one way to redeem a promissory note of the kind I have issued, owing to the fact that there is generally more than one kind of object that can serve as a proxy object. For example, the note that is issued by the philosopher who talks of merely possible objects may be redeemed in either maximally consistent sets of properties or in haecceities. And I might have redeemed my note in other ways; one rather elegant way would have been to press lives, or, rather, borderline lives, into service as proxy borderline objects: The extension of the predicate 'weighs four pounds at noon', for example, would be assigned the case B if no event that is definitely a life at noon is such that the simples then caught up in it collectively weigh four pounds, and some event of which it is neither definitely true nor definitely false that it is a life at noon is such that the simples then caught up in it collectively weigh four pounds. (To avoid making the example hard to follow by mixing two kinds of vagueness in it, I have treated "being caught up in" as if it were not a matter of degree.)

This is perhaps as good a place as any to take note of an important difference between our treatment of the vagueness of existence and identity in the present (and the previous) section and our treatment of the vagueness of the part-whole relation in Section 17. Our treatment of the vagueness of existence and identity has been coarse-grained: We have only the sentence-operator 'indef', which applies or fails to apply, without qualification, to any given sentence, and which is therefore of no use to us if we wish to discuss degrees of vagueness. This is clearly a limitation. For two different settings for the dials on the Cabinet, A and B, we might well want to be able to say that the person who emerged when the dials were set at B, though not definitely nonidentical with the person who entered, was further from being definitely identical with the person who entered than was the person who emerged when the dials were set at A. Our treatment of the vagueness of the part-whole relation, on the other hand, was fine-grained: We treated "is a part of" as a matter of degree, and, indeed, as a matter of continuous degree, as something whose continuity could be modeled on the continuity of the real numbers. Why the different treatments? The difference was partly a matter of convenience and partly imposed by the topics I was discussing. It was natural, in discussing Unger's "problem of the many," to treat the part-whole relation not in any simplified form but as what it manifestly is if parthood is (as I maintain) a matter of being caught up in the life of an organism: a matter of continuous degree. And doing this raised no very great difficulties of statement or exposition, since the idea of a fuzzy set, which seems tailor-made for the purpose, lies ready to hand. On the other hand, Evans's argument involves no more sophisticated device for making assertions of vagueness than the sentence-operator 'indef'. And to treat the vagueness of existence and identity as admitting of continuous degree would have necessitated constructing a semantics according to which there are as many values as there are real numbers. But the three-valued semantics I have constructed is already much more complex than I like. Nevertheless, the vagueness of existence and the vagueness of identity *are*, in my judgment, matters of continuous degree, and a fully satisfactory account of vagueness would have to reflect that fact. I shall not, in this book, attempt a more sophisticated treatment of the vagueness of existence and identity.

Even our three-valued semantics is incomplete. Our very sketchy semantics of vague existence statements would require a little development before it could be applied to inferences that involved sentences in which a negation sign was prefixed to a predicate. We have not attempted to integrate our semantics of vague identity and our semantics of vague existence, and neither of these semantics treats either polyadic predicates or binary connectives. We therefore leave open the possibility that, even if our treatments of Evans's argument and "Lewis's paradox" are satisfactory, some other argument can be constructed that (apparently) deduces some embarrassing consequence from some (apparently) true sentence by means of logical devices on which our two semantical fragments are not equipped to pass judgment. One might wonder, for example, what the enemies of vague identity and existence could do with multiply quantified sentences that have 'indef' interspersed among their quantifiers. I will leave this problem to real logicians, however, for I have come to—I have perhaps passed—the limits of my logical abilities. In any case, sufficient unto the day is the evil thereof. I do think that the semantics I have constructed probably blocks all "logical" objections to the idea of "real vagueness in the world," provided these objections can be stated using only the resources of monadic first-order logic with identity and property abstraction.

It has been the thesis of the final part of this book that the theses on composition and identity that were introduced and defended earlier in the book (the Proposed Answer and *Life*) make it almost impossible for their adherents to deny that there is real vagueness in the world—that is, vagueness that cannot be accounted for by the Linguistic Theory of Vagueness. It has been our thesis, moreover, that this is no idiosyncrasy of *our* answer to the Special Composition Question: It is a consequence of any interesting Moderate answer to the Special Composition Question. This consequence of our own and other Moderate answers to the Special Composition Question is likely to be unpalatable to a great many philosophers. These philosophers will almost certainly object to the revision of standard logic that this consequence (apparently) requires. But there is a different, if not wholly distinct, reason for finding "objective" vagueness unpalatable: The Linguistic Theory of Vagueness just seems *right*. When we think about vagueness, don't we see that it just *is* a product of language, a product of the way we talk about the world, having no foothold in the world we talk about?

I feel the pull of this thesis very strongly, as I suspect you do. But a recent episode in the history of philosophy ought to make us at least a bit suspicious of convictions that a certain sort of phenomenon *must* be a "product of language, a product of the way we talk about the world, having no foothold in the world we talk about." I am just old enough to have felt the pull of, and indeed once to have accepted, the thesis that modal phenomena like necessity are a product of language, a product of the way we talk about the world, having no foothold in the world we talk about. The Linguistic Theory of Necessity has had a very hard time of it during the last twenty-five years. As I try to think through the implications of questions like "Must the man who emerges from the Cabinet be either definitely the same man as the man who entered it, or else definitely not the same man as the man who entered it?" and as I remember my attempts of twenty years ago to think through the implications of questions like "Could this lectern have been made of frozen Thames-water?" I discover a growing conviction that the Linguistic Theory of Vagueness deserves to be in for a hard time of it.

Notes

1. "Plantinga and the Philosophy of Mind," in James E. Tomberlin and Peter van Inwagen, eds., *Alvin Plantinga* (Dordrecht: D. Reidel, 1985), pp. 199–223. The quoted passage occurs on p. 220.

2. A representative list of works: Cartwright, "Scattered Objects," in Keith Lehrer, ed., *Analysis and Metaphysics* (Dordrecht: D. Reidel, 1975), pp. 153–72; Chisholm, *Person and Object: A Metaphysical Study* (LaSalle, Ill.: Open Court, 1976); Heller, *The Ontology of Physical Objects*, forthcoming from Cambridge University Press; Hirsch, *The Concept of Identity* (New York: Oxford University Press, 1982); Johnston, "Is There a Problem about Persistence?" *Proceedings of the Aristotelian Society*, suppl. vol. 61 (1987): 107–35, and "Human Beings," *Journal of Philosophy* 84 (1987): 59–83; Parfit, *Reasons and Persons* (Oxford: The Clarendon Press, 1984); Quine, "Identity, Ostension, and Hypostasis," in *From a Logical Point of View* (Cambridge: Harvard University Press, 1953), pp. 65–79; Salmon, *Reference and Essence* (Princeton: Princeton University Press, 1981); Simons, *Parts: A Study in Ontology* (Oxford: The Clarendon Press, 1987); Sosa, "Subjects among Other Things," *Philosophical Perspectives* 1 (1987): 155–87; Thomson, "Parthood and Identity across Time," *Journal of Philosophy* 80 (1983): 201–20; Van Cleve, "Mereological Essentialism, Mereological Conjunctivism, and Identity through Time," *Midwest Studies in Philosophy* 11 (1986): 141–56; Wheeler, "On That Which Is Not," *Synthese* 41 (1979): 155–73; Wiggins, *Sameness and Substance* (Cambridge: Harvard University Press, 1980).

Two of the authors on this list, Johnston and Wiggins, say many things that I find very congenial. But I have grave difficulties in understanding many of the other things they say, and I find myself unable to decide whether, in the end, I have understood their theories. I have twice heard Saul Kripke lecture on identity across time, and each time I was (characteristically) fascinated. But since my only record of Kripke's ideas is in the form of notes (my own and others'), I have decided to say nothing about them.

3. Gerhardt 75–77; H. T. Mason, ed. and trans., *The Leibniz-Arnauld Correspondence* (Manchester: Manchester University Press, 1967), pp. 92–95.

4. Or this is what I want to say if it is strictly true that there are such things as temperatures and average ages, and that they can alter. It is a plausible position

that there really are no such things; it is also a plausible position that, although there are such things, they are really mathematical objects and thus cannot alter. The thesis that 'John's body temperature in degrees C at noon' denotes one real number and '. . . at one P.M.' denotes another is an example of one form the second position can take. We may note that if this thesis is correct, the case of "alteration of temperature" is not thereby shown to be radically unlike all cases of "parthood": just as (on the thesis we are considering) the idea that the objects called 'temperatures' *alter* is an illusion, so perhaps it is an illusion that the objects called 'curves' have *parts*. Perhaps "curves" are really only functions; perhaps the statement 'the part of the curve that lies below the x-axis contains two minima' should receive an "official" formulation that contains no primitive mereological language: a "part" of a function f is a function which is defined for *some* of the arguments for which f is defined, and which takes, for those arguments, the same values as f.

5. I use 'part' in the conveniently inclusive sense in which everything is a part of itself. A *proper* part of an object is a part of that object other than the object itself. Thus, everything has exactly one *improper* part: itself.

6. This will be true as long as we assume that the part-whole relation is not vague. In Section 17 we shall examine the consequences of the assumption that there are borderline cases of parthood. As we shall see, we shall be forced to employ certain set-like objects ("fuzzy sets") in order to achieve the kind of collective reference that will be needed for a discussion of "fuzzy composition."

7. See Max Black, "The Elusiveness of Sets," *Review of Metaphysics* 24 (1971): 614–36; Adam Morton, "Complex Individuals and Multigrade Relations," *Nous* 9 (1975): 309–18. Morton's paper contains an alternative approach to the logical problems discussed in the present section.

8. Or, at least, they will contain quantifier words only in subordinate clauses, as 'the men who own all the coal mines'.

9. (Cambridge: Harvard University Press, 1940), pp. 65–71.

10. A set-theoretical semantics for plural quantification, like a set-theoretical semantics for ordinary quantification, can yield the right results only in a limited domain. Consider, for example, 'For any xs, if the ordinal numbers are among the xs, then the xs do not form a set'.

11. The reader may find it a useful exercise to write out the *definiens* of our formal definition of composition using only logical constants (quantifiers, variables, truth-functional connectives, the identity sign, 'is one of') and the predicate 'x is a part of y'.

12. In "Is a Thing Just the Sum of Its Parts?" *Proceedings of the Aristotelian Society* n.s. 86 (1985–86): 213–33, Christopher Hughes uses 'A composite object is just the mereological sum of its parts' to express the following thesis: For any xs, there is necessarily a unique object that is the sum of those xs; and if y is the sum of the xs, then y is the sum of the xs at every time and possible world at which y exists, and at every time and possible world at which the xs exist. This is an important metaphysical thesis—which I reject, root and branch—but I do not see why the words 'A composite object is just the mereological sum of its parts' should be thought to express it.

13. The thesis that a whole is a, or the, sum of its parts may be the thesis (briefly touched on in the Preface) that some philosophers have tried to express by the words 'A whole *is* its parts'. This sentence seems to me to be syntactically radically defective. There is the predicate 'is identical with', which yields a sentence when flanked by singular terms or singular variables. There is the predicate 'are identical with', which yields a sentence when flanked by plural referring expressions or plural variables. I do not see how there could be any sort of "identity" predicate that yielded a sentence by being put between a singular term (or variable) and a plural referring expression (or variable). *A* thing is *a* thing. Thing*s* are thing*s*.

14. I credit H. Scott Hestevolt with being the first philosopher—at least, the first present-day philosopher—to ask the Special Composition Question, although I cannot agree with the answer he proposes. See his "Conjoining," *Philosophy and Phenomenological Research* 41 (1980–81): 371–83.

15. I shall so use the word 'answer' that there can be wrong answers. Thus, by 'answer' I shall generally mean 'proposed answer, right or wrong'—unless I speak of *the* answer to a question, by which of course I mean the *right* answer.

16. Except one very special one: the one that tells us that proper composition never occurs (or, equivalently, that nothing is a proper part of anything). See Section 8.

17. The mereological language we sometimes use when talking about the regions of space occupied by objects can be dispensed with if we have the notion of a point in space *falling inside* an object. For example, instead of saying 'y occupies the sum of the regions of space occupied by the xs', we can say 'a point in space falls inside y if and only if it falls inside one of the xs'.

18. For an account of the Leonard-Goodman calculus, see Rolf Eberle, *Nominalistic Systems* (Dordrecht: D. Reidel, 1970), sec. 2.4.

19. Roderick M. Chisholm, *The First Person: An Essay on Reference and Intentionality* (Minneapolis: University of Minnesota Press, 1981), pp. 7–9.

20. For a possible solution to this problem, see Jonathan Bennett's discussion of "positive and negative instrumentality" in the first of his Tanner Lectures. These three lectures are printed under the title "Morality and Consequences," in Sterling M. McMurrin, ed., *The Tanner Lectures on Human Values, Volume II* (Salt Lake City: University of Utah Press, 1981), pp. 49–116.

21. Try to imagine bringing something into existence by gluing hamsters or snakes together.

22. The clause 'or there is only one of the xs' is needed to preserve the convention that every object is a part of itself. Suppose we had neglected to include that clause, and suppose that the two atoms x and y are fastened. Since fastening was introduced on the model of contact, each thing is by definition fastened to itself, and, hence, the things identical with x are fastened; but, because x is fastened to y, the things identical with x are not *maximally* fastened. Hence, they do not compose anything. But if x is a part of x, the things identical with x compose x. Therefore, x is not a part of x.

23. See "There Are No Ordinary Things," *Synthese* 41 (1979): 117–54, and "Skepticism and Nihilism," *Nous* 14 (1980): 517–45.

24. See the remarks on parthood and analogy in Section 1.

25. I mean chemical atoms—atoms in the modern, scientific sense—not mereological atoms. The argument could as easily be stated in terms of mereological atoms or "simples" as in terms of chemical atoms. I state the arguments in terms of atoms in the usual present-day sense of the word because we are familiar with the idea that we are all constantly "changing our atoms." In any case, Universalism presumably entails the existence of atoms, since it entails that two up-quarks, a down-quark, and an electron will have a sum, and (if these particles are properly arranged) that sum would certainly be a hydrogen atom. Hence, we cannot be faulted for assuming the existence of chemical atoms in an argument against Universalism.

26. Well, not quite. Organisms have parts that overlap no atom, such as ions, free electrons, and photons. A few of the atoms that composed me ten years ago were unstable (carbon-14 atoms, for example) and no longer exist. The atoms that ten years ago made up the cholesterol molecules in the myelin sheaths around the neurons in my brain are mostly still there, and a few of the atoms expelled from my system ten years ago have no doubt wandered back into it during the last few weeks and are still there. Let us ignore these subtleties.

27. See my "Philosophers and the Words 'Human Body'," in Peter van Inwagen, ed., *Time and Cause: Essays Presented to Richard Taylor* (Dordrecht: D. Reidel, 1980), pp. 283–99. See also Michael Tye, "In Defense of the Words 'Human Body'," *Philosophical Studies* 38 (1980): 177–82.

28. This argument can be evaded by the philosopher who believes that enduring objects are four-dimensional (extended in time as well as in the three spatial dimensions) and who also accepts (1) the thesis that if a four-dimensional object x occupies a certain region R of space-time, then every subregion of R (or every subregion that satisfies certain reasonable topological requirements) is occupied by a part of x, and (2) "Four-dimensional Universalism": the thesis that for any four-dimensional objects, the ys, the ys have a sum. Such a philosopher can argue as follows: "There are certain atoms such that I am a proper part of the sum of those atoms. For any atom that I overlap, that atom and I will be related as follows: it will have a temporal extension of (say) millions of years, and I will have a temporal extension of (say) seventy years; there will be a brief interval t—a few days in length, perhaps—such that the t-part of that atom, and no other part of that atom (except *parts* of its t-part) is a part of me."

I touch on my reasons for rejecting "four-dimensionalism" in the Preface and in the article "Four-Dimensional Objects" cited there.

29. The parenthetical disjunct is included to secure the reflexivity of parthood. In the sequel I shall often ignore this refinement.

30. *An Essay Concerning Human Understanding* II.27.6.

31. "According to the Proposed Answer, the nuts and bolts and diodes that most people would say composed an automaton do not compose anything, since their activity does not constitute a life. But if they do not compose anything, what can be meant by calling them 'parts'?" What is essentially this question will be addressed in Sections 10 and 11.

32. Young, *An Introduction to the Study of Man* (Oxford: The Clarendon Press, 1971), pp. 86–87.

33. *The Body in Question* (New York: Random House, 1978), pp. 140–41.

34. This wording presupposes that an organism is not caught up in its *own* life. Whether one talks of an organism's being caught up in its own life is presumably a matter of convention. If we adopted the convention that an organism was caught up in its own life, we should have to say that a thing was a proper part of something just in the case that it was caught up in a life other than its own. In the sequel I shall adopt the convention that an organism is not caught up in its own life. The opposite convention would require a few trivial modifications in the wording of various statements and definitions.

35. As we have seen, the conjunct 'y is an organism' is redundant, and the preposition 'of' is a disguised mereological term.

36. Or we might say that all physical objects are living organisms, some of them (the simples) having "degenerate" *lives*. If we adopted both this convention and the convention mentioned in n. 34—that every organism is caught up in its own life—then the following three biconditionals will hold (according to the Proposed Answer) without the annoying "special case" qualifications that are necessary in the absence of the two conventions:

$\exists y$ (the xs compose y) iff the activity of the xs constitutes a life.

The xs compose y iff the activity of the xs constitutes the life of y.

x is a part of y iff x is caught up in the life of y.

37. "The Doctrine of Arbitrary Undetached Parts," *Pacific Philosophical Quarterly* 62 (1981): 123–37.

38. See Haim Harani, "The Structure of Quarks and Leptons," *Scientific American*, April 1983, pp. 56–68.

39. Saul A. Kripke, *Wittgenstein on Rules and Private Language: An Elementary Exposition* (Cambridge: Harvard University Press, 1982), p. 65.

40. Some of those who have read drafts of this book have told me that they doubted whether one could understand 'are arranged tablewise' unless one first understood 'table'. I do not see that this thesis would have any untoward consequences for the present study if it were true. In any case, it seems to me to be rather implausible. Why, in general, can't we teach children to use 'are arranged wuffishly' without going through the step of teaching them a noun ('wuff', say) that is supposed to denote the mereological sum of things arranged wuffishly? If "wuffs" are recognizable, must not occasions of the wuffish arrangement of things be recognizable?

41. Cf. Jay Rosenberg's explanation of his term "nominal object" in *Thinking Clearly about Death* (Englewood Cliffs, N.J.: Prentice Hall, 1983), p. 10.

42. See John R. Searle et al., "Minds, Brains, and Programs," commentaries by various hands, and reply by Searle, *Behavioral and Brain Sciences* 3 (1980): 417–56.

43. Reported by Morton White in "Memories of G. E. Moore," *Journal of Philosophy* 57 (1960): 805–10. The attribution is on p. 806. I am grateful to José Benardete for this reference.

44. But consider the following quotation from a book by the chemist Robert Shapiro, *Origins: A Skeptic's Guide to the Creation of Life on Earth* (New York: Bantam Books, 1986): "The smallest free-living organisms are probably the mycoplasmas, tiny bacteria. . . . As we shall see, viruses are generally smaller than mycoplasmas, but they are not separate living beings. They function as parts of organisms, not as complete ones" (pp. 117–18).

45. One argument that will probably occur to us, since we are so intelligent, is that—granted that the mental supervenes upon the physical—if there is a hammock distinct from a snake, it has all the same beliefs as the snake (leaving aside niceties about indexical beliefs). Like the snake, it believes that it existed before the snake was woven into a hammock and that it will continue to exist after the snake is unwoven. Unlike the snake, however, it is wrong in these beliefs. It is, for example, blissfully unaware that it will cease to exist when the snake is unwoven. Given that no *snake* goes out of existence when the snake is unwoven, it is wrong in thinking that it is a snake.

46. Note that one's hesitation about how to answer the question 'Is the house that stands here now the same one that stood here then?' is not to be accounted for by reference to one's hesitation about whether to apply some vague general term—not unless that term is 'same'. Although 'house' is certainly a vague general term, this fact would seem to be irrelevant to one's hesitation, since—we may so stipulate—the house that stands here now and the house that stood here then are both central, perfectly clear cases of houses. Or at least this is true if houses are three-dimensional objects. If houses are four-dimensional objects, extended in time as well as in space, then we may account for hesitation about how to answer the question whether the "now" house and the "then" house are the same by reference to hesitation over whether to apply a vague general term. This point will be developed in detail in Section 18, which also includes a discussion of vagueness and the Law of the Excluded Middle.

47. I do not say that the theory of artifacts I have proposed makes the sentence 'Uncle Henry's old Ingersol is now in pieces on the jeweler's worktable' "come out true." Whether that is so would depend on what proposition was, according to our theory, expressed by that sentence. It is certainly *not* true that the pieces on the worktable are now arranged watchwise, and it can plausibly be argued that the quoted sentence expresses a truth (according to our theory) only if those pieces are now arranged watchwise. I say only that this theory of artifacts explains our tendency to utter that sentence and the corresponding lack of any tendency to utter any similar sentence with respect to the parts in the scrap bin.

48. I concede, however, that our theory does nothing to explain our at least equally strong tendency to say that the ship reconstructed from the "original" planks is the original ship.

49. My own views about counterfactual event-identity can be found in "Ability and Responsibility," *Philosophical Review* 87 (1978): 201–24, and *An Essay on Free Will* (Oxford: The Clarendon Press, 1983), pp. 167–70.

50. This question was put to me by Eric Olson.

51. This is perhaps too simple. What is certainly true is this: at least the layer of atoms virtually composing the *surface* of the appendage right at the flesh-

appendage interface would have to be a perfect duplicate of the corresponding layer of atoms in the severed ear, if the appendage were really perfectly to duplicate the causal powers of the severed ear. But then those atoms would be assimilated by the organism. We may apply this reasoning over and over again, one layer of atoms at a time, till the whole of the appendage has been assimilated—and is, in fact, an ear.

52. *Essay* II.27.4.

53. *Essay* II.27.8.

54. Or it may be that Locke is a Universalist and accepts both the principle that I argued in Section 8 was an obvious adjunct to Universalism (namely, that if the xs compose y, then, necessarily, if the xs exist, the xs compose y) and mereological essentialism.

55. *The Virtues* (Cambridge: Cambridge University Press, 1977), p. 30. In verifying this reference, I was surprised to find that the phrase "mere blob of slime" does not occur there. It has a very secure place in my memory, however. I think I must have heard Professor Geach use the phrase in an oral presentation of the same material in lectures he gave at Calvin College in 1973. If my memory has played me false, I apologize to Professor Geach for attributing the phrase to him.

56. Michael Denton, *Evolution: A Theory in Crisis* (Bethesda, Md.: Adler & Adler, 1986), p. 220.

57. A very interesting case of this is discussed in Stephen Jay Gould's "This View of Life" column in *Natural History* for December 1984 ("A Most Ingenious Paradox," pp. 20–29): the Portuguese man-of-war, which is a plausible candidate for a borderline case between "organism" and "mass of fused organisms." (Or one might say that one of the tentacles of the man-of-war was a borderline case between "organism" and "organ.") I thank Peter Unger for sending me a copy of this article.

58. See the article cited in note 38.

59. See my paper "Plantinga on Trans-World Identity," in Tomberlin and van Inwagen, eds., *Alvin Plantinga*, pp. 101–20. Since I wrote that paper, I have accepted David Lewis's point that "trans-world identity" is a barbarism. I ought to have said "identity across worlds" or "interworld identity."

60. "Where Am I?" in *Brainstorms: Philosophical Essays on Mind and Psychology* (Montgomery, Vt.: Bradford Books, 1978), pp. 310–23.

61. The constitution of the Dual Monarchy was actually rather more complicated than this example suggests.

62. In conversation.

63. Nevertheless, these functions are localized in different parts of the brain. I have read a newspaper account of a child who (if the personal relative pronoun is appropriate) was born without a cerebrum—his, or its, cranial cavity was filled with fluid—and who, or which, nevertheless functioned normally as regards heartbeat, respiration, metabolism, and bodily growth for at least a few years. It is possible, therefore, that the thinking part of the brain might be "preserved" by a wholly external life-support system and in no way constitute an organism. I should have to say that the events inside such a brain-part (a mere virtual object) that would be identical with thoughts and experiences if they occurred within

an organism would not be identical with thoughts and experiences—since there would be no one for them to be the thoughts and experiences *of*. This, I concede, is a highly counterintuitive position. For an attempt to undermine some of the convictions and presuppositions that lead us to find this position counterintuitive, see the case of "flickering Alice" in the next section (pp. 209–10).

64. The ribonucleic acid is as mythological as the Springs of Lethe—mere corroborative detail, as Pooh-Bah would say. (The idea that RNA played some central role in the physical basis of memory once enjoyed a brief vogue.)

65. *Collected Papers*, vol. 5 (Cambridge: Harvard University Press, 1935), p. 355. The argument I attribute to Peirce includes some improvements due to Roderick Chisholm. See his *Person and Object: A Metaphysical Study* (LaSalle, Ill.: Open Court, 1976), p. 110.

66. *Essay* II.27.15.

67. "Brain Bisection and the Unity of Consciousness," *Synthese* 22 (1971): 396–413. For a very clear and sensible monograph-length discussion of the problem, see Charles E. Marks, *Commissurotomy, Consciousness, and Unity of Mind* (Cambridge, Mass.: MIT Press, 1981).

68. See note 49.

69. This discussion of the metaphysics and logic of the surgical division of thinking organisms has been conducted on the supposition that the "classical" or "absolute" view of identity is correct. (Compare the remarks earlier in the present section concerning absolute versus relative identity and memory.) One who took seriously the idea of relative identity, however, might want to explore the idea that Alpha and Beta were two persons, that they existed before the division when they were the same organism and existed after the division when they were different organisms.

70. See "The Problem of the Many," *Midwest Studies in Philosophy* 5 (1980): 411–67.

71. *Word and Object* (Cambridge: Harvard University Press, 1960), p. 203.

72. Cf. Robert Stalnaker, "Vague Identity," in David F. Austin, ed., *Philosophical Analysis: A Defense by Example* (Dordrecht: Kluwer Academic Publications, 1988), pp. 349–60.

73. Strictly speaking, we need to add the disjunct 'or a simple is a member of x to the degree 1 and x has no other members'.

74. This thesis could be disputed. See the discussion of the "Duplication Principle" in Section 13.

75. *On the Plurality of Worlds* (Oxford: Basil Blackwell, 1986), p. 212.

76. But see the quotation in note 44. (The author is not a biologist, but a chemist specializing in DNA and the genetic effects of environmental chemicals.)

77. 'Alpha' and 'Omega' are pure or "Kripkean" proper names. They are thus wholly unlike 'the tallest man Sally knows' and 'the distance from Chicago to Salt Lake City', which contain vague predicates. We may also suppose that when they were conferred, no borderline cases of any predicates used in the acts of conferring them ("I name this *man* 'Alpha' . . .") were present. Or we may suppose this if we are taking the extensions of these predicates to be three-dimensional objects

that endure through time. If, however, the extension of, for instance, 'man' comprises four-dimensional objects, objects extended in time as well as in space, it may well be that (owing to the actions of the Cabinet) it will be indeterminate what 'this man' denotes. We shall take this point up in the text.

78. "Can There Be Vague Objects?" *Analysis* 38, no. 4 (1978): 208. Nathan Salmon has a similar argument for the same conclusion: see his *Reference and Essence*, pp. 243–45. At one time I assumed (as did several other philosophers) that Evans's and Salmon's arguments were equivalent. Correspondence with Salmon, however, has convinced me that the question of the equivalence of his and Evans's arguments is a delicate one. Accordingly, I do not claim that the arguments of the present section constitute an adequate reply to *Salmon's* argument for the impossibility of vague identity. I hope to examine Salmon's argument elsewhere.

79. Evans, "Can There Be Vague Objects?". Evans's puzzling words make sense if we postulate that he supposes that the dual of 'indef' is 'it is definitely true that'. But this, of course, is false: the dual of 'indef' is 'it is either definitely true or definitely false that'. How to expand a valid deduction of '$\sim\alpha = \omega$' from 'indef $\alpha = \omega$' into a valid deduction of '$\sim$indef $\alpha = \omega$' from that premise is by no means the trivial problem it might at first glance appear to be. In an unpublished paper, "The Good, The Bad, and The Ugly," F. J. Pelletier presents a proof of '$\sim$indef $\alpha = \omega$' from 'indef $\alpha = \omega$', a proof that (essentially) contains Evans's deduction as a part. But this proof depends on some strong second-order principles, such as 'indef $\forall_x F_x \cdot \leftrightarrow \cdot \exists_x$ (indef F_x) & $\sim \exists_x$ deff F_x'. (Here 'deff' means 'it is definitely false that'.) In this proof 'F' is not a predicate-letter but a true variable (both '$\forall$F' and '$\exists$F' occur in the proof).

80. In writing names of models in this form, we adopt the convention that 'A', 'B', 'C', and so on always have distinct referents when they are used within the name of a given model.

81. They will not, if they are wise, claim even to have presented an argument for the conclusion that Evans's reasoning is invalid—or not simply in virtue of having constructed a formal semantics according to which that reasoning is invalid. But here is an outline of an argument for that conclusion: (1) The "Cabinet" case makes it plausible to suppose, antecedently to any argument, that there could exist cases of vague identity, and hence that any argument for the impossibility of such cases contains an error. (2) The semantic fragment presented herein puts forward a reasonably plausible candidate for the office "error in Evans's reasoning"—at least (I predict) it will be regarded as a reasonable candidate by someone who antecedently believes that there probably is such an error; I do not predict that it will be regarded as a plausible candidate by those who accept Evans's conclusion. This, of course, is only an argument. It is not a proof. There are, I think, few if any proofs of interesting philosophical theses. The argument could be replied to, like (almost?) all philosophical arguments, and the reply could be replied to, and so on, ad infinitum. What someone said of the study of history can with at least equal justice be said of philosophy: philosophy is argument without end. But I don't think that the above argument is a bad argument—as philosophical arguments go. A philosophical argument does not

count as a failure if it does not force assent to its conclusion. It is enough that it lend some support to that conclusion.

82. "Supervalues" are the invention of Bas van Fraassen. See "Presupposition, Implication, and Self-Reference," *Journal of Philosophy* 65 (1968): 136–52.

83. More exactly: to no philosophical need having to do with vagueness. Supervalues may have their place if one is evaluating sentences in a language having "truth-value gaps" (a language in which no value at all is assigned to some sentences), or if the intended interpretation of the "intermediate" value has some other basis than vagueness. (Consider, for example, the semantic problem facing an Aristotelian who believes that the sentence 'There will either be a sea battle tomorrow or there will not' is true and who also believes that both of its disjuncts have the intermediate value.)

84. This paragraph contains the germ of what I would say in reply to Salmon's argument against the possibility of vague identity (see note 78), but I do not claim that it will do as it stands as a criticism of his argument.

85. "The Doctrine of Arbitrary Undetached Parts," *Pacific Philosophical Quarterly* 62 (1981): 123–37. See p. 128.

86. Doesn't rejecting the transitivity of identity violate my "proposed strategy" of assigning ½ to a sentence if there is the least excuse for doing so? If '$a = b$' and '$b = c$', both have the value ½; doesn't their both having that value constitute a good reason for not assigning 0 to '$a = c$'? This question misconstrues the strategy I have proposed. The misconstrual is facilitated by my occasional use of the graphic but imprecise wording "assign the value ½ if there is the least excuse for doing so." Here is a statement of the strategy that is less open to misconstrual: Given the information contained in a model (given certain objects, given a specification of which objects are paired, and given an assignment to constants of referents drawn from among those objects), assign the value ½ to a sentence on that model if there is the least excuse for doing so. The strategy, in other words, constrains the use made of the information contained in a model and does not constrain what information may be contained in a model; if a model does contain the information that 'a' and 'c' denote distinct objects that are not paired, there can be no excuse for assigning any value but 0 to '$a = c$', no matter what other information may be contained in the model. One could, of course, adopt an extension of the "proposed strategy," one that constrained the information contained in a model in the following way: if some of the information contained in a model provides the least excuse for assigning ½ to a sentence, then the rest of the model must be "filled in" in such a way that ½ is assigned to that sentence by the model. This extended strategy would, I suppose, lead us to adopt the constraint on the pairings included in a model that is mentioned in the paragraph to which this note is attached.

87. This is an adaptation of a point made by Terence Parsons in his important paper "Entities without Identity," *Philosophical Perspectives* 1 (1987): 1–19. I say "an adaptation" because Parsons's point is made in relation to "the contrapositive of Leibniz's Law" and "Leibniz's Law," which correspond to, but are not the same as, what I call "the Principle of the Nonidentity of Discernibles" and "Liebniz's Law." What Parsons calls "Leibniz's Law" is a more general principle than the one I call by that name.

Let me take this opportunity to commend Parsons's paper, which contains a different approach to the problem of vague identity from mine, one that in many respects I like better than my own. Parsons's approach has the consequence that the property abstracts in Evans's argument fail to denote anything. And this is not the result of an ad hoc stipulation but is extremely well motivated.

Much of the material in the present section (up to this point) was published as a paper, "How to Reason about Vague Objects," *Philosophical Topics* 16 (1988): 255–84. In the interest of brevity, I have omitted in the present work several very long notes to that article. The reader who is specially interested in vague identity may find some of them to be worth looking at.

88. The interlocutor might be identified with Frances Howard, although she is not to be held responsible for his *ipsissima verba*.

89. *The Nature of Necessity* (Oxford: The Clarendon Press, 1974). See particularly p. 132.

90. Pp. 212–13. This paragraph immediately follows the paragraph quoted in the preceding section. (See note 75.)

91. A second tautological "principle of composition" is: Anything the xs compose exists. Thus, every proxy borderline object has existence as an associated property. If there are both definite and borderline cases of composition, then 'x exists' has both full and borderline objects in its extension and an empty frontier. (Compare our stipulation in Section 18 that '$x = x$'—which is extensionally equivalent to 'x exists'—has in any model the universe of that model as its extension and an empty frontier.) This might seem paradoxical. Should not a borderline object fall within the frontier of 'x exists'? Did we not talk in just that way when we were attempting to provide an intuitive sense for 'borderline object'? In the end, I believe, there is no way to make sense of the idea of a thing's belonging to the frontier of existence—just as there is no way to make sense of a nonexistent object, an object that falls outside both the extension and the frontier of existence. If we did somehow modify our semantics so that the frontier of 'x exists' comprised all and only borderline objects, this modification would have the not implausible consequence that—if there are borderline cases of composition—'$\exists x$ indef x exists' had the value $\frac{1}{2}$. (As things stand, this sentence can have no value but 0.) But it is unclear whether any modification that satisfied this description could avoid contradiction. In standard logic, 'x is round$\lor \sim x$ is round' is equivalent to '$\exists y\, y = x$'. Suppose there were a borderline object z that belonged to the extension of 'x is round'. Surely an object that belonged to the extension of a predicate would belong to the extension of the disjunction of that predicate with some other predicate? Surely an object that belonged to the frontier of a predicate would belong to the frontier of any logically equivalent predicate? But then, it would seem, z must belong both to the extension and to the frontier of 'x is round$\lor \sim x$ is round'.

Index

Italicized entries (e.g., *Cohesion*) are names of principles.

Library of Congress Cataloging-in-Publication Data

Van Inwagen, Peter.
  Material beings / Peter van Inwagen.
    p. cm.
  Includes bibliographical references and index.
  ISBN 0-8014-1969-7 (alk. paper)
    1. Ontology. 2. Identity. I. Title.
BD311.V35   1990
111—dc20   90-55125

84565   111
                        V31

		DATE DUE	